Meaning and Reference

Meaning
and
Reference

EDITED BY
ALI A. KAZMI

University of Calgary Press
Calgary, Alberta, Canada

ISSN 0229-7051   ISBN 0-919491-23-5

© 1998 The Canadian Journal of Philosophy
ISBN 0-919491-23-5
ISSN 0229-7051
CJP Supplementary Volume 23 (1997)

University of Calgary Press
2500 University Drive NW
Calgary, Alberta
Canada T2N 1N4

Canadian Cataloguing in Publication Data

Main entry under title:
    Meaning and reference

    (Canadian Journal of Philosophy. Supplementary volume,
ISSN 0229-7051 ; 23)
    Includes bibliographical references and index.
    ISBN 1-919491-23-5

    1. Meaning (Philosophy) 2. Reference (Philosophy) 3. Language
and languages—Philosophy. I. Kazmi, Ali A., 1947– II. Series.

B105.M4M392 1998   121'.68   C98-910688-8

Printed and bound in Canada.
♾This book is printed on acid-free paper.

iv

Table of Contents

CANADIAN JOURNAL OF PHILOSOPHY
Supplementary Volume 23

Missing Modes of Supposition

TERENCE PARSONS
University of California, Irvine

I The Modes of Common Personal Supposition

Supposition theory is a medieval account of the semantics of terms as they function in sentences. The word 'supposition' is probably interchangeable with our word 'reference,' but I'll leave it as 'supposition' so as to identify the medieval source of the theory I discuss here. Medieval writers had a great deal to say about supposition; this paper focuses on only one part of the theory, the study of what is now generally called the theory of *modes of common personal supposition*. The word 'common' is used here as in 'common term,' as opposed to 'singular term,' but in fact, the theory focuses on common terms *along with the quantifiers that accompany them*. The word 'personal' is a technical term indicating that the word in question is used in its normal way to refer to the things it is true of, as distinguished from occurrences in which it refers to itself (as in "Giraffe' is a noun') or refers to a particular thing intimately related to the things it is true of (as in 'Giraffe is a species'). So we might describe this as a theory of the *modes of reference of quantified common terms used normally*. There are three such modes, illustrated as follows:

Determinate: The term 'dingo' has determinate supposition in:
    Some *dingo* is a predator.

Determinate supposition has something to do with existential quantification. Exactly what it has to do with existential quantification is a question to be discussed.

Distributive: The term 'dingo' has distributive supposition in:
    Every *dingo* is an animal.

Distributive supposition has something to do with universal quantification.

Merely Confused: The term 'dingo' has merely confused supposition in:
    Every predator is a *dingo*.

Merely confused supposition has something to do with existential quantification that occurs within the scope of a universal quantification.

Among twentieth century commentators, the major outstanding questions regarding the theory of the modes of common personal supposition are:
What is it a theory of?
What is it intended to accomplish?
This paper addresses only the first question: what is the theory of modes of common personal supposition a theory of?[1]

II The Fourteenth Century Theory

Following Spade (1988), I see two quite different accounts of personal supposition, an early account and a later one.[2] The early account is found in the late twelfth and thirteenth centuries in the writings of Peter of Spain, William Sherwood, Lambert of Auxerre, and several anonymous theorists.[3] I see this account as an (obscure) account of

---

1 I make some comments about the second question in Terence Parsons, 'Supposition as Quantification or as Global Quantificational Effect?' *Topoi* **16** (1997) 41-63.

2 Paul Vincent Spade, 'The Logic of the Categorical: The Medieval Theory of Descent and Ascent,' in Norman Kretzmann, ed., *Meaning and Inference in Medieval Philosophy* (Dordrecht: Kluwer 1988), 187-224

3 There are English translations of Peter in Francis P. Dinneen, *Peter of Spain: Language in Dispute* (Amsterdam/Philadelphia: John Benjamins Publishing Com-

quantification. A term has determinate supposition, essentially, if it is existentially quantified; it has distributive supposition if it is universally quantified; and something a bit more complicated needs to be said about merely confused supposition. I will not be talking about this early account at all.

In the fourteenth century a new account was developed by Walter Burley, William Ockham, John Buridan, Albert of Saxony, and others.[4] It replaced the obscurity of the earlier account with clarity, relatively speaking. It also changed it into a different theory. At least that is what I have claimed in the past (following Spade (1988) in general, though not in detail), and that is part of the theme of this paper: what is the fourteenth century theory of the modes of personal supposition a theory of?

First we have to see what the account is. Here is Ockham's version, which is very close to versions given by Burley, Buridan, and Albert.[5] The theory itself consists of three definitions; they give necessary and

---

pany 1990), and Joseph P. Mullally, *The* Summae Logicales *of Peter of Spain* (Notre Dame: University of Notre Dame Press 1945); of Sherwood in Norman Kretzmann, *William of Sherwood's Introduction to Logic* (Minneapolis: University of Minnesota Press 1966) and *William of Sherwood's Treatise on Syncategorematic Words* (Minneapolis: University of Minnesota Press 1968); of Lambert in Norman Kretzmann and Eleonore Stump, *The Cambridge Translations of Medieval Philosophical Text*, vol. 1 (Cambridge: Cambridge University Press 1988); and of a typical anonymous writer in Steve Barney, Wendy Lewis, Calvin Normore, and Terence Parsons (trans.), 'On the Properties of Discourse,' *Topoi* **16** (1997) 77-93.

4 There are English translations of Burley in Paul Vincent Spade, 'Walter Burley, From the Beginning of his *Treatise on the Kinds of Supposition (De Suppositionibus),' Topoi* **16** (1997) 95-102, and *Walter Burley: On the Purity of the Art of Logic, the Shorter and the Longer Treatises* (New Haven: Yale University Press, forthcoming), of Ockham in Alfred J. Freddoso and Schuurman (trans.), William Ockham, *Summa Logicae, Part II* (Notre Dame: University of Notre Dame Press 1980), and Michael J. Loux, *Ockham's Theory of Terms: Part I of the Summa Logicae* (Notre Dame: University of Notre Dame Press 1974), and of Buridan in Peter King *Jean Buridan's Logic: The Treatise on Supposition, The Treatise on Consequences* (Dordrecht: D. Reidel 1985).

5 See §§70-74 of Loux, *Ockham's Theory of Terms*.

sufficient conditions for a term's having determinate, distributive, or merely confused supposition. Beginning with determinate:

(A)   A term *F* has *determinate* supposition in a proposition *S* if and only if
        Descent: you may descend under *F* to a disjunction of propositional instances of all the *F*'s, and
        Ascent: from any such instance you may ascend back to the original proposition *S*.

A 'propositional instance' of a proposition with respect to *F* is the proposition you get by replacing the denoting phrase containing *F* with one of the form 'this *F*' or 'that *F*.'[6] 'Descent' and 'ascent' are simply valid inferences, picturesquely expressed in terms of the directions in which the inferences go. So we validate the claim that 'dingo' has determinate supposition in 'Some dingo is spotted' by establishing these two claims:

Descent: You may descend under 'dingo' in 'Some dingo is spotted' to a disjunction of instances of all dingo's. That is, from:

> Some dingo is spotted

you may infer:

> This dingo is spotted *or* that dingo is spotted *or* ... and so on for all the dingos.

Ascent: You may ascend back to the original proposition, because from any instance of the form:

> This dingo is spotted

you may infer the original proposition:

---

6   Sometimes other adjustments are required. For example, an instance of 'No dingo is spotted' will be 'this dingo is not spotted,' not 'this dingo is spotted.'

4

Some dingo is spotted.

Distributive supposition has a parallel explanation:

(B)   A term F has *distributive* supposition in a proposition S if and
      only if
      Descent: you may descend under F to a conjunction of
      propositional instances of all the F's, and
      Ascent: from any one instance you may not ascend back to the
      original proposition S.

So 'dingo' has distributive supposition in 'Every dingo is spotted' because

Descent: You may descend under 'dingo' in 'Every dingo is spotted' to
a conjunction of instances of all dingo's. That is, from:

      Every dingo is spotted

you may infer:

      This dingo is spotted *and* that dingo is spotted *and* ... and so on
      for all the dingos.

Ascent: You may not ascend back to the original proposition; from an
instance of the form:

      This dingo is spotted

you may not infer the original proposition:

      Every dingo is spotted.

Finally, merely confused supposition:

(C)   A term F has *merely confused* supposition in a proposition S if
      and only if

Descent: you may not descend under *F* to either a conjunction or a disjunction of propositional instances of all the *F*'s, but
You may descend to a disjunctive term, and
Ascent: from any instance you may ascend back to the original proposition *S*.

The term 'mammal' has merely confused supposition in 'Every dingo is a mammal' because:

Descent: You may not descend under 'mammal' in 'Every dingo is a mammal' to either:

> Every dingo is this mammal *and* every dingo is that mammal *and* ... , and so on for all the dingos.

or to:

> Every dingo is this mammal *or* every dingo is that mammal *or* ... , and so on for all the dingos.

But you may descend to a disjunctive *term*:

> Every dingo is this-mammal-or-that-mammal-or-that-mammal ... , and so on for all the mammals.

Ascent: You may ascend back to the original proposition from any instance. From:

> Every dingo is this mammal[7]

you may infer the original proposition:

> Every dingo is a mammal.

---

7 This is the claim that every dingo is this *particular* mammal, not the claim that every dingo is a mammal of this *kind*.

III Modes are Kinds of Global Quantificational Effect

The definitions of the modes of common personal supposition look
something like twentieth century truth conditions for quantifiers,
though for restricted quantifiers like 'every dingo' instead of for 'every
thing' or 'everything.' This led some twentieth century authors to suggest that the descended forms are meant to provide truth conditions
for the quantifiers occurring in the original forms.[8] But this is not right,
for two reasons. First, as was noted decades ago,[9] the descended forms
are not equivalent to the original forms; they follow from the original
forms, but in the case of distributive supposition, for example, the descended forms do not always entail the originals.[10] And so they cannot
be analyses. The second reason, bears on the topic of this paper. I'll
begin explaining it by using a modern parallel. Suppose we ask what
the sign '$\exists x$' is doing here:

$\exists x Px.$

An accurate answer is: It's an existential quantifier. It makes a sentence
that is true if the part following the quantifier is satisfied by at least
one thing.

Now let us ask what the sign '$\exists x$' is doing here:

$\sim\exists x Px.$

One natural response would be:

---

8 Principally, Philotheus Boehner, *Medieval Logic* (Manchester: Manchester
University Press 1959), and Ernest Moody, *The Logic of William of Ockham* (New
York: Russell and Russell 1955 [reissued 1965]).

9 E.g. in Gareth B. Matthews, 'Ockham's Supposition Theory and Modern Logic,'
Philosophical Review 73 (1964) 91-99; '*Suppositio* and Quantification in Ockham,'
Noûs 7 (1973) 13-24; and 'A Note on Ockham's Theory of the Modes of Common
Personal Supposition,' *Franciscan Studies* 44 (1984) 81-86.

10 'Dingo' is distributed in 'Some predator is not a dingo,' but that proposition
may not be inferred from 'Some predator is not this dingo, and some predator is
not that dingo, and ..., and so on for all the dingos.'

Response 1: We already answered that question: it's an existential quantifier. The negation sign doesn't change that answer. The quantifier behaves as we said above, and the negation reverses the truth value of the resulting sentence.

That response is correct. But so is this response:

Response 2: In this context the sign is, in effect, a *universal* sign. It makes the sentence true if the part of the sentence without the quantifier — namely, this part:

$$\sim Px$$

(the part with the quantifier removed) — is satisfied by everything.

That response is also correct. The first response is a part of a typical twentieth century theory of quantifiers; it explains what quantifiers do locally. (This is like the earlier, thirteenth century account.) It analyses sentences modularly, with bigger modules produced from smaller ones; you analyze how quantifiers behave in their own local modules, and a recursive semantics takes care of the rest. The second response looks at quantifiers in terms of their global context, and says what they do to their global context — including parts of that context, such as the negation sign above, that are not even within the scope of the quantifier. You *can* look at things this way. What you get is a theory of what I call *global quantificational effect*. It's the effect a quantifier *actually* has, described in terms of the effect it *would* have if it had scope over the whole global context, or almost the whole context.

This idea can be made precise within the theory of 'prenex normal forms.' If no biconditional sign appears in a formula of quantification theory, then you can take any quantifier in that formula and move it in stages toward the front of the formula, each stage being equivalent to the original formula, provided that you switch the quantifier from universal to existential (or *vice versa*) whenever you move it past a negation sign or out of the antecedent of a conditional, and provided that you do not move it past a quantifier of opposite quantity (i.e. you don't move a universal past an existential, or *vice versa*). For example, you can take the universal quantifier in:

$$\sim(Gy \rightarrow \underline{\forall x}Px)$$

and move it onto the front of the conditional to get:

$\sim\underline{\forall x}(Gy \rightarrow Px),$

and then the resulting universal sign can be moved further front, turning into an existential:

$\underline{\exists x}\sim(Gy \rightarrow Px).$

This chain of equivalences

$\sim(Gy \rightarrow \underline{\forall x}Px)$

$\sim\underline{\forall x}(Gy \rightarrow Px),$

$\underline{\exists x}\sim(Gy \rightarrow Px).$

can be interpreted as the *movement* of a single quantifier to the front, retaining its identity while changing its quantity.[11]

If you do this systematically to all the quantifiers in a formula, the result is a formula in 'prenex normal form,' in which the quantifiers are all on the front in a row, each of them having scope over the rest of the formula to its right. In terms of these prenex forms you can define the *global quantificational effect* of any quantifier in any formula: when it moves to the front it ends up being either universal or existential, and

---

11 The process of forming prenex normal forms is well-known; cf. George Boolos and Richard Jeffrey, *Computability and Logic* (Cambridge: Cambridge University Press 1974), 112-113. The fact that the formation of a prenex normal form can be viewed as the *movement* of quantifiers to the front of the formula depends on the fact that the steps do not introduce new quantifiers or lose old ones. Such steps are available when the connectives in the formula are negation, conjunction, disjunction, and the material conditional. This is not so if the formula contains biconditional signs (see *ibid*, page 113); fortunately, medieval theorists did not employ unitary biconditional signs. It is clear from their practice that they would have seen a proposition of the syntactic form 'A if and only if B' as consisting of a conjunction of 'A if B' and 'A only if B,' neither of which contains a biconditional.

it may or may not be able to move to the front of all the *other* quantifiers in the sentence.

Let us take this idea and use it to analyze the terminology of supposition theory. The subject matter here is terms, not quantifiers, but each term comes with its own quantifier, so we can treat the theory as if it is a theory of restricted quantification. We then give this account:

A term is *determinate* in a formula if it becomes a wide scope existentially quantified term in (one of) the prenex normal form(s) of that formula.

A term is *distributive* in a formula if it becomes a universally quantified term in (one of) the prenex normal form(s) of that formula.

A term is *merely confused* in a formula if it becomes an existentially quantified term in (one of) the prenex normal form(s) of that formula, but it can't get wide scope in any such form.

Illustration: Let us test 'dingo' for its mode of supposition in 'Some *dingo* is a predator.' Using well-known symbolizations for categorical sentences in modern notation, we see that 'dingo' has determinate supposition here, because it is already in prenex form, existentially quantified:

> Some *dingo* is a predator
> (for some dingo x)(for some predator y)[x is y]

It has distributive supposition here, for the same reason:

> Every *dingo* is a predator
> (for every dingo x)(for some predator y)[x is y]

The term 'predator' in the sentence just displayed has merely confused supposition because it is existentially quantified with scope inside that of 'for every dingo', and it cannot be moved further to the front while preserving equivalence.

Now consider:

Some predator is not a *dingo*
(for some predator *x*) not (for some dingo *y*)[*x* is *y*]

Here the 'not (for some dingo *y*)' is equivalent to '(for every dingo *y*) not,' yielding:

(for some predator *x*) (for every dingo *y*) not [*x* is *y*]

The original 'some dingo' has now become universal, thus classifying it as having distributive supposition, which is the mode that the theory described in terms of ascent and descent says it has. This illustrates the importance of looking at things globally; although 'dingo' is existentially quantified here, it has universal *effect*. For example, you could 'universally specify' it. This is why it is classified in this theory as distributive.

These are simple examples; as the sentences get more complex, so do the examples. To be sure how it all works, you need to develop a precise syntax and define these notions carefully. For the rest of this paper I will take for granted that the theory of ascent and descent and the theory of these prenex normal forms is clearly worked out; this should not be problematic for the simple examples discussed here.[12]

Taking this for granted, the thesis to be examined is that the later theory of supposition, explained in terms of ascent and descent, is a theory of global quantificational effect, a theory that can be made precise in a mechanical way in terms of the theory of prenex forms for quantifiers.

IV   Gaps in the Accounts?

In Parsons (1997) I argued that textual evidence supports the claim that the fourteenth century theory of supposition is essentially a theory of global quantificational effect (and that the thirteenth century theory is different, more like our modern recursive theories of quantifiers).[13]

---

12   I have done that in work in draft form; I am relying on it here.

13   Parsons, 'Supposition'

But two issues (not discussed there) threaten this conclusion. Each has to do with gaps in the accounts.

Gap 1: First, there is a problem about the prenex normal forms alluded to above. In the predicate calculus with unrestricted variables, any quantifier not in a biconditional moves into prenex form as described. But the medieval theory uses *restricted* quantification; instead of 'for every *x*,' or 'for every *thing x*,' one has 'for every *dingo x*.' And in the restricted version of quantification theory the version of the prenex normal form theorem I have alluded to does not hold. It holds for some occurrences of restricted quantifiers, but not for all. For example, in this disjunction:

Snow is white ∨ For some dingo *x*: *x* is spotted

you cannot move the 'for some dingo' so as to have scope over the whole disjunction, as in:

For some dingo *x*:[Snow is white ∨ *x* is spotted].

This is because if there are no dingos, the former is true and the latter false.[14] This means that there are terms for which the notion of global quantificational effect is not defined. There are terms that *do not have* global quantificational effect. This is the first gap in the account.

Gap 2: Looking at the medieval theory of ascent and descent, there is a similar problem. Here too, not all terms fit the definitions of the modes. If the modes are defined as above, there are terms that *do not have* any mode of supposition at all. (Examples will be given below.)

I suppose you can see what is coming. Perhaps the gap in the one account matches the gap in the other account? That is a thesis to be explored in this paper: *the gaps match*. This requires qualification, since (i) there was not one theory of supposition; each author had his own version, and (ii) there are a number of details that need to be worked

---

14 If you separate the restricted quantifier from its restriction, you can move the quantifier alone:

∃*x*[Snow is white ∨ [*x* is a dingo & *x* is spotted]]

but this does not result in the whole 'some dingo' moving.

out in all the accounts. I will consider specifically whether it is possible to formulate a theory of supposition that is very close to Ockham's account (and also close to the accounts of others, a kind of compromise version) that is equivalent to an account of global quantificational effect. A rigorous formulation will not be given here; the point of this paper is rather to explain what the issues are as clearly as possible without getting bogged down in details. For the remainder of this paper I will talk almost entirely in terms of the medieval theory of ascent and descent, returning specifically to the issue of global quantificational effect in the last section.

V   Terms with no Mode of Supposition

In order to investigate the accounts in a manageable fashion, we need to limit the domain of applicability in a clear way. So for the time being, I exclude plural terms, and I consider only the quantifier words 'every,' 'some,' and 'no' and their synonyms. I also for the time being ignore all examples containing non-extensional contexts. Even within these strict limits, the modes of supposition are not complete.

Let us look at a term with no mode of supposition. Consider the term 'human' in the following simplification of a sentence from William of Sherwood:[15]

Every thing that sees every human is running,

If you represent this sentence in terms of restricted quantifiers in predicate calculus notation, the step to any kind of prenex position for the term 'human' is blocked. The term cannot be moved into a prenex position.[16] And if you test for mode of supposition by appeal to ascent

---

15 Kretzmann, *William of Sherwood's Treatise on Syncategorematic Words*, 35-36. Sherwood's sentence is 'Every human who sees every human is running'; I have changed the first 'human' to 'thing' to avoid the complication of the same term being used twice; this is not essential to the point Sherwood is illustrating.

16 I assert this without proof; the reader is invited to try to find an equivalent normal form. The original sentence is a universal affirmative, and requires for

and descent, it has no mode of supposition either. It is not determinate because the ascent condition fails:

The original sentence:

> Every thing that sees every human is running

is not entailed by

> Every thing that sees this human is running.

This is because the original sentence is affirmative, and so its subject has existential import; the sentence cannot be true unless there is a 'thing that sees every human.' But this is not guaranteed by the truth of 'Every thing seeing this human runs.'[17] The term is not distributive because descent to an arbitrary conjunction of singulars fails:

The original sentence does not entail:

> Every thing that sees this human is running *and* every thing that sees that human is running *and* ... and so on for all humans.

Finally, the term 'human' is not merely confused, because both the ascent and descent conditions for merely confused supposition also fail.

---

its truth that there be a thing that sees every human; this aspect of it will be lost in most prenex forms. (If you decide to ignore this medieval doctrine about universal affirmatives and instead hold that universal affirmatives with empty subject terms are vacuously true, then the vacuous truth of the original sentence when there is no thing that sees every human is lost in most prenex forms.)

17 It might appear that this is a peculiar result, dependent on a special view about existential import of subject terms. But the same result follows if we take the modern view that universal affirmatives are vacuously true when their subject terms are empty. For on that view the original proposition is true if nothing sees every human; thus the descent condition for determinate supposition fails: the original proposition does not entail that 'Every thing that sees this human is running' for some particular case of 'this human'. (Just imagine that each thing sees some human, but nothing sees every human, and nothing is running.)

Thus there are common terms suppositing personally that have no defined mode of supposition. Yet, so far as I know, this is not a possibility that is discussed by any author before 1370.[18] So perhaps we might be mistaken, either in articulating the theory or in applying it. The question of whether the modes are complete has been discussed quite a bit in recent literature, and there are some suggestions along these lines that should be considered. I will discuss three of them.

Suggestion 1: One obvious idea to consider is that we should not try to assign supposition to terms that are parts of other terms. If the theory is not intended to apply to terms that are parts of larger terms, then perhaps there is no gap in the theory *so far as its intended application is concerned.*

Spade shows that the modes of supposition are complete (there are no gaps) for a certain class of sentences.[19] Spade is liberal in what he takes to be the scope of the theory, but not libertine. One of his constraints is that the terms for which supposition is to be defined obey what he calls the 'rule of scope': that the scope of that term's denoting phrase extends to the end of the whole proposition under consideration. Terms that occur within other terms violate this constraint, and the test case we are discussing is one of these: 'every human' in 'Every thing seeing every human runs' is part of the complex term 'thing seeing every human,' and its scope is limited to the relative clause.

However, in practice authors did not stick to this constraint. Examples exist throughout the tradition of discussions of terms that violate it. They include:

Dialectica Monacensis:[20]
  'Every[thing] seeing *every human* runs.'

---

18 I rely here on Stephen Read, 'Thomas Cleves and Collective Supposition,' *Vivarium* **29** (1991) 50-84.

19 Spade, 'The Logic of the Categorical'

20 L.M. De Rijk, *Logica Modernorum*, vol. II part 2 (Assen, The Netherlands: Koninklijke Van Gorcum & Company N.V. 1967), 615

Sherwood:[21]

> 'Every human who sees *every human* is running,'

Buridan:[22]

> 'Seeing *any/every ass* is an animal,'

Paul of Venice:[23]

> 'Seeing *every human* is an animal,'
> 'A donkey of *any human* runs'
> 'A donkey of *no one* is an animal.'

These discussions are mostly not accompanied by a classification of terms with regard to their modes of supposition, so there is room for debate over intent. But Buridan clearly means to discuss supposition of terms that violate the rule of scope. In discussing the sentence:

> An animal which is not a human is a substance

he says that 'human' has distributive supposition.[24]

Notice that if we apply the tests of ascent and descent to 'human' in 'An [= some] animal which is not a human is a substance' they classify it as having distributive supposition, as Buridan says. So at least some terms that violate the rule of scope were assigned supposition, and the theory of ascent and descent does naturally apply to them. (Even if such terms had not been discussed it would be interesting to ask what the theory *could* have said about them.)

---

21 Kretzmann, *William of Sherwood's Treatise on Syncategorematic Words*, 35-6

22 King, *Jean Buridan's Logic*, 141

23 Alan Perreiah, *Logica Parva: Translation of the 1472 Edition* (München: Philosophia Verlag 1984), 152-53

24 He says, "... 'man' is properly distributed here, since part of the sentence is 'which is not a man.' Even though this is not a sentence (since it is part of a sentence) it nevertheless has a likeness to a sentence with respect to the distribution and supposition of the terms; such terms supposit and appellate in an expression which is part of a sentence and which taken of itself is a sentence as they would in a sentence taken *per se*." King, *Jean Buridan's Logic*, 138.

Suggestion 2: Several twentieth century authors (motivated in part by Geach[25]) have speculated about a missing 'fourth mode' of supposition. The speculation is prompted by a lack of symmetry among the extant modes. We have descent to a disjunctive proposition, descent to a conjunctive proposition, and descent to a disjunctive term, but no descent to a conjunctive term. Perhaps that is what needs to be provided to fill the gap we are discussing. In fact, this proposal seems to work beautifully for the example we are discussing. For you can descend in our example from:

Every thing seeing every human runs

to:

Every thing seeing this-human-and-that-human-and-that-one-and-so-on, runs.

However, the proposal to complete the modes by adding descent to a conjunctive term only continues a slippery slope. This is because the proposed fourth mode does not complete the modes either. Consider this example:

Every thing not seeing a dingo runs.

The occurrence of 'dingo' in this example is not determinate because descent fails to the disjunction:

Every thing not seeing this dingo runs *or ...*

It is not distributive for the same reason. And it is not merely confused because ascent fails: an instance of the descended form:

Every thing not seeing this dingo runs

---

25 Peter Geach, *Reference and Generality* (Ithaca, New York: Cornell University Press 1962)

does not entail that there is a thing not seeing any dingo, and thus the existential import for the original proposition is not guaranteed. Finally, the fourth mode under discussion does not apply either, because one cannot descend to a conjoint term. Such a descent would produce:

> Every thing not seeing this-dingo-and-that-dingo-and-that-one-and-so-on, runs,

and this is a synonym of 'Every thing not seeing *every* dingo runs,' which does not follow.[26] So the popularly suggested fourth mode does not fill the gap.

Suggestion 3: Read discusses an idea pursued by John Dorp to avoid this consequence.[27] It is an attempt to avoid having to posit a fourth mode in addition to the standard three. Dorp suggests that if a proposition does not pass any of the tests under consideration as worded, then we need to find an equivalent form of the proposition containing the same terms, and test for its mode of supposition in the equivalent form. He thinks that this may capture the recalcitrant cases. For example, although one may not descend to a disjunctive term under 'human' in 'No animal is every human,' one can do so in the equivalent 'Every animal some human is not' (*Omne animal homo non est*), thereby showing that 'human' has merely confused supposition in the original proposition.

This is an enticing idea, but it is not clear whether it works. First, it seems to be based on the principle that terms must have the same supposition in equivalent propositions containing them. But there are counter-examples to that principle. Consider the sentence:

> Every animal is an animal.

---

26 If you want to make a conjoint something-or-other, you need to make a conjoint negative predicate in the twentieth century meaning of 'predicate':
'Every[thing] not seeing this dingo and not seeing that dingo and … runs.'
But this is not the test; the test is descent to a conjoint *term*.

27 Read, 'Thomas Cleves and Collective Supposition'

From the medieval perspective there are two equiform terms here, one in the subject and one in the predicate. The first has distributive supposition, and the second has merely confused supposition.[28] Now consider the proposition you get when the terms are interchanged. The terms have each switched supposition, but the new proposition is equivalent to the original. So we cannot assume that a term has not changed supposition merely because the new proposition is equivalent to the old. This consideration may not be persuasive, since it seems to be a rather special case, unlike those that Dorp had in mind. Maybe the idea works when no term is repeated? I am not sure.

The more important problem with this proposal is that it is a *speculation* that every term will receive one of the three modes of supposition by finding an equivalent form that passes the tests of ascent and descent. I don't know how to do this for 'human' in our test example:

Every thing seeing every human runs.

I have no proof that it cannot be done, but I am doubtful.

I think it is a mistake to focus on descents to disjoint or conjoint terms. In ordinary extensional contexts, 'some A' is always equivalent to 'this A or that A or that one, …', and 'every A' is always equivalent to 'this A and that A and that one, …', and 'no A' is always equivalent to 'every A, not.'[29] So some kind of local descent of this kind is always possible in extensional contexts. It indicates only that the term is singular and occurs in an extensional context. Requiring any particular kind of descent — to a disjoint, or a conjoint, term — would be logically capricious. Since this is so, it is better ignored altogether for

---

28 This requires a slight refinement of the theory concerning how to treat repeated terms; you have to test for supposition on the assumption that repeated terms are logically independent of one another. This fine tuning adjustment must be made both in the formal account for global quantificational effect, and in the theory couched in terms of ascent and descent.

29 This is subject to the grammatical idiosyncrasies of individual languages; sometimes in ordinary language it is not clear whether such descent is possible, or exactly how it is to be formulated.

purposes of the present discussion. We should instead take the explanation of the modes of common personal supposition and do with them what Buridan and Burley both did: *omit* the condition in merely confused supposition that requires descent to a disjoint term. The simplified condition then becomes:

(D)   A term *F* has *merely confused* supposition in a proposition *S* if and only if
      Descent: you may not descend under *F* to either a conjunction or a disjunction of propositional instances of all the *F*'s, but
      Ascent: from any instance you may ascend back to the original proposition *S*.

This automatically takes care of Dorp's example, 'No animal is every human,' *without* having to rephrase it; 'human' automatically has merely confused supposition by the definition, because no descent is possible, and ascent is possible from any instance. If we make this modification, then, so far as I can see, the modes of common personal supposition correspond to the kinds of global quantificational effect discussed earlier. The gaps remain unfilled, but the gaps that we have surveyed so far in supposition theory appear to match those in the theory of global quantificational effect.

VI   Completing the Modes

Suppose that modes of supposition *are* kinds of global quantificational effect, corresponding to positions in prenex normal form. Then there cannot be any more modes than the original three. This is because the modes correspond to

> wide scope existential,
> any scope universal, and
> non-wide scope existential.

But there are no more options than these. So the modes must be complete. And if some terms have no mode, then it is in principle impossible to change this. No modes are missing, but there are terms without modes. So if there are terms that are not classifiable in these ways, as I have argued, they cannot be assigned new modes without changing the idea of mode of common personal supposition to something quite different in kind.

But suppose one *is* willing to 'change the subject,' by allowing modes that do *not* correspond to kinds of global quantificational effect. Then it is easy to complete the modes. In fact, it has already been done, by Buridan. This is because Buridan defines merely confused supposition in such a way that it simply means "neither determinate nor distributive."[30] *All* terms used personally now have one of the modes, because any term not passing the tests for determinate or distributive supposition goes into the official leftover category *merely confused*. So I was not accurate in saying that *Buridan's* theory is a theory of global quantificational effect, because the leftover category includes all the rest.

However, even Buridan is uneasy about this. He goes on to note that terms classified in his leftover mode are of two sorts: the sort we thought we were discussing, and ones of a quite different kind. He says:[31]

> The verbs 'to know,' 'to comprehend,' 'to understand,' and many others ... confuse without distributing the terms following them which terminate their action.
>
> For example, if I say "I know a triangle" it does not follow that therefore I know an isosceles triangle or I know an equilateral triangle, and so on. So too "I owe you a horse" does not entail that therefore I owe you Brunellus, or I owe you Favellus, and so on.
>
> It seems to me that this kind of confusion is quite different from the preceding modes, although they are each called 'confusion without distribution.'

(He goes on to discuss a number of ways in which these examples with nonextensional contexts differ from others.)

---

30   King, *Jean Buridan's Logic*, 130. Buridan adds to the definition that "perhaps a sentence with a disjunctive extreme follows," but he makes clear in other discussion that the 'perhaps' means that some terms with merely confused supposition satisfy this *and some do not*. So it is not a requirement. (See discussion below.)

31   King, *Jean Buridan's Logic*, 145

The problem of completing the modes by making the third mode a grab-bag, including all other ways in which terms with personal supposition may function, is that it lumps together quite unlike phenomena. In particular, it lumps together the terms I have been discussing that lack global quantificational effect because of their quantificational scope with terms that lack global quantificational effect because they are in opaque contexts.

I think it is possible to provide a maximally refined classification of the modes of functioning of terms with common personal supposition, using only ingredients of the medieval theory of ascent and descent. This classification will cut at the joints, in a way that Buridan's does not. Recall our temporary restriction from above, where we excluded plural terms, and we limited consideration to the quantifier words 'every,' 'some,' and 'no' and their synonyms, occurring in extensional contexts. Call terms occurring in such restricted contexts 'ordinary.' Then consider the following categories. There are six categories: four categories of terms that have prenex positions, a category for ordinary terms without prenex position, and a sixth category for non-ordinary occurrences of terms. They go as follows, with the understanding that each entry below presupposes that the conditions for higher entry have not been met. 'GQE' abbreviates 'Global Quantificational Effect.'

Determinate: Existential wide scope GQE.
Descent to and ascent from a disjunction of propositional instances.

> Example: 'Some *dingo* is a predator'

Strong Distributive: Universal wide scope GQE.
Descent to and ascent from a conjunction of propositional instances.[32]

> Example: Every *dingo* is a predator

---

32 This descent and ascent condition means descent to and ascent from the whole conjunction of instances, not just to/from a single instance. This is the condition used by Paul of Venice; see Alan Perreiah, *Logica Magna (Tractatus de Suppositionibus)* (St. Bonaventure, NY: The Franciscan Institute 1971).

Weak Distributive: Universal non-wide scope GQE.
Descent to a conjunction of propositional instances without ascent from an arbitrary single instance.

> Example: Some predator is not a *dingo*

Merely Confused ('Weak Determinate'): Existential non-wide scope GQE. Ascent from an arbitrary instance.

> Example: Every predator is a *dingo*

Left-over Ordinary: Terms in 'Ordinary' contexts without any GQE.
Descent to and ascent from a conjunction or disjunction of terms.

> Examples: Every thing seeing every *dingo* runs
> Every thing not seeing a *dingo* runs

Non-Ordinary: None of the above

> Examples: The *apostles* are twelve
> Necessarily, a *dingo* runs
> Socrates believes a *dingo* runs

Is this proposal at all in the spirit of the medieval tradition? I think so. For the additional distinctions made in this classification were made by Paul of Venice.[33] The additional distinctions are the distinction between strong and weak distributive, and the distinction between ordinary and non-ordinary. Paul calls my *Determinate* 'Determinate,' he calls my *Strong Distributive* 'Mobile Distributive,' which he distinguishes from the amalgam of my *Weak Distributive, Merely Confused,* and *Left-over Ordinary* (which he calls 'Mobile Merely Confused'). His category of 'Immobile' cases include some (but perhaps not all) of my *Non-Ordinary* category. So he singles out wide scope existential and wide

---

33 In his *Logica Magna,* translated in Perreiah, 89-121. This account differs from that in the *Logica Parva,* translated in Perreiah.

scope distributive (the first two above) for special consideration; these would be the ones that a twentieth century logician would want to figure in truth conditions for quantified terms in a recursive semantics; he then uses 'Mobile' versus 'Immobile' to distinguish ordinary terms in extensional contexts without wide scope from the rest. (He also distinguishes between immobile distributive and immobile merely confused; I have not tried to capture this.)

If we compare Paul, Buridan, and Ockham (revised) with one another, we see that among them they made exactly the distinctions suggested above, though no one of them made all the distinctions:

	All Common Terms Used Personally					
	Ordinary Terms					Others
	Terms with Prenex Position				Terms Without Prenex Position	
	Wide Scope		Narrow Scope			
	∃	∀	∀	∃		
Proposed Above	Determinate	Strong Distributive	Weak Distributive	Weak Determinate	Left-Over Ordinary	Non-Ordinary
Paul of Venice	Determinate	Mobile Distributive	Mobile Merely Confused			Immobile
Buridan	Determinate	Distributive		Merely Confused		
Ockham (revised)	Determinate	Distributive		Merely Confused	<no mode>	

So perhaps the classification given above, which seems to cut at the joints from a twentieth century perspective, is close to what supposition theory matured into. The classification is of interest because it is equivalently explainable in modern terms, or in terms of the medieval notions of ascent and descent.

CANADIAN JOURNAL OF PHILOSOPHY
Supplementary Volume 23

Quinus ab Omni Nævo Vindicatus[1]

JOHN P. BURGESS
Princeton University

I   Quine's Critique

I.1 Quine and his critique:

Today there appears to be a widespread impression that W. V. Quine's notorious critique of modal logic, based on certain ideas about reference, has been successfully answered. As one writer put it some years ago: "His objections have been dead for a while, even though they have not yet been completely buried."[2] What is supposed to have killed off the critique? Some would cite the development of a new 'possible-worlds' model theory for modal logics in the 1960s; others, the development of new 'direct' theories of reference for names in the 1970s.

These developments do suggest that Quine's unfriendliness towards any formal logics but the classical and indifference towards theories of reference for any singular terms but variables were unfortunate. But in

---

1   This paper is a completely rewritten version of an unpublished paper, 'The Varied Sorrows of Modality, Part II.' I am indebted to several colleagues for information used in writing that paper, and for advice given on it once written, and I would like to thank them all — Gil Harman, Dick Jeffrey, David Lewis — even if the portions of the paper with which some of them were most helpful have disappeared from the final version. But I would especially like to thank Scott Soames, who was most helpful with the portions that have *not* disappeared.

2   J. Hintikka, 'Is Alethic Modal Logic Possible?', *Acta Philosophica Fennica* **35** (1982) 89-105, opening paragraph. In context it is clear this is a description, not an endorsement, of a widespread impression.

this study I will argue, first, that Quine's more specific criticisms of modal logic have *not* been refuted by either of the developments cited, and further, that there was much that those who did not share Quine's unfortunate attitudes might have learned about modality and about reference by attention to that critique when it first appeared, so that it was a misfortune for philosophical logic and philosophy of language that early reactions to it were as defensive aand uncomprehending as they generally were. Finally, I will suggest that while the lessons of Quine's critique have by now in one way or another come to be absorbed by many specialists, they have by no means been fully absorbed by everyone, and in this sense there is still something to be learned from Quine's critique today.

Section III below will list some lessons from Quine's critique, after Section II has examined the early responses to it. Since I will be arguing that most of these simply missed the point, I should say at the outset that this is easier to see by hindsight than it was from expositions of the critique available at the time, and that the early responses were useful insofar as they provoked new expositions. That there are flaws in Quine's own presentations is conceded even by such sympathetic commentators as Dagfinn Føllesdal and Leonard Linsky, and at least as regards his earliest presentations by Quine himself.[3] To remove flaws is the aim of the present section, and the aim suggested by my title, which readers familiar with the history of mathematics will recognize as echoing Saccheri's *Euclides ab Omni Nævo Vindicatus* or *Euclid Freed from Every Blemish*. Such readers will also recall that though

---

3 The most important of Quine's presentations is 'Reference and Modality,' in *From a Logical Point of View* (Cambridge: Harvard University Press, three editions, 1953, 1961, 1980). Citations of this twice-revised work here will be by internal section and paragraph divisions, the same from edition to edition. This work supersedes the earlier 'The Problem of Interpreting Modal Logic,' *Journal of Symbolic Logic* **12** (1947) 43-8. For commentary see Linsky, editor's introduction to *Reference and Modality* (Oxford: University Press 1971), and 'Reference, Essentialism, and Modality,' therein 88-100. See also D. Føllesdal, 'Quine on Modality,' in D. Davidson and J. Hintikka, eds., *Words and Objections: Essays on the Work of W. V. Quine* (Dordrecht: Reidel 1969), 175-85; and 'Essentialism and Reference,' in L. E. Hahn and P. A. Schilpp, eds., *The Philosophy of W. V. Quine* (La Salle: Open Court 1986), 97-113.

Saccheri's aim was to defend Euclid, ironically his work is today remembered as a contribution to *non*-Euclidean geometry. While I hope to avoid a similar irony, I do not hesitate to depart from Quine on occasion, and begin with two limitations that I think need more explicit emphasis than they get from Quine.

I.2 Non-trivial de re modality:

A first restriction is that Quine's critique is limited to predicate as opposed to sentential modal logic, his complaint being that modal predicate logic resulted from mechanically combining the apparatus of classical predicate and modal sentential logic, without thinking through philosophical issues of interpretation.[4] Quine does sometimes suggest that engaging in modal logic would be pointless unless one were eventually going to go beyond the sentential to the predicate level, so that though his critique deals explicitly only with predicate modal logic, it is tantamount to a critique of all modal logic; but the suggestion is not strenuously argued.[5]

The restriction to predicate logic has two aspects. First, the critique is limited to *de re* as opposed to *de dicto* modality, to modalities within the scope of quantifiers as opposed to quantifiers within the scope of modalities, to modalities applying to open formulas as in $\exists x \Box Fx$, rather than modalities applying to closed formulas as in $\Box \exists x Fx$. Second, the critique is limited to *non-trivial de re* modality. The first point has been generally understood. Not so the second, which calls for some explanation.

I begin with an analogy. One can contrive systems of sentential modal logic that admit modalities notationally, but that make every modal formula more or less trivially equivalent to a non-modal formula. It

---

4 A theme in his reviews in the *Journal of Symbolic Logic* **11** (1946) 96-7 and **12** (1947) 95-6

5 See the last paragraph of the third section of 'Reference and Modality,' ending: "… for if we do not propose to quantify across the necessity operator, the use of that operator ceases to have any clear advantage over merely quoting a sentence and saying that it is analytic."

suffices to add as a further axiom the following, whose converse is already a theorem in the common systems:

(1) $P \rightarrow \Box P$

This corresponds to a definition according to which P holds necessarily just in case P holds — a definition that could silence any critic who claimed the notion of necessity to be unclear, but would do so only at the cost of making the introduction of the modal notation pointless.

Analogously, one can contrive systems of predicate modal logic that admit *de re* modalities notationally, but that make every *de re* formula more or less trivially equivalent to a *de dicto* formula. The precise form a *trivialization axiom* would take depends on whether one is considering monadic or polyadic predicate logic, and on whether one is admitting or excluding an existence predicate or an identity predicate or both. In the simplest case it suffices to add as a further axiom the following, whose converse is already a theorem in the common systems:

(2) $\forall x(\Box Fx \rightarrow \Box \forall y Fy)$

This corresponds to the *trivializing definition* according to which F holds necessarily of a thing just in case it is necessary that F holds of everything — a definition that could silence any critic who claimed the notion of *de re* modality to be more obscure than that of *de dicto* modality, but would do so only at the cost of making the introduction of *de re* notation pointless.

When Quine complains of the difficulty in defining *de re* modality, he is tacitly assuming the trivializing definition above has been rejected; so his critique is tacitly limited to systems that, like all the common ones, do *not* have the trivialization axiom as a theorem. To accept such a system as the correct system, the one whose theorems give all and only the general laws necessarily holding in all instances, is to reject the trivialization axiom as not being a such a general law, and hence is to reject the trivializing definition, which would make it one. Note that Quine's objection is thus to the *un*provability of something, namely trivialization, not the *provability* of anything.

I.3 Strict necessity:

A second restriction is that Quine's critique is limited to what he calls 'strict' necessity, identified with analyticity, as opposed to what may be called 'subjunctive' necessity, involved in counterfactuals. For Quine the former belongs to the same circle of ideas as *synonymy* and *definition*, and the latter to the same circle as *similarity* and *disposition*. Quine sometimes explicitly states this limitation; but he also often suggests that his argument generalizes to all intensional operators, or at least that there is an *obstacle* to making sense of quantification into intensional contexts in general (an obstacle that is *insurmountable* in the case of quantification into contexts of strict modality in particular).[6] Insofar as I wish to defend it, I take Quine's critique to be limited to strict modality, and his suggestion about generalization to be an attachment to it, not a component of it.

In connection with different senses of necessity there is a feature of the terminology current in the 1940s through 1960s that needs to be explicitly emphasized, lest one fall into anachronistic misreadings: the tendency to use interchangeably with each other, as adjectives modifying the noun 'truth,' all the expressions in the left-hand column below (and similarly for the right-hand column).[7] Each row merits separate comment:

Necessary	Contingent
Linguistic	Empirical
Apriori	Aposteriori
Analytic	Synthetic
Logical	Non-logical

---

6 Contrast the opening section of 'Reference and Modality,' on knowledge and belief contexts, with the antepenultimate paragraph of the paper, beginning: "What has been said in these pages relates only to strict modality...."

7 For a contemporary account deploring such tendencies, see W. Kneale and M. Kneale, *The Development of Logic* (Oxford: Clarendon Press 1962), 628ff. Such tendencies are exemplified by the usage of *all* the participants in the exchange discussed in section II below.

Logical truth and analytic truth. Quine distinguished a narrower notion of 'logical' truth, roughly truth by virtue of syntactic form alone, from a broader notion of 'analytic' truth, roughly truth by virtue of this plus semantic factors such as definition and synonymy. He notoriously thought the latter, broader notion unclear, and so had a *double* objection to the first of the following formulations:

(3)   It is analytically true that all bachelors are unmarried.
(4)   It is logically true that all unmarried men are unmarried.
(3′)   "All bachelors are unmarried" is analytically true.
(4′)   "All unmarried men are unmarried" is logically true.

One objection was to the common feature of (3) and (3′), involvement with broadly analytic rather than narrowly logical truth; another, to the common feature of (3) and (4), treatment of modality as a connective in the object language applying to sentences, rather than a predicate in the meta-language applying to quotations. What is important to understand is that in his critique of modal logic Quine presses only his objection to the second feature — a feature presupposed by quantified modal logic, since quantification into quotation contexts is obvious nonsense — waiving his objection to the first for the sake of argument. Others of the period shared neither Quine's worries about the broad, semantic notion, nor his concern to distinguish it from the narrow, syntactic notion, and often wrote 'logical' when they meant 'analytic.'

Analytic truth and apriori truth. Quine's first and foremost target, Rudolf Carnap, and others of the period, took the distinction between analytic and synthetic to be central to epistemology because they took it to coincide with the distinction between apriori and aposteriori. They recognized not a trichotomy of 'analytic' and 'synthetic apriori' and 'aposteriori,' but a dichotomy of 'analytic' and 'aposteriori.'

Apriori truth and linguistic truth. Quine often complained that others were sloppy about distinguishing use and mention. If one is sloppy, quibbles and confusions can result if, as was commonly done, one uses 'linguistic' interchangeably with 'analytic' or 'apriori' and 'empirical' interchangeably with 'synthetic' or 'aposteriori' respectively. For consider:

(5)   Planetoids are asteroids.
(6)   Ceres is the largest asteroid.

(5′)   In modern English, 'planetoids' and 'asteroids' refer to the same things.

(6′)   In modern English, 'Ceres' and 'the largest asteroid' refer to the same thing.

As to (5), discovery that planetoids are asteroids requires (for a fully competent speaker of modern English) mere reflection, not scientific investigation. As to (6), discovery that Ceres is the largest asteroid requires natural-scientific investigation of the kind engaged in by astronomers. Discovery that (5′) is the case (understood as about the common language, not just one's personal idiolect) requires social-scientific investigation of the kind engaged in by linguists. Discovery that (6′) is the case requires both kinds of scientific investigation. Since linguistics is an empirical science, using 'linguistic' and 'empirical' for 'analytic' and 'aposteriori' can be confusing when dealing with metalevel formulations like (5′) and (6′) rather than object-level formulations like (5) and (6); but such usage was common.

Linguistic truth and necessary truth. Quine distinguished strict and subjunctive modality, but whereas the default assumption today might be that someone who writes 'necessary' *sans phrase* intends subjunctive necessity, this was not so for Quine, let alone modal logicians of the period. Originally the primitive notion of modal logic was 'implication' $P \Rightarrow Q$, with 'necessity' defined as $\sim P \Rightarrow P$; later necessity $\Box P$ was taken as primitive, with implication defined as $\Box \sim (P \wedge \sim Q)$. But even then, the notion of implication of primary interest was strict, so that the notion of necessity of primary interest also had to be, and was often enough explicitly stated to be, strict. It was commonly assumed, if not that *all* necessity is linguistic or semantic or verbal necessity, then at least that the *primary* notion of necessity was that of verbal necessity. In reading the older literature, the default assumption must be that strict necessity is intended when one finds *sans phrase* the word 'necessary.'

I.4 'Aristotelian essentialism':

Preliminary restrictions having been enumerated, the critique proper begins by indicating what would have to be done to make sense of such notation as $\exists x \; Fx$. Given that '∃' is to be read in what has always been the standard way, as an existential quantifier, and that '$\square$' is to be read in what was at the time the prevailing way, as a strict modality, the following are equivalent:

(7a) $\exists x \square Fx$ holds
(7b)   there is some thing such that $\square Fx$ holds of it
(7c)   there is some thing such that Fx holds necessarily of it
(7d)   there is some thing such that Fx holds analytically of it

The commitment then is to making sense (in a non-trivial way) of the notion of an open formula or open sentence Fx holding analytically of a thing.

Now traditional accounts of analytic truth in philosophy texts provide only an explanation of what it is for a closed sentence to be analytically true, and do not even purport to provide any explanation of a notion of an open sentence being analytically true *of a thing*. (And rigorous analyses of logical truth in logic texts again supply only a definition of what it is for a closed formula to be logically true, and do not even purport to supply any definition of a notion of an open formula being logically true *of a thing*.) The notion of analyticity as it stands simply does not apply *literally* to an open sentence or formula relative *to a thing*, and the most one can hope to do is to extend the traditional notion from *de dicto* to *de re* — or to put the matter the other way round, reduce the notion for *de re* modality to the traditional one for *de dicto* — while remaining faithful to the *spirit* of strict modality. This presumably means remaining attached to a conception of necessity as purely *verbal* necessity, and confined within the circle of ideas containing *definition* and *synonymy* and the like, not bringing in physical notions of *disposition* or *similarity*, let alone Peripatetic or Scholastic metaphysical notions of *matter* and *form* or *potency* and *act* or *essence* and *accident*. Quine expresses pessimism about the prospects for defining *de re* modality subject to this restriction by suggesting that quantified modal logic is committed to 'Aristotelian essentialism.'

While Quine's own approach is resolutely informal, there is a technical result of Terence Parsons that is illuminating here, even though Parsons's usage of 'commitment to essentialism' differs in a potentially confusing way from Quine's. Roughly speaking, Parsons shows that though the common systems are, in the sense indicated earlier, committed to the failure of trivialization *as a general law,* yet no *specific instance* of such failure is provable in the common systems *even with the addition of any desired consistent set of de dicto assumptions.*[8] (On Parsons's usage the result is somewhat confusingly stated as saying that though the common systems are 'committed to essentialism' in one, weaker sense, essentially Quine's, they are not 'committed to essentialism' in another, stronger sense, Parsons's own.) This being so, any attempt to make sense of *de re* strict modality by reducing it to *de dicto* faces a dilemma.

On the one hand, if one adopts some *general* law permitting passage from *de dicto* to *de re,* one will in effect be adding a new general passage law as an axiom to the common systems. But with any such addition of a new formal axiom one is already rejecting the common systems as incomplete if not as incorrect. Worse, there is a threat that the new axiom will yield the trivialization; or worse still, will yield a contradiction. On the other hand, if one allows passage from *de dicto* to *de re* only *selectively,* one will in effect be adding a new selection principle as an ingredient to the concept of modality. But with any such addition of a new intuitive ingredient there is a danger that one will be making one's conception no longer one of merely *verbal* necessity; or worse, that one will be making it arbitrary and incoherent.

This abstract dilemma is concretely illustrated by Quine's *mathematical cyclist* example, an elaboration of an old example of Mill's, and his *morning star* example, an adaptation of an old example of Frege's. The only obvious approach to reducing the application of modal notions *to a thing,* to an application of modal notions *to words,* would be to represent or replace a thing by a word or verbal expression appropriately related to it. In fact, there are two strategies here, the most obvious one being to take the expression to be a *term referring to* the thing, and an only slightly less obvious one being to take the expression to be a *predicate satisfied by* the thing. Hence the need for two examples.

---

8 For a less rough formulation, see Parsons, 'Essentialism and Quantified Modal Logic,' *The Philosophical Review* **78** 35-52, reprinted in Linsky, 73-87.

I.5 The mathematical cyclist:

One strategy would be to count Fx as holding necessarily of a thing just in case F is necessarily implied by some predicate(s) P satisfied by the thing.

On the one hand, if we are non-selective about the predicates, this leads to contradiction with known or plausible non-modal or *de re* premises, such as the following:

(8a)   It is necessarily the case that all mathematicians are rational.
(8b)   It is at best contingently the case that all mathematicians are bipeds.
(8c)   It is necessarily the case that all cyclists are bipeds.
(8d)   It is at best contingently the case that all cyclists are rational.

(These are plausible at least if we take rationality to mean no more than capability for verbal thought, and bipedality to mean no more than having at least two legs, and count mathematicians who have lost limbs as non-bipeds, and count bicycle-riding circus animals as cyclists.) Non-selective application of the strategy to (8a-d) yields:

(9a)   Any mathematician is necessarily rational.
(9b)   Any mathematician is at best contingently a biped.
(9c)   Any cyclist is necessarily a biped.
(9d)   Any cyclist is at best contingently rational.

Together (9a-d) contradict the known actual existence of persons who are at once mathematicians and cyclists.

More formally, allowing non-selective application of the strategy amounts to adopting the following as an axiom, which can be seen to collapse modal distinctions all by itself:

(10) $\forall x(Px \rightarrow (\Box Fx \leftrightarrow \Box \forall y(Py \rightarrow Fy)))$

This is the first horn of the dilemma.

On the other hand, the obvious fall-back would be to allow (10) to apply only selectively, only to certain selected 'canonical' predicates. In order for (10), restricted to canonical predicates, to give an adequate definition of *de re* modality, it would suffice for two things to hold. It would suffice to have first that for each thing there is (or can be introduced) some canonical predicate it satisfies; and second that for any two canonical predicates *A*, *B* we have:

(11) $\quad \exists x(Ax \wedge Bx) \rightarrow \Box \forall y(Ay \leftrightarrow By)$

This condition would preclude taking both '*x* is a mathematician' and '*x* is a cyclist,' or both the Plato's '*x* is a featherless biped' and Aristotle's '*x* is a rational animal,' as canonical. But how is one to select what predicates *are* admitted as canonical? It seems that making a selection, choosing for instance between Plato and Aristotle, would require reviving something like the ancient and mediæval notion of 'real definitions' as opposed to 'nominal definitions'; and this is something that seems impossible to square with regarding the necessity with which we are concerned as simply *verbal* necessity.

I.6 The morning star:

The second strategy would be to count *Fx* as holding necessarily of a thing just in case *Ft* holds necessarily for some term(s) *t* referring to the thing.

On the one hand, if we are non-selective about the terms, applying the strategy to all terms equally, then whenever two terms *s* and *t* refer to the same thing, *Fx* holding necessarily of that thing will be equivalent to *Fs* holding necessarily and equally to *Ft* holding necessarily, so that *Fs* holding necessarily and *Ft* holding necessarily will have to be equivalent to each other. But this result leads to inferences from known or arguably true premises to known or arguably false conclusions, even in the very simple case where *Fx* is of the form $x = t$, since $t = t$ will in all cases be necessarily true though $s = t$ may in some cases be only contingently true.

For instance, the following are true:

(12)   The evening star is the morning star.
(13)   Necessarily, the morning star is the morning star.

And the following false:

(14)   Necessarily, the evening star is the morning star.

More formally, allowing non-selective application of the strategy amounts to adopting the following as an axiom:

(15) $\forall x(x = t \rightarrow (\Box Fx \leftrightarrow \Box Ft))$

And this can be seen to collapse modal distinctions (at least if enough apparatus for converting predicates to terms is available). This is the first horn of the dilemma.

On the other hand, the obvious fall-back would be to allow (15) to apply only selectively, only to certain selected 'canonical' terms. In order for (15), restricted to canonical predicates, to give an adequate definition of *de re* modality, two things would be required to hold. It would suffice to have first that for each thing there is (or can be introduced) some canonical term referring to it; and second that for any two canonical terms a, b we have:

(16) $(a = b) \rightarrow \Box(a = b)$.

Now the following is a theorem of the common systems:[9]

(17) $(x = y) \rightarrow \Box(x = y)$

---

9 It may be worth digressing to mention that Quine's one and only contribution to the formal side of modal logic occurred in connection with this law, though the history does not always emerge clearly from textbook presentations. The earliest derivations of the law took an old-fashioned approach on which identity is a defined second-order notion, and on such an approach the derivation was anything but straightforward, and only went through for systems at least as strong as the second-strongest Lewis system **S4**. Quine was one of the first to note that on a modern approach with identity a primitive first-order notion, the derivation becomes trivial, and goes through for all systems at least as strong as the minimal normal system **K**. This is alluded to in passing in the penultimate paragraph of the third section of 'Reference and Modality.' For the original presentation see R. Barcan (Marcus), 'Identity of Individuals in a Strict Functional Calculus of Second Order,' *Journal of Symbolic Logic* **12** (1947) 3-23. For a modern textbook presentation see G. E. Hughes and M. J. Creswell, *An Introduction to Modal Logic* (London: Methuen 1968), 190.

But (17) involves only variables $x, y, \ldots$, corresponding to pronouns like 'he' or 'she' in natural language, not constants $a, b, \ldots$ or function terms $fc, gc, \ldots$, corresponding to names like 'Adam' and 'Eve' or descriptions like 'the father of Cain' and 'the mother of Cain.' So (17) leaves open what terms should be allowed to be substituted for variables.[10]

What (16) says is that for the fall-back strategy being contemplated to work, we must be able to go beyond (17) to the extent of allowing canonical terms to be substituted for the variables. This condition would preclude taking both 'the morning star' and 'the evening star' as canonical. But owing to the symmetry involved, it would be entirely arbitrary to select 'the morning star' as canonical and reject 'the evening star' as apocryphal (or the reverse), and it would seem almost equally arbitrary to reject both and select some other term such as 'the second planet.' This is the second horn of the dilemma.

And with this observation Quine rests his case, in effect claiming that since the obvious strategies for doing what needs to be done have been tried and found to fail, the burden of proof is now on the other side to show, if they can, just how, in some unobvious way, what needs to be done can be. And with this observation, I too rest my case for the moment.

I.7 Coda:

Quine's critique was directed towards the strict kind of modality and towards quantification over ordinary sorts of objects: persons, places, things. Much of his discussion generalizes to other kinds of modal or intensional operators and other sorts of objects, to show that for them, too, the most obvious strategy for making sense of quantifying over such objects into such modal or intensional contexts faces an obstacle. But whether this obstacle can be surmounted, by the most obvious fall-back strategy of identifying an appropriate class of canonical terms

---

10 In the original paper where (17) was derived there were no singular terms but variables, and nothing was said about application to natural language. For an idea of the range of options formally available, see the taxonomy in J. Garson, 'Quantification in Modal Logic,' in D. Gabbay and F. Guenthner, eds., *Handbook of Philosophical Logic* II (Dordrecht: Reidel 1984) 249-308.

or in some other way, needs to be considered case-by-case. The most important case of a non-strict modality for which a reasonable choice of canonical terms seems to be available (for almost any sort of objects) will be mentioned at the very end of this study. Here I want to mention a case of a special sort of objects for which a reasonable choice of canonical terms seems to be available (for almost any kind of intensional operator).

Several writers, beginning with Diana Ackerman, have pointed out that *numerals* suggest themselves as non-arbitrary candidates for canonical terms if one is going to be quantifying only over natural *numbers*. And the numerals are in effect taken as canonical terms in two flourishing enterprises, *intensional mathematics* and *provability logic*, where the modality in question is a version or variant of strict modality.[11]

Still, natural numbers are a *very* special sort of object. Workers in the cited fields have noted the difficulty of finding canonical terms as soon as one goes beyond them even just to other sorts of mathematical objects, such as sets or functions. To avoid difficulties over there simply being *too many* objects to find terms for them all, let us restrict attention to recursively enumerable sets of natural numbers and recursive partial functions on natural numbers, where there is actually a standard way of *indexing* the objects in question by natural numbers or the numerals thereof. Even here there does not seem to be any non-arbitrary way of selecting canonical terms, since there will be many indices for any one set or function, and two indices for the same object will not in general be *provably* indices for the same object.[12]

---

11 See Ackerman, '*De Re* Propositional Attitudes Toward Integers,' in R. W. Shahan and C. Swoyer, eds., *Essays on the Philosophy of W. V. Quine* (Norman: University of Oklahoma Press 1979). Lectures of Kripke have brought this formerly underappreciated paper to the attention of a wider audience. See also S. Shapiro, ed., *Intensional Mathematics* (Amsterdam: North Holland 1985); and especially G. Boolos, *The Logic of Provability* (Cambridge: Cambridge University Press 1993), *xxxiv* and 226.

12 Workers in the cited fields have in effect suggested that something like indices can serve as canonical terms for more fine-grained intensional analogues of recursive sets and functions. But these too would be very special objects. The best discussion of these matters known to me is in some papers of Leon Horsten still at the time of this writing 'forthcoming.'

Whatever successes have been or may be obtained for non-strict modalities and ordinary objects, or for strict modalities and non-ordinary objects, they only make it the more conspicuous how far we are from having any reasonable candidates for canonical terms in the case to which Quine's critique is directed.

II   Quine's Critics

II.1 *Quine and his critics:*

Today when one thinks of model theory for modal logic, or the application of theories of reference to it, one thinks first of Saul Kripke, whose relevant work on the former topic only became widely known after his presentation at a famous 1962 Helsinki conference,[13] and on the latter only after his celebrated 1970 Princeton lectures.[14] But the impression that somehow an appropriate theory of models or of reference can refute Quine's critique can be traced back a full half-century. For less sophisticated model theories for quantified modal logic go back to some of the first publications on the subject, by Rudolf Carnap, in the 1940s;[15] while the application of less sophisticated theories of reference to modal logic goes back to one of the first reviews of Quine's critical writings, by Arthur Smullyan, again in the 1940s.[16]

---

13   Whose published proceedings make up one issue of *Acta Philosophical Fennica* **16** (1963), and include not only Kripke's 'Semantical Considerations on Modal Logic,' 83-94, but also Hintikka's 'Modes of Modality,' 65-82.

14   'Naming and Necessity: Lectures Given to the Princeton University Philosophy Colloquium, January, 1970,' in D. Davidson & G. Harman, eds., *Semantics of Natural Language* (Dordrecht: Reidel 1972), 253-355 and 763-9; reprinted with a new preface (Cambridge: Harvard University Press 1980).

15   'Modalities and Quantification,' *Journal of Symbolic Logic* **11** (1946) 33-64; *Meaning and Necessity: A Study in Semantics and Modal Logic* (Chicago: University of Chicago Press 1947).

16   *Journal of Symbolic Logic* **12** (1947) 139-41; with elaboration in his paper 'Modality and Description,' *Journal of Symbolic Logic* **13** (1948) 31-7. Smullyan's priority for his particular response to Quine has been recognized by all competent and

For purposes of examining the main lines of response to Quine's critique prior to the new developments in model theory and the theory of reference in the 1960s and 1970s, and Quine's rebuttals to these responses, it is almost sufficient to consider just three documents, together constituting the proceedings of a notorious 1962 Boston colloquium. The main talk, by Quine's most vehement and vociferous opponent, Ruth (Barcan) Marcus, was a compendium of almost all the responses to Quine that had been advanced by over the preceding fifteen years, plus one new one. The commentary, by Quine himself, marked an exception to his apparent general policy of not replying directly to critics, and gives his rebuttal to almost all early objections to his critique. An edited transcript of a tape recording of a discussion after the two talks among the two invited speakers and some members of their audience, notably Kripke, was published along with the two papers, and clarifies some points.[17]

II.2 Potpourri:

A half-dozen early lines of response to the critique may be distinguished. Most appear with differing degrees of explicitness and em-

---

responsible commentators. See note 15 in Linsky, 'Reference, Essentialism, and Modality,' and Føllesdal, 'Quine on Modality,' 183.

17 Thus the items are: (i) the compendium, 'Modalities and Intensional Languages'; (ii) the 'Comments' later retitled 'Reply to Professor Marcus'; and (iii) the edited 'Discussion.' They appear together in the official proceedings volume, M. W. Wartofsky, ed., *Proceedings of the Boston Colloquium for the Philosophy of Science 1961/1962* (Dordrecht: Reidel 1963), 77-96 (compendium), 97-104 (commentary), 105-16 (edited discussion). The same publisher had printed them in 1962 in *Synthese* in a version that is textually virtually identical down to the placement of page breaks, (i) and (ii) in a belated issue of the volume for 1961, and (iii) in an issue of the volume for 1962. (There have been several later, separate reprintings of the different items, but these incorporate revisions, often substantial.) Two of the present editors of *Synthese*, J. Fetzer and P. Humphreys, have proposed publishing the *unedited, verbatim* transcript of the discussion, with a view to shedding light on some disputed issues of interpretation; but according to their account, one of the participants, Professor Marcus, has objected to circulation of copies of the transcript or the tape.

phasis in the compendium, and most are rebutted in the commentary thereupon. They all involve essentially the same error, confusing Quine's philosophical complaint with some formal claim. Since — despite the best efforts of Quine himself in his rebuttal and of subsequent commentators — such confusions are still common, it may be in order to review each response and rebuttal briefly.

(A) *The development of possible-worlds semantics shows that there is no problem of interpreting quantified modal logic.* This response is represented in the compendium by the suggestion that disputes about quantified modal logic should be conducted with reference to a 'semantic construction,' in which connection the now-superseded approach of Carnap is expounded (with the now-standard, then-unpublished approach of Kripke being alluded to as an alternative in the discussion). Perhaps Quine thought the fallacy in this response obvious, since he makes no explicit response to it in his commentary; but it has proved very influential, albeit perhaps more as an inchoate feeling than as an articulate thought. The fallacy is one of equivocation, confusing 'semantics' in the sense of a mathematical theory of models, such as Carnap and Kripke provided, with 'semantics' in the sense of a philosophical account of meaning, which is what Quine was demanding, and thus neglecting the dictum that "there is no mathematical substitute for philosophy."[18] A mathematical theory of models could refute a technical claim to the effect that the common systems are formally inconsistent, but without some further gloss it cannot say anything against a philosophical claim that the common systems are intuitively unintelligible. In the case of Carnapian model theory this point perhaps ought to have been obvious from the specifics of the model, which validates some highly dubious theses.[19] In the case of Kripkean model theory

---

18 These are the closing words of Kripke, 'Is There a Problem about Substitutional Quantification?' in G. Evans and J. McDowell, eds., *Essays in Semantics* (Oxford: Oxford University Press 1976). The fallacy recurs again and again in other contexts in the literature. See B. J. Copeland, 'On When a Semantics Is Not a Semantics: Some Reasons for Disliking the Routley-Meyer Semantics for Relevance Logic,' *Journal of Philosophical Logic* 8 (1979) 399-413.

19 Notably the Barcan or Carnap-Barcan formulas, which give formal expression to F. P. Ramsey's odd idea that whatever possibly exists actually exists, and

the point perhaps ought to be obvious from the generality of the theory, from its ability to accommodate the widest and wildest variety of systems, which surely cannot *all* make good philosophical sense.

(B) *Quantified modal logic makes reasonable sense if '∀' and '∃' are read as something other than ordinary quantifiers, such as Lesniewski-style substitution operators Π and Σ.* This is the one substantial novelty in the compendium. One rebuttal, of secondary importance to Quine, is that if one allows oneself to call substitution operators 'quantifiers,' one can make equally good or poor sense of 'quantification' not only into modal but into absolutely any contexts whatsoever, including those of quotation. But quantification into quotation contexts is obvious nonsense — on any *reasonable* understanding of 'quantification.'[20] Still, the rebuttal of primary importance to Quine is a different and more general one, applying also to the next response.

(C) *Quantified modal logic makes reasonable sense if '□' and '◊' are read as something other than strict modalities, such as Prior-style temporal operators G and F.* This response is represented in the compendium by the suggestion, made passing in the introduction, that modal logic is worth

---

whatever actually exists necessarily exists. (The 'Barcan' label is the more customary, the 'Carnap-Barcan' label the more historically accurate according to N. Cocchiarella, 'Philosophical Perspectives on Quantification in Tense and Modal Logic,' in D. Gabbay and F. Guenthner, eds., *Handbook of Philosophical Logic* II (Dordrecht: Reidel 1984) 309-53, which also explains the connection with Ramsey.) If these formulas are rejected, one must distinguish a thing's having a property *necessarily* (for every possible world it exists there and has the property there) from its having the property *essentially* (for every possible world, *if* it exists there, *then* it has the property there). I have slurred over this distinction so far, and will for the most part continue to do so.

20 As shown by examples in the opening section of 'Reference and Modality.' This point seems to be conceded even by some who otherwise take an uncritically positive view of the compendium, as in the review by G. Forbes, *Notre Dame Journal of Formal Logic* **36** (1995) 336-9. The last sections of 'Is There a Problem about Substitutional Quantification?' in effect point out that the claim that the ordinary language 'there is' in its typical uses is a 'substitutional quantifier' devoid of 'ontological commitment' is absurd, since 'ontological commitment' is *by definition* whatever it is that the ordinary language 'there is' in its typical uses conveys.

pursuing because of the value of studies of various non-alethic 'modalities.' The specific example of temporal 'modalities' was suggested by Quine in his last remarks in the discussion, his purpose being to bring out his primary point of rebuttal to the previous response, that Lesniewski's devices are just as irrelevant as Prior's devices, given the nature of his complaint. If his complaint had been that there is a formal inconsistency in the common systems, then it would have been cogent to respond by considering those systems as wholly uninterpreted notations, and looking for some reading of their symbolism under which they would come out saying something true or plausible. But the nature of the critique is quite different, the complaint being that the combination $\exists x\Box$ is philosophically unintelligible *when the components '∃' and '$\Box$' are interpreted in the usual way*.[21]

(D) *Quantified modal logic is not committed to essentialism because no formula expressing such a commitment* (no instance of the negation of (2)) *is deducible in the common systems, even with the addition of any desired set of consistent de dicto axioms.* This response does not explicitly occur as such in the compendium, and would have been premature, since the results of Parsons which it quotes did not come until a few years later. But it is advanced in a slightly later work of the same author, and has been influential in the literature.[22] It could be construed as merely a generalization of the next response on the list, and Quine's rebuttal to the next response would apply to this one, too. Basically, the response is the result of terminological confusion, since its first clause is only *relevant* if 'commitment to essentialism' is understood in Quine's sense, but its second clause is only *true* if 'commitment to essentialism' is

---

21   "What I've been talking about is quantification, in a quantificational sense of quantification, into modal contexts, in a modal sense of modality," Wartofsky, 116

22   'Essentialism in Modal Logic,' *Noûs* **1** (1967) 90-6. And about the same time we find even the usually acute Linsky (editorial introduction, 9) writing: "Terence Parsons bases his search for the essentialist commitments of modal logic on Kripke's semantics, and he comes up (happily) empty-handed.... He finds modal logic uncontaminated." The continuation of this passage better agrees with Parsons' own account of his work and its bearing on Quine's critique.

understood in a different sense partly foreshadowed in the compendium and explicitly introduced as such by Parsons. It has already been noted in the exposition of the critique both that Quine's complaint is not about the *provability* of anything, and that Parsons's results *substantiate* some of Quine's suspicions.

(E) *The mathematical cyclist example does not show there is any problem, because no de re conclusions of the kind that figure in the example* (conclusions (9a-d)) *provably follow in the common systems from such de dicto premises as figure in the example* (premises (8a-d)). *While the example gives a legitimate counter-instance to the law that figures in it* (law (10)), *that law is not a theorem in the common systems.* This response occurs in a section of the compendium where Quine's criticisms are said to "stem from confusion about what is or isn't provable in such systems," and where it is even suggested that Quine believes $\Box(P{\to}Q){\to}(P{\to}\Box Q)$ to be a theorem of the common systems![23] This response, which accuses Quine of committing a howler of a modal fallacy, it is itself a howler, getting the point of Quine's example exactly backwards. The complaint that we can't deduce examples of non-trivial *de re* modality from plausible examples of non-trivial *de dicto* modality by taking something like (10) as an axiom, because we would get a contradiction, is misunderstood as a formal claim that something like (10) *is* an axiom, and we *do* get a contradiction. Quine's rebuttal in his commentary borders on indignation: "I've never said or, I'm sure, written that essentialism could be proved in any system of modal logic whatsoever."[24]

(F) *The morning star example does not show there is any problem, because while the law that figures in the example* (law (17)) *is a theorem of the common systems, the example does not give a legitimate counter-instance, as can be seen by applying an appropriate theory of reference.* This response is

---

23 See Wartofsky, 90-2. It is just conceivable that this is deliberate exaggeration for effect, a rhetorical flourish rather than a serious exegetical hypothesis. 'Essentialism in Modal Logic' cites some other authors who have written in a similar vein about the example.

24 And "I did not say that it could ever be deduced in the S-systems or any systems I've ever seen," Wartofsky, 113. Despite these forceful remarks, the understanding of Quine's views has not much improved in the later 'Essentialism in Modal Logic.'

repeated, with elaboration but without expected acknowledgments — it is described as 'familiar,' but no specific citation is given — in the compendium. The citation ought to have been to Smullyan.[25] This response again mistakenly takes Quine to be claiming to have a counter-example to a formal theorem of the common systems. (And if Quine *had* claimed that (12) and (14) constitute a counter-example to (17), it would have sufficed to point out that one is not required, just because one recognizes an expression to be a real singular term, to recognize it as legitimately substitutable for variables in all contexts. This point has been noted already in the exposition of the critique, but the response under discussion seems to miss it.) Nonetheless, response (F) is worthy of more extended attention.

II.3 Smullyanism or neo-Russellianism:

While responses (A)-(E) are entirely skew to Quine's line of argument, response (F) (when fully articulated) makes tangential contact with it, and shows that a minor addition or amendment to critique as expounded so far is called for. Another reason response (F) calls for more attention than the others is that for a couple of decades it was the conventional wisdom among modal logicians. It was endorsed not only by (in chronological order) Smullyan, Fitch, and Marcus, but also by Arthur Prior and others. It was the topic of two talks at the famous 1962 Helsinki conference and was put forward in major and minor encyclopedias.[26] Yet another reason response (F) calls for more attention than the

---

25 An earlier paper by the author of the compendium, 'Extensionality,' *Mind* **69** (1960) 55-62, reprinted in Linsky, ed., gives a more concise statement of the response in its last paragraph, where a footnote acknowledges the author's teacher Frederic Fitch. The latter, in his 'The Problem of the Morning Star and the Evening Star,' *Philosophy of Science* **16** (1949) 137-41, and 'Attribute and Class,' in M. Farber, ed., *Philosophic Thought in France and the United States* (Buffalo: University Press 1950), 640-7, acknowledges Smullyan. (See footnote 4 in the former, footnote 12 in the latter, and the text to which they are attached.)

26 The major one being P. Weiss, ed., *The Encyclopedia of Philosophy*, six volumes, (New York: MacMillan 1967), and the minor one the collection of survey articles, R. Klibansky, ed., *Contemporary Philosophy*, four volumes (Firenze: Editrice

others is that it represents an early attempt to apply a theory of reference distinguishing names from descriptions to the interpretation of
modal logic; understanding why this attempt was unsatisfactory should
lead to increased appreciation of more successful later attempts.

The ideas on reference involved derive from Russell. The writings
of Ramsey, alluded to in passing in the compendium, and of Carnap,
with whom the author of the compendium at one time studied, may
have served to transmit Russell's influence, though of course Russell
himself was still writing on reference in the 1950s, and still living in
the 1960s, and should not be considered a remote historical figure like
Locke or Mill. But whether his influence on them was direct or indi-
rect, Smullyan's disciples are unmistakably Russell's epigones, even
though they seldom directly quote him or cite chapter and verse from
his writings.[27]

The Smullyanite response, it will be seen, splits into two parts, one
pertaining to descriptions, the other to names. The theory of descriptions presupposed by the Smullyanites is simply the very well known
theory of Russell. The theory of names presupposed is the less well
known theory Russell always took as a foil to his theory of descriptions.
This is perhaps best introduced by contrasting it with the theory of
Frege, according to which the reference of a name to its bearer is *descriptively mediated*, and accomplished by the name having the same meaning as some description uniquely true of the bearer. The theory of Russell
is the diametrically opposed one whereby the reference of a name to
its bearer is *absolutely immediate*, in a sense implying that the meaning
of a name is simply its bearer, from which it follows that two names
having the same bearer have the same meaning. It is taken to follow

---

Nuova Italia 1968). The former contains Prior, 'Logic, Modal,' **V** 5-12; while the
latter contains Marcus, 'Modal Logic,' **I** 87-101. The conference talks are to be
found in the previously cited proceedings, Marcus' 'Classes and Attributes in
Extended Modal Systems,' 123-36, and Prior's 'Is the Concept of Referential
Opacity Really Necessary?,' 189-99. Another advocate of closely related ideas
has been J. Myhill.

27 Let me not fail to cite chapter and verse myself. For the most relevant pages of
the most recently reprinted work, see *The Philosophy of Logical Atomism*, (La Salle:
Open Court 1985), 113-5.

('compositionality' being tacitly assumed) that two sentences involving two different names with the same bearer, but otherwise the same, have the same meaning, and hence the same truth value (with one sole exception, usually left tacit, the exception for meta-linguistic contexts; that is, for those sentences, usually involving quotation, where the names are being mentioned as words rather than being used to refer).

This theory is Russell's account of how names *in an ideal sense* would function. While Russell illustrated his theory by examples involving names *in the ordinary sense*, he actually more or less agreed with Frege about their meaning (so that the Fregean theory is often known as the Frege-Russell theory). Moreover, he held that ordinary, complex things are *not even capable of being given* names in his ideal sense; that names in the ideal sense could be given only to special, simple things (such as sense data). There is an ambiguity running through the writings of all the Smullyanites as to whether they do or do not wish to claim that names in the ordinary sense function as names in the ideal sense. But they do unambiguously wish to claim, contrary to Russell, that whether or not they are already in existence, names in an ideal sense *can at least be introduced* for ordinary things. For this reason, while the Smullyanites may be called 'Russellians,' it is perhaps better to add the distinguishing prefix 'neo-.'

So much for the background assumptions of response (F). Its further articulation has several components:

(F0)   *Quine's example is ambiguous, since the key terms 'the morning star' and 'the evening star' might be either mere definite descriptions or genuine proper names.*

(F1a)   *If the key phrases are taken to be descriptions, then they are only apparently and not really singular terms, and (12) is only apparently and not really a singular identity, so one gets only an apparent and not a real counter-example to (17).*

(F1b)   *Moreover, though the foregoing already suffices, it may be added that (13) and (14) are ambiguous, and it is not unambiguously the case that they are of opposite truth value, the former true and the latter false, as the example claims.*

(F2)   *If the key phrases are taken to be names, then (14) means the very same thing as, and is every bit as true as, (13), contrary to what the example claims.*

47

To dispose of the issue (F0) of ambiguity, the example may be re-stated twice:

(12a) Hesperus is Phosphorus.
(13a) Necessarily, Phosphorus is Phosphorus.
(14a) Necessarily, Hesperus is Phosphorus.
(12b) The brightest star of the evening is the brightest star of the morning.
(13b) Necessarily, the brightest star of the morning is the brightest star of the morning.
(14b) Necessarily, the brightest star of the evening is the brightest star of the morning.

II.4 Quine's rebuttal to neo-Russellianism on descriptions:

The main claim (F1a) of the descriptions side of the Smullyanite response is immediate from Russell's theory, on which (12b) really abbreviates something more complex involving quantifiers:

(12c) There exists a unique brightest star of the evening and
       there exists a unique brightest star of the morning, and
       whatever is a brightest star of the evening and
       whatever is a brightest star of the morning,
       the former is the same as the latter.

The subsidiary claim (F1b) is also almost immediate, since on Russell's theory in all but the simplest cases expressions involving descriptions involve ambiguities of 'scope,' and for instance there is one disambiguation of (14b) that follows by (17) from (12c):

(14c) There exists a unique brightest star of the evening and
       there exists a unique brightest star of the morning, and
       whatever is a brightest star of the evening and
       whatever is a brightest star of the morning,
       necessarily the former is the same as the latter.

In rebuttal to all this, the main point is that the example was *not* intended as a counter-instance to (17) or any other theorem of the common systems, but as an illustration of an obstacle to reducing *de re* to *de dicto* modality, so that response (F1a) is wholly irrelevant.

Response (F1b) is partly relevant, however, because it does show that the example needs to be worded more carefully if the Russellian theory of descriptions is assumed. The strategy against which the example was directed was that of defining $\Box Fx$ to hold of a thing if and only if $\Box Ft$ holds where t is a term referring to that thing. But assuming the Russellian theory of descriptions, there is actually more than one strategy here (when t is a description) because $\Box Ft$ is ambiguous between a 'narrow' or a 'wide' reading.

Also the predicate $\Box Fx$ used in the example, 'Necessarily x is the brightest star of the morning' is similarly ambiguous. To eliminate this last ambiguity, take the predicate to be something like 'Necessarily, (if x exists then) x is the brightest star of the morning.' Then on the narrow-scope reading $\Box Ft$ and $\Box Fs$ boil down to:

(13c)   Necessarily, if there exists a unique brightest star of the morning then it is the brightest star of the morning.

(14c)   Necessarily, if there exists a unique brightest star of the evening then it is the brightest star of the morning.

So in this case the reduction strategy fails for *the reason originally given*, since (13c) and (14c) are of opposite truth-value, the former being true and the latter false. But on the wide-scope reading $\Box Ft$ and $\Box Fs$ boil down instead to:

(13d)   There exists a unique brightest star of the morning and necessarily, (if it exists then) it is the brightest star of the morning.

(14d)   There exists a unique brightest star of the evening and necessarily, (if it exists then) it is the brightest star of the morning.

In this case the reduction strategy fails for *a more basic reason*, since (13d) and (14d) themselves still involve unreduced *de re* modalities. The claim that the strategy breaks down thus does not have to be retracted, though the explanation *why* it does so needs to be reworded.

Response (F1b) is almost the only significant response to Quine in the early literature not reproduced in the compendium, and for Quine's own statement of a rebuttal to it we need to look beyond his commentary at the colloquium. We find the following formulation, where "nonsubstitutive position" means a position, such as that of x in $\square Fx$, where different terms referring to the same thing are not freely intersubstitutable:

> [W]hat answer is there to Smullyan? Notice to begin with that if we are to bring out Russell's distinction of scopes we must make two contrasting applications of Russell's contextual definition of description [as in the (c) versions versus the (d) versions]. But, when the description is in a non-substitutive position, one of the two contrasting applications of the contextual definition [namely, the (d) versions] is going to require quantifying into a non-substitutive position. So the appeal to scopes of descriptions does not justify such quantification, it just begs the question.[28]

II.5 Neo-Russellianism on Names:

Response (F2) is immediate assuming the neo-Russellian theory of names. Indeed, what neo-Russellianism assumes about names is more than enough to guarantee that they would have all the properties required of canonical terms.[29] Thus whereas in rebuttal to (F1) Quine did not have to reject Russell's theory of descriptions, he does have to reject the neo-Russellian theory of names.

Response (F2) is *so* immediate assuming the neo-Russellian theory that it is stated without elaboration by Smullyan and his early disciple Fitch as if it were supposed to be self-evident.[30] Elaboration is provided by later disciples in the compendium and elsewhere. The elaboration in Prior's talk at the 1962 Helsinki conference is of especial interest

---

28 Reply to Sellars, in Davidson and Hintikka, 338. This 1969 formulation is the earliest adequate one known to me, the rebuttal even in the 1961 version of 'Reference and Modality' being inadequate.

29 As was pointed out in Kripke's last few remarks in the discussion at the colloquium. Quine seems to accept the observation in his last remark. Marcus had apparently ceased to follow by this point.

30 Fitch, 'The Problem of the Morning Star and the Evening Star,' explicitly claims that Quine's contention is "clearly" false if the key expression are taken to be names.

because it anticipates in a partial way a significant later contribution to the theory of reference.

Since this has not hitherto been widely noted, I digress to quote the relevant passage:

> It is not necessary, I think, for philosophers to argue very desperately about what is in fact 'ordinary' and what is not; but let us say that *a name in Russell's strict sense* is a simple identifier of an object ...
>
> [T]here is no reason why the same expression, whether it be a single word like 'This' or 'Tully,' or a phrase like 'The man who lives next door' or 'The man at whom I am pointing,' should not be used sometimes as a name in Russell's strict sense and sometimes not. If 'The man who lives next door' is being so used, and successfully identifies a subject of discourse, then 'The man who lives next door is a heavy smoker' would be true if and only if the subject thus identified *is* a heavy smoker, even if this subject is in a fact a woman and doesn't live next door but only works there. And if 'Tully,' 'Cicero,' 'The Morning Star' and 'The Evening Star' are all being so used, then 'Tully is Cicero' and 'The Morning Star is the Evening Star' both express necessary truths, to the effect that a certain object is identical with itself.[31]

The distinctive part of the passage, not in the founder or other members of the Smullyanite school, is the middle, where it is suggested that even an expression that is *not* a name in the ordinary sense may sometimes *function as* a name. This is a different point from the trivial observation that names often have descriptive *etymologies*, and those familiar with the later literature will recognize how what is said about 'the man who lives next door' partially anticipates what was later to be said about 'referential' as opposed to 'attributive' uses of descriptions.

II.6 Quine's rebuttal:

The elaboration in Marcus's talk at the same conference, a kind of sequel to the compendium, is of especial interest because it makes more explicit than any other published Smullyanite work the implication

---

31 Prior, 'Is the Concept of Referential Opacity Really Necessary?,' 194-5. Prior was from Balliol, and I have heard it asserted — though I cannot confirm it from my own knowledge — that there was a tradition of setting examples of this kind on undergraduate examinations at Oxford in the 1960s.

that was to be most emphatically rejected by later work in the theory of reference: the *epistemological* implication that discoveries like (14a) are not 'empirical' (at least not in a non-quibbling sense), and are not properly *astronomical* discoveries:

> [T]o discover that we have alternative proper names for the same object we turn to a lexicon, or, in the case of a formal language, to the meaning postulates.... [O]ne doesn't investigate the planets, but the accompanying lexicon.[32]

The same thought had been expressed in slightly different words — 'dictionary' for 'lexicon,' for instance — in the discussion at the colloquium.[33] The picture underlying such remarks had been sketched in the compendium itself:

> For suppose we took an inventory of all the entities countenanced as things by some particular culture through its own language ... And suppose we randomized as many whole numbers as we needed for a one-to-one correspondence, and thereby tagged each thing. This identifying tag is a proper name of the thing.[34]

To talk of an 'inventory,' and especially to presuppose that we know how many numbers would be 'needed for a one-to-one correspondence,' is to assume that we are dealing with a known number of unproblematically identifiable items. If it is a matter of applying tags to such items, then of course we should be able to keep a record of when we have assigned multiple tags to a single one of them, though our record would perhaps more colloquially be called a 'catalogue' than an 'accompanying lexicon' or set of 'meaning postulates.'

---

32 'Classes and Attributes in Extended Modal Systems,' 132. Note the characteristically Carnapian expression "meaning postulates."

33 For the published version, too familiar to bear quoting again, see Wartofsky, 115. This is one of the parts of the discussion where comparison with the *verbatim* transcript could be most illuminating. It is a shame that the scholarly public should be denied access to so significant an historical document.

34 Wartofsky, 83-4. This passage has sometimes been misleadingly cited in the later literature as if it were unambiguously about ordinary names in ordinary language.

The rebuttal to the Smullyanites on names consists in observing that what is said in the last few quotations is false. Take first Prior. If one defines 'names in the strict sense' as expressions with the magical property of presenting their bearers so absolutely immediately as to leave no room for empirical questions of identity, then there never have been in any historically actual language and never can be in any humanly possible language any such things as 'names in the strict sense.' As Russell himself noted, even '*this* is the same as *this*,' where one points to the same object twice, is not a linguistic and non-empirical truth, if the object in question is complex, and one points to a different component each time.

Take now the compendium and its sequel. Assigning names to heavenly bodies may be like tagging, but it is not like tagging individuals *from among a known number of unproblematically identifiable items*, since we always have unresolved questions before us about the identity of asteroids or comets, as Frege noted long ago. And to resolve such questions one must investigate not some 'accompanying lexicon' or 'meaning postulates,' but the planet(oid)s themselves.

In brief, the following have the same status as (6) and (6') respectively, and not as (5) and (5'):

(12a)   Hesperus is Phosphorus.
(12a') In modern English, 'Hesperus' and 'Phosphorus' refer to the same thing.

Quine's own formulation of this rebuttal is almost too well known to bear quotation. But while what Quine *means* is what I have just said, what Quine *says* may be open to quibbles, since taken with pedantic literalness it would seem to be about (12a') rather than (12a):

> We may tag the planet Venus, some fine evening, with the proper name 'Hesperus.' We may tag the same planet again, some day before sunrise, with the proper name 'Phosphorus.' When at last we discover that we have tagged the same planet twice, our discovery is empirical. And not because the proper names were descriptions.[35]

---

35 Wartofsky, 101. Quine surely means that (12a') is not just a *linguistic* empirical discovery but a properly *astronomical* empirical discovery. By contrast, Marcus

III Quine's Lessons

III.1 Hints from Quine for the formal logic of modalities:

With the wisdom of hindsight it can be seen that there are several important lessons about modality and reference directly taught or indirectly hinted at in Quine's critique. For modal logic, the first lesson from Quine is that strict or (as many have called it) 'logical' modality and subjunctive or (as we now call it) 'metaphysical' modality are distinct. A further lesson is that quantification into contexts of strict modality is difficult or impossible to make sense of. A yet further lesson is that quantification into contexts of subjunctive modality is virtually indispensable.

This last lesson is not as explicitly or emphatically taught as the other two, and moreover Quine's remarks are flawed by a tendency to conflate subjunctive or 'metaphysical' modality with scientific or 'physical' modality — as if we could not speak in the subjunctive of counterfactual hypotheses to the effect that the laws of science or physics were violated. But due allowance being made for this flaw, I believe that the work of Quine, supplemented by that of his student Føllesdal, gives a broad hint pointing in the right direction.

Føllesdal's treatment of the topic begins by quoting and stressing the importance of some of Quine's remarks about the question of the meaningfulness of quantification into contexts of subjunctive modality:

> It concerns ... the practical use of language. It concerns, for example, the use of the contrary-to-fact conditional within a quantification.... Upon the contrary-to-fact conditional depends in turn, for instance, this definition of solubility in water: To say that an object is soluble in water is to say that it would dissolve if it were in water. In discussions in physics, naturally, we need quantifications containing the clause 'x is soluble in water.'[36]

---

in Wartofsky, 115, distinguishes "such linguistic" inquiry as leads to discoveries like (12a′) from "properly empirical" methods such as lead to discoveries about orbits.

36 The quotation from Quine is from 'Reference and Modality,' antepenultimate paragraph. The work of Føllesdal where it is quoted is 'Quantification into Causal Contexts,' in R.S. Cohen and M.W. Wartofsky, eds., *Boston Studies in the Philosophy*

Such passages stop just short of saying, what I think is true, that while quantification into contexts of strict modality may be nonsense, quantification into contexts of subjunctive modality is so widespread in scientific theory and commonsense thought that we could not abandon it as nonsensical even if we wanted to.

Putting the lessons cited together, it follows that there is a difference between strict and subjunctive modality as to what expressions should be accepted as meaningful formulas and so *a fortiori* as to what formulas should be accepted as correct laws. The strictly or 'logically' possible, *what it is not self-contradictory to say actually is,* and the subjunctively or 'metaphysically' possible, *what could potentially have been,* differ in the *formalism* appropriate to each.

III.2 *A hint from Quine for the theory of reference of names:*

The article on modal logic in the minor encyclopedia alluded to earlier devotes a section to objections, of which the very first (3.1) is Quine's morning star example. In the next section the following is said:

> Before proceeding to a summary of recent work in modal logic which is directed toward clear solutions to [such] problems ... it is important to realize that the perplexities about interpretation can only be understood in terms of certain presuppositions held by Quine and others which I will call "the received view" (rv).

A bit later one finds the assertion that: "The Russellian theory of descriptions and the distinction between proper names and descriptions is rejected by rv." This is immediately followed by the assertion that the morning star example (3.1) is "resolved on Russellian analysis as was shown by Smullyan ... and others," and somewhat later by the insistence that "The usefulness of the theory of descriptions and the distinction between descriptions and purely referential names was

---

of Science, II (New York: Humanities Press 1965), 263-74; reprinted in Linsky, ed., 52-62. Føllesdal's final footnote suggests that "causal essentialism" is better off than "logical essentialism," and that Quine's own proposal to treat dispositions as inhering structural traits of objects is a form of "causal essentialism."

argued long before it proved applicable to modal logic," so that one cannot simply reject them, as Quine is alleged to do.[37]

Now some of this account is quite correct, since the theory of descriptions and of the distinction between them and names as one finds it in the compendium, for instance, did not originate there, or even with Smullyan, who first applied it to the interpretation and defense of modal logic, but was indeed argued by Russell long before. But some of this account is quite incorrect. It is *not* true that Quine's rebuttal to Smullyan on descriptions requires rejection of Russell's theory of descriptions.[38] And it is not unambiguously true that Quine's rebuttal to Smullyan on names requires rejection of "the distinction between descriptions and proper names". It is true that it requires rejection of *the neo-Russellian conception* of that distinction, but it is *not* true that Quine insists rejecting *any* distinction between descriptions and proper names. This should be clear from the last half-sentence of the rebuttal quoted earlier: "And not because the proper names were descriptions."

Before Quine, difficulties with the theory that the reference of a name to its bearer is absolutely immediate had been recognized by Føllesdal and Alonzo Church.[39] And before Quine, difficulties with the theory that the reference of a name to its bearer is descriptively

---

37 Klibansky, 91ff. This echoes Fitch, 'Attribute and Class,' where it is said (553) that: "Smullyan has shown that there is no real difficulty if the phrase [*sic*] 'the Morning Star' and 'the Evening Star' are regarded either as proper names or as descriptive phrases in Russell's sense." The syntactic ambiguity in this last formulation as to whether "in Russell's sense" is supposed to modify "proper names" as well as "descriptive phrases" matches the ambiguity in the formulation quoted earlier as to whether "Russellian" is supposed to modify "the distinction between proper names and descriptions" as well as "theory of descriptions." The ambiguity is appropriate, since the theory of names in question is *neo*-Russellian.

38 Though this may not yet have been made clear at the time the encyclopedia article was written, since the formulation of the rebuttal I have quoted dates from two years later.

39 See Føllesdal, §17, 96ff. of *Referential Opacity and Modal Logic*, doctoral dissertation, Harvard, 1961; reprinted as *Filosofiske Problemer*, **32** (Oslo: Universitetsforlaget 1966). Church, review in the *Journal of Symbolic Logic* **15** (1950) 63. Both address Smullyan and Fitch.

mediated had also been recognized.[40] But before Quine, those who recognized the difficulties with the absolute immediacy theory generally either did not take them to be decisive or took them to be arguments for the descriptive mediation theory, and vice versa. But if the first lesson of Quine's critique for the theory of reference is that the neo-Russellian theory of names is untenable, the last-half sentence of his rebuttal suggests a second lesson, that this first lesson is *not* in and of itself an argument for the Fregean theory. Putting these lessons together, it is *not* to be assumed that there are just two options; there is space for a third alternative.

III.3 Formal differences between logical and metaphysical modality:

A few words may be in order about post-Quinine work on 'logical' or strict versus 'metaphysical' or subjunctive modalities. The *locus classicus* for the distinction is of course 'Naming and Necessity,' but my concern here will be with *formal* differences, which are not what was of primary concern there. Three apparent such differences have emerged.

First, there is the difference at the predicate level. The conventional apparatus allows *de re* modalities, as in $\Box Rxy$, but does not allow application of different modalities to the different places of a many-place relation. The conclusion that, if one is concerned with logical modality, then the conventional apparatus *goes too far* when it allows *de re* modality, has been endorsed on lines not unrelated to Quine's by a number of subsequent contributors to modal logic, a notable recent example being Hartry Field.[41] The complementary conclusion that, if one is con-

---

40 For work on difficulties with the Fregean theory in the 1950s and early 1960s, see the discussion in 'Naming and Necessity,' and J. Searle's article on 'Proper Names and Descriptions' in Weiss, **VI** 487-91. The doctrines in 'Naming and Necessity' were first presented in seminars in 1963-64, and whereas that work apologizes for being spotty in its coverage of the literature of the succeeding years, it is pretty thorough in its discussion of the relevant literature (work of P. Geach, P. Strawson, P. Ziff, and others) from the immediately preceding years. (Searle discusses work of yet another contributor, Elizabeth Anscombe.)

41 In, *Realism, Mathematics and Modality* (Oxford: Basil Blackwell 1989), chapter 3. Field also cites several expressions of the same or related views from the earlier

cerned with metaphysical modality, then the conventional apparatus of quantified modal logic *does not go far enough*, when it disallows the application of different modalities to the different places of a many-place relation, has also been advanced by a number of modal logicians, a notable recent example being Max Creswell.[42] (What is at issue in the latter connection is that a two-place predicate *Rxy* may correspond to a phrase with two verbs, such as '*x* is richer than *y* is,' each of which separately can be left in the indicative or put in a non-indicative mood, as in '*x* would have been richer than *y* is' contrasting with '*x* would have been richer than *y* would have been,' so as to allow *cross-comparison* between how what is is, and how what could have been would or might have been.)

Second, there may well be a formal difference already at the sentential level. For logical modality, at least in some of its versions or variants, *iterated* modalities make good sense. I allude here again to work on intensional mathematics and provability logic, where being unprovable is to be distinguished from being *provably* unprovable. For metaphysical modality, it is much less clear that iteration makes sense. In Prior's well-known work on systems combining subjunctive mood operators with past and future tense operators, for instance, iterated modal operators collapse, unless separated by temporal operators: There is no distinction recognized between what is as of today possibly possible and what is as of today possible, though there is a distinction between what as of yesterday it was possible would be possible as of today and what after all is possible as of today. In later work also on the inter-

---

literature, and such citations could in a sense be carried all the way back to the 'principle of predication' in G. H. von Wright, *An Essay in Modal Logic* (Amsterdam: North Holland 1951).

42 In *Entities and Indices* (Dordrecht: Kluwer 1990). Cresswell also cites several expressions of the same or related views from the earlier literature, and such citations could in a sense be carried all the way back to D. K. Lewis, 'Anselm and Actuality,' *Noûs* 4 (1970) 175-88. This is the earliest relevant publication known to me, but its author has suggested that there was very early unpublished work on the topic by A. P. Hazen and by D. Kaplan. The parallel phenomenon for tense in place of mood was noted even earlier by P. Geach.

action of mood and tense the purely modal part of the logic adopted amounts to S5, which collapses iterated modalities.[43]

Third, there is the difference that while logical possibility does not admit of degrees — a theory cannot be just a little bit inconsistent — metaphysical possibility seems to, with some possibilities being more remote than others. At any rate, this is the thought that underlies theories of counterfactuals since the pioneering work of R. Stalnaker.[44] In particular, miraculous possibilities, involving violations of the laws of physics, are in general more remote than non-miraculous possibilities, a fact that may make the error of earlier writers in associating counterfactuals with *physical* necessity in some respects a less serious one.

Thus there is a fair amount of work that has been — or can be construed as — exploration of the formal differences between the two kinds of modality. As apparent formal differences accumulate, the situation comes to look like this: There is one philosophically coherent enterprise of logical modal logic, attempting to treat in the object language what classical logic treats in the meta-language; there is another philosophically coherent enterprise of metaphysical modal logic, attempting to do for grammatical mood something like what temporal logic does for grammatical tense; there is a mathematically coherent field of non-classical logics dealing with technical questions about both these plus intuitionistic, temporal, and other logics; but there is no coherent field broad enough to include both kinds of 'modal logic,' but still narrower than non-classical logic as a whole. In this sense, *there is no coherent enterprise of 'modal logic'* — a conclusion that may be called Quinesque.

---

43 See Prior, *Past, Present, and Future* (Oxford: Clarendon Press 1967), chapter VII, and among later work R. H. Thomason, 'Combinations of Tense and Modality,' in Gabbay and Guenthner, 135-65. The purely modal part is also S5 for virtually all the workers there cited, as well as later ones like A. Zanardo.

44 'A Theory of Conditionals,' in N. Rescher, ed., *Studies in Logical Theory* (Oxford: Basil Blackwell 1968), 98-112. This feature becomes even more prominent in later work on the same topic by D. K. Lewis and others.

III.4 New alternatives in the theory of reference for names:

A few words may also be in order about post-Quinine work on theories of reference for names that reject both the Fregean *descriptive mediation* and the neo-Russellian *absolute immediacy* views. The *locus classicus* for such an alternative is of course again 'Naming and Necessity.' One can perhaps best begin to bring out how the new theory of that work relates to the old theory of Quine's opponents by considering what similarities and differences are emphasized in the only early extended response to the new theory by the one former adherent of the old theory who remained living and active in the field through the 1970s and 1980s and beyond.[45]

First, the one area of real agreement between the new theory and the old is emphasized, that both are 'direct' (in the minimal sense of 'anti-Fregean') theories; and the new theory is praised for providing additional arguments:

> Kripke's criticism of the 'Frege-Russell' view ... is presented ... Among the arguments he musters are that competent speakers communicate about individuals, using their names, without knowing or being able to produce any uniquely identifying conditions short of circular ones ... Unlike descriptions, proper names are indifferent to scope in modal ('metaphysical') contexts.... Contra Frege he points up the absurdity of claiming that counterfactuals force a shift in the reference of a name.

Second, another area of apparent agreement, over the 'necessity of identity' (in some sense), is also emphasized, with the new theory again being praised for providing additional arguments:

> It is one of the achievements of Kripke's account, with its effective use of the theory of descriptions, the theory of proper names, the distinction between metaphysical and epistemological modalities (for example, necessary vs. a priori), that it provides us with a more coherent and satisfactory analysis of statements which appear to assert contingent identities.

---

45 Unfortunately this comes in the form of a review of a book by a third party, and is subject to the limitations of such a form. The third party is Linsky; the book is his *Names and Descriptions* (Chicago: University of Chicago Press 1977); the review is by Marcus, *Philosophical Review* **87** 497-504. The three quotations to follow come from 498, 501, and 502-3.

Third, the contribution most praised is the provision of a novel account of the mechanism by which a name achieves reference to its bearer:

> Kripke provided us with a 'picture' which is far more coherent than what had been available. It preserves the crucial differences between names and descriptions implicit in the theory of descriptions. By distinguishing between fixing the meaning and fixing the reference, between rigid and nonrigid designators, many nagging puzzles find a solution. The causal or chain of communications theory of names (imperfect and rudimentary as it is) provides a plausible genetic account of how ordinary proper names can acquire unmediated referential use.

All this amounts to something approaching an adequate acknowledgment of substantial *additions* by the new theory to the old, but what needs to be understood is that the new theory in fact proposes substantial *amendments* also. The new theory is not 'direct' in anywhere near as extreme a sense as the old. On the new theory, which is a 'third alternative,' the reference of a name to its bearer is neither descriptively mediated nor absolutely immediate, but rather is *historically mediated*, accomplished through a chain of usage leading back from present speakers to the original bestower of the name. Also the new theory does not endorse the 'necessity of identity' in anything like so broad a sense as does the old theory, or on anything like the same grounds. On the new theory, 'Hesperus is Phosphorus' is only subjunctively or metaphysically necessary — not strictly or logically necessary like 'Phosphorus is Phosphorus.' And moreover the metaphysical necessity of identity is the conclusion of a separate argument involving considerations peculiar to subjunctive contexts, about *cross-comparison* between actual and counterfactual situations — not an immediate corollary or special case of some general principle of the intersubstitutability of coreferential names in all (except meta-linguistic) contexts.[46]

---

46 In this connection mention may be made of one serious historical inaccuracy — of a kind extremely common when authors quote themselves from memory decades after the fact — to be found in the book review, where it is said that the compendium maintained "that unlike different but coreferential descriptions, two proper names of the same object were intersubstitutable in modal contexts" (502). In actual fact, in the compendium it is *repeatedly* asserted that two proper names of the same object are intersubstitutable in *all* contexts.

The gap between the old, neo-Russellian theory and the new, anti-Russellian theory is large enough to have left space for the development of several even newer fourth and fifth alternatives, semi-, or demi-semi-, or hemi-demi-semi-Russellian intermediate views, of which the best known is perhaps Nathan Salmon's.[47] These differ from the Kripkean, anti-Russellian theory in that they want to say that in *some* sense 'Hesperus is Phosphorus' and 'Phosphorus is Phosphorus' have the same 'semantic content.'[48] They differ from the Smullyanite, neo-Russellian theory in that there is full awareness that in *some* sense assertive utterance of 'Hesperus is Phosphorus' can make a difference to the 'epistemic state' of the hearer in a way that assertive utterance of 'Phosphorus is Phosphorus' cannot. How it could be that utterances expressing the same semantic content have such different potential effects on epistemic states is in a sense the *main* problem addressed by such theories. My concern here is not to offer any evaluation, or even any exposition, of the solutions proposed, but only to point out that they all operate in the space between Fregeanism and neo-Russellianism — and therefore in a space of whose existence Quine was one of the first to hint.

III.5 Have the lessons been learned?

It would be absurd to claim that Quine anticipated all the many important developments in modal logic or the theory of reference to which I have been alluding. But it is not absurd to suggest that some of them might have been arrived at sooner if the reaction to Quine's critique had been more attentive.

Is the matter of more than antiquarian interest today? Well, certainly there are many workers in philosophical logic and philosophy of lan-

---

47 *Frege's Puzzle* (Cambridge, MA: MIT Press 1986). While the early Marcus followed Smullyan, the later Marcus has developed in response to Kripke an idiosyncratic theory that may be described as intermediate in degree of Russellianism between Salmon's and Smullyan's. See her 'Some Revisionary Proposals about Belief and Believing,' *Philosophy and Phenomenological Research* **50** (Supplement) 133-53.

48 For Kripke's rejection of this view, see the closing paragraphs of the preface to the second edition of 'Naming and Necessity.'

guage (only a few of whom I have had occasion to mention) who have long since fully absorbed every lesson there was to be learned from Quine. And yet, scanning the literature, it seems to me that specialists in the relevant areas do not always clearly express these lessons in their writings, and that (surely partly in consequence) many non-specialists interested in *applying* theories of modality or reference to other areas have not yet fully learned these lessons.

Take modal logic first. It is said that when Cauchy lectured on the distinction between convergent and divergent series at the Académie des Sciences, Laplace rushed home to check the series in his *Mécanique Céleste*. But when Kripke lectured on the distinction between logical and metaphysical modality, modal logicians did not rush home to check which conclusions hold for the one, which conclusions hold for the other, and which result from a fallacious conflation of the two. It is a striking fact that the basic article — an article written by two very eminent authorities — on modal logic in that standard reference work, the multi-volume encyclopedia mistitled a 'handbook' of philosophical logic makes no mention at all of any such distinction and its conceivable relevance to choosing among the plethora of competing modal systems surveyed.[49]

No wonder then that workers from other areas interested in *applying* modal logic seem often not fully informed about formal differences between the two kinds of modality. To cite only the example I know best, consider philosophy of mathematics, and debates over nominalist attempts to provide a modal reinterpretation of applied mathematics, where quantification into modal contexts is unavoidable. Those on the nominalist side have quite often supposed that they could get away with quantifying into contexts of *logical* modality, while those on the anti-nominalist side have quite often supposed that anyone wishing to make use of modality must stick to the traditional formal systems, which *do not allow for cross-comparison*. Both suppositions are in error.[50]

---

49 R. A. Bull and K. Segerberg, 'Basic Modal Logic,' in Gabbay and Guenthner, 1-88. Other articles in the same work, some of which I have already cited, *do* recognize the importance of the distinction.

50 It would be out of place to enter into technicalities here. See J. Burgess and G. Rosen, *A Subject with No Object* (Oxford: Oxford University Press 1997).

Take the theory of reference now. Here a great many people seem to have difficulty discerning the important differences among distinct anti-Fregean theories. To mention again the example I know best, many nominalists seem to think that the work of Kripke, David Kaplan, Hilary Putnam, and others has established something implying that it is impossible to make reference to mathematical or other causally inert objects.[51]

Such misunderstandings are encouraged by the common sloppy use by specialists of ambiguous labels like 'causal theory of reference,' and even those who carefully avoid 'causal theory' in favor of 'direct theory' are often sloppy in their usage of the latter, encouraging other confusions. Of late, not only has the confused opinion become quite common that Quine's critique has somehow been answered by the new theory of names (the one coming from 'Naming and Necessity'); but so has the even more confused opinion that Quine's critique was already answered by an old theory of names (the one coming from Russell through Smullyan to the compendium); and so too has the most confused opinion of all, that there is no important difference between the old and new theories. Confusion of this kind is found both among those who think of themselves as sympathizers with 'the' theory in question,[52] and among those who think of themselves as opponents of 'it.'[53] The latter cite weaknesses of the old theory as if pointing them out

---

51 In actual fact, on Kripke's theory, for instance, a name can be given to any object that can be described, not excluding mathematical objects. But again see Burgess and Rosen. (The theory of P. Geach probably deserves and the theory of M. Devitt certainly deserves the label 'causal,' and does have nominalistic implications.)

52 For comparatively moderate instance see the review by S. Lavine, *British Journal for the Philosophy of Science* **46** (1995) 267-74.

53 For an extreme instance see J. Hintikka and G. Sandu, 'The Fallacies of the New Theory of Reference,' *Synthese* **104** (1995) 245-83. This work acknowledges no important differences among: (i) the neo-Russellian theory of Smullyan as expounded by the early Marcus (which incidentally is erroneously attributed to Marcus as something original, ignoring the real authors Smullyan and Russell); (ii) theories adopted in reaction to Kripke by the later Marcus; and (iii) the theory of Kripke.

could refute the new theory — a striking example of how confusion over history of philosophy can lead to confusion in philosophy proper.

There is hardly a better way to sort out such confusions than by considering the relations of the old and the new theory to Quine's critique, from which therefore some people still have something to learn. Neither the old theory nor the new provides a refutation of that critique, but the reasons why are radically different in the two cases. The old theory *attempted* to refute that critique, but in doing so it arrived at consequences, notably the one made explicit in the 'lexicon' passage quoted earlier, that reduced the theory to absurdity. Quine's rebuttal, pointing out the untenability of these consequences, refuted the old theory. Quine's critique does *not* refute the new theory, but then neither does the new theory refute Quine's critique, nor does it even *attempt* to do so. The new theory *would* refute any incautious claim to the effect that 'quantification into any intensional context is meaningless,' since it shows that proper names have all the properties required of canonical terms for contexts of *subjunctive* modality. But Quine's critique was addressed to *strict* modality, and as for that, the main creator of the new theory of names has said as I do: "Quine is right."[54]

---

54 In context, what is said to be right is specifically the rebuttal to Smullyanism on names quoted earlier. See 'Naming and Necessity,' 305.

CANADIAN JOURNAL OF PHILOSOPHY
Supplementary Volume 23

On Singular Propositions

RICHARD L. CARTWRIGHT
Massachusetts Institute of Technology

I

A designator a of an object x is *rigid* in Kripke's sense if and only if (i) for every possible world w, if x exists in w, then a designates x with respect to w and (ii) there is no possible world with respect to which a designates something other than x.[1] Alternatively, but to the same effect, a is rigid just in case neither the sentence:

> a might have existed and not have been a

nor the sentence:

> Something other than a might have been a

has an interpretation on which it is true.[2] This alternative seems to me preferable: the concept of designation *with respect to a world* is difficult

---

1 I rely here on David Kaplan, 'Afterthoughts,' in Joseph Almog, John Perry, and Howard Wettstein, eds., *Themes from Kaplan* (New York/Oxford: Oxford University Press 1989), 565-614, at 569, where Kaplan quotes from a letter written by Kripke in clarification of earlier formulations. For these, see: Saul A. Kripke, *Naming and Necessity* (Cambridge, MA: Harvard University Press 1980) and 'Identity and Necessity,' in Milton K. Munitz, ed., *Identity and Individuation* (New York: New York University Press 1971), 135-64.

2 The conditions are independent: 'the actor Paul Newman' satisfies the second but not the first, and 'the x such that x = Paul Newman if he exists and x = 9 otherwise' satisfies the first but not the second.

and occasions certain problems (about which something will be said later), but these problems do not arise on this explanation. As an example of a rigid designator, Kripke cites 'Nixon': neither 'Nixon might have existed and not have been Nixon' nor 'Something other than Nixon might have been Nixon' has an interpretation on which it is true. And as it is with 'Nixon,' so it is according to Kripke with proper names in general. 'Wade Boggs' and 'William Weld,' for instance, are rigid designators; the former contrasts with 'the American League batting champion of 1987,' and the latter with 'the governor of Massachusetts in July 1997,' in the way that 'Nixon' contrasts with 'the president of the U.S. in 1970.'

Certain points must be borne in mind concerning the concept of rigid designation and the associated thesis that proper names are rigid designators.

(a) 'Designates' is to be understood in a sense according to which every result of putting a name or description for the dots in

> If and only if ... exists, then '...' designates ...

expresses a true proposition.[3] Note that this a weak sense, for it is one in which definite descriptions may designate even if, as is sometimes held, they are properly regarded as "quantified noun phrases."[4]

(b) Kripke intends the thesis that proper names are rigid designators to be compatible with the fact that most proper names are names of more than one thing. Thus it is irrelevant to the contention that 'Nixon' is a rigid designator that it designates with respect to the actual world, and hence with respect to some possible world, things other than the president of the United States in 1970. Indeed, Kripke's entire discussion of these matters proceeds under the simplifying pretence, common in philosophical discussions of reference, than no proper name designates more than one thing.[5]

---

3 The schema is a modification of one given by Kripke. See *Naming and Necessity*, 25 *n* 3.

4 For an explanation of the phrase, and of the associated view, see Stephen Neale, *Descriptions* (Cambridge, MA: MIT Press 1990), Chapter 2.

5 See *Naming and Necessity*, 7-8. Kripke does allow that a terminology "according

(c) Neither of the explanations given above is intended to make provision for terms that vary in designation with variations in context. An explanation that accommodates such terms — indexical and demonstrative expressions, for example — would be complicated, and cannot be undertaken here.

(d) When it is said e.g. that there is a possible world with respect to which 'the president of the U.S. in 1991' designates Dukakis rather than Bush, the point being made concerns the description 'the president of the U.S. in 1991' *as it is used in our language*; how, if at all, the description would be used by speakers in the circumstances envisaged is irrelevant. Consider a possible world in which 'president' means *chief justice*. What does 'the president of the U.S. in 1991' designate with respect to such a world? We are of course in no position to say, for the world has not been specified in enough detail. But notice: among such worlds is one in which 'president' means *chief justice*, and with respect to such a world 'the president of the U.S. in 1991' designates Bush.

(e) Not *only* proper names are rigid designators. In particular, some descriptions are rigid — for example, 'the even prime number,' 'the sum of 2 and 3,' 'the actual president of the U.S. in 1991,' 'the x such that $x =$ Boggs.'

(f) The classification of designators into rigid and nonrigid is of course a classification of elements of language, of certain linguistic expressions. But to determine whether a designator is rigid it is necessary to engage in reflection about the object designated. The *name* 'Shakespeare' is rigid only if the *man* Shakespeare could not have existed without being Shakespeare — or, as we might equally well say, only if it is essential to Shakespeare that he is Shakespeare. The *description* 'the author of *Hamlet*' is nonrigid if the *object* described might have existed and yet not alone have written *Hamlet* — if, that is, it is not essential to that object that it and it alone have written *Hamlet*.

(g) To be a rigid designator of an object x a term must designate x with respect to every world in which x exists, but it need not designate

---

to which uses of phonetically the same sounds to name distinct objects count as distinct names ... may have a great deal to recommend it for theoretical purposes," even though it "certainly does not agree with the most common usage."

x with respect to worlds in which x does not exist. Thus a rigid designator need not be "obstinate," in Salmon's sense.[6] A case in point is 'the actual president of the U.S. in 1991.' If Bush does not exist in a world w, nothing in w fits the description as we use it and hence it designates nothing with respect to w.[7] But what about the proper name 'Bush'? We may be inclined to say the same about it: that nothing in w fits the name as we use it, and hence that it designates nothing with respect to w. On the other hand, we may be inclined to yield to the following argument: w is a possible world in which Bush does not exist only if the sentence 'Bush does not exist' is true at w; but that in turn requires that 'Bush' designate Bush with respect to w.[8] The idea is that although nothing in w is designated by 'Bush,' something in the actual world is; we have a name for Bush, namely 'Bush,' and it is our terms whose designations are to be assessed with respect to w.[9]

This second argument demands that in assessing designation with respect to possible worlds, proper names be treated differently from descriptions. Otherwise one might equally well argue: w is a possible world in which the actual president of the U.S. in 1991 does not exist only if the sentence 'the actual president of the U.S. in 1991 does not exist' is true at w; but that in turn requires that 'the actual president of the U.S. in 1991' designate the actual president of the U.S. in 1991 with respect to w. But what is the relevant difference between proper names and descriptions? Presumably it will be said that in our use a name, in contrast with a description, has no other linguistic function than to des-

---

6 Nathan Salmon, *Reference and Essence* (Princeton, NJ: Princeton University Press 1981), 34

7 Compare Salmon, *Reference and Essence*, 35, where it is said that "singular terms formed from the variable-binding definite descriptions operator ... can denote something with respect to a given possible world only if that thing exists in the given possible world."

8 See A.D. Smith, 'Semantical Considerations on Rigid Designation,' *Mind* 96 (1987) 83-92, at 86.

9 Thus David Kaplan, 'Bob and Carol and Ted and Alice,' in J. Hintikka, J. Moravcsik, and P. Suppes, eds., *Approaches to Natural Language* (Dordrecht: Reidel 1973), 490-518, at 503.

ignate its bearer and hence is used, with respect to a possible world, as it is used in our language only if it designates with respect to that world its bearer in the actual world. And that may be true. Still, it is perhaps just there that Kripke wants to be noncommittal; for his intention is to remain neutral on the question whether e.g. 'Bush' designates Bush with respect to a world in which Bush does not exist, and yet he would acknowledge that 'Bush does not exist' is true at such a world.[10]

I think neutrality is more easily maintained by avoiding the difficult concept of designation with respect to a possible world. It was pointed out above that we may say that a designator *a* of an object *x* is *rigid* just in case neither the sentence:

> *a* might have existed and not have been *a*

nor the sentence:

> Something other than *a* might have been *a*

has an interpretation on which it is true. Let us say, analogously, that a designator *a* of *x* is *obstinate* just in case the sentence:

> *a* must have been *a*

has no reading on which it is not true. It is evident that with these definitions one may say that proper names are rigid without thereby being committed to their being obstinate.

(h) It does not follow from the thesis that proper names are rigid designators that they are mere labels, or tags — that they are "unmeaning," as Mill claimed.[11] It is compatible with Kripke's thesis that a proper name of an object should 'connote' a purely qualitative essence that distinguishes the object from all others. Such a proper name would in effect be a rigid definite description.

------

10 See *Naming and Necessity*, 78-9.

11 *A System of Logic*, I, ii, 5

The last point deserves emphasis, because it seems sometimes not to be appreciated. Kripke is sympathetic to the doctrine that proper names are mere labels, or tags. Thus in 'Identity and Necessity' he writes:

> At least if one is not familiar with the philosophical literature about this matter, one naively feels something like the following about proper names. First, if someone says "Cicero was an orator," then he uses the name 'Cicero' in that statement simply to pick out a certain object and then to ascribe a certain property to the object, namely, in this case, he ascribes to a certain man the property of having been an orator. If someone else uses another name, such as say 'Tully,' he is still speaking about the same man. One ascribes the same property, if one says "Tully was an orator," to the same man. So to speak, the fact, or state of affairs, represented by the statement is the same whether one says "Cicero is an orator" or one says "Tully is an orator." It would, therefore, seem that the function of names is *simply* to refer, and not to describe the objects so named by such properties as "being the inventor of bifocals" or "being the first Postmaster General."[12]

Nevertheless, he does not in this essay or in *Naming and Necessity* officially endorse this naive view. But his extended criticism of views according to which (roughly) proper names are disguised definite descriptions has been taken to indicate that he holds it. However that may be, what needs emphasis is that the naive view is not a consequence of the doctrine that proper names are rigid designators. Perhaps the tendency to think otherwise is encouraged by the ease with which one moves in the other direction: if proper names are mere tags, if their only semantic function is to designate their bearers, then it is hard to see how they can fail to be rigid. For consider: If anything at all is essential to an object, it is surely essential to it that it be the object it is; *it* could not have exited without being *it*. And surely also nothing other than it could have been it. So if e.g.'Shakespeare' is a mere tag, without descriptive content, then 'Shakespeare might not have been Shakespeare' will be false simply because the object designated by 'Shakespeare' could not have existed without being that object, and 'Something other than Shakespeare might have been Shakespeare' will be false simply because nothing other than that object could have been that object. It thus takes a minimum of metaphysical commitment to move from the doctrine that proper names are mere tags to the doctrine that they are rigid designators.

---

12   140

According to the naive view proper names are, as some say, directly referential, or as I prefer to say, purely designative. Whether or not Kripke held the view, a number of other philosophers have. Mill, of course; it was Russell's view prior to 1905;[13] and more recently Ruth Marcus has advocated it.[14] Even more recently a number of writers, too numerous to be cited here, have advocated it under the label 'the New Theory of Reference' or 'the Direct Reference Theory.' David Kaplan has nicely formulated what is evidently to be regarded as a consequence of the view, namely, that

> we can meaningfully speak of a thing itself — without reference either explicit, implicit, vague, or precise to individuating concepts (other than being *this* thing), defining qualities, essential attributes, or any other of the paraphernalia that enable us to distinguish one thing from another.[15]

And when in thus speaking of a thing itself, without any descriptive apparatus, we say something about the thing, we assert what Kaplan calls a *singular proposition*. The doctrine that there are such propositions is a consequence of the view that proper names are purely designative. But again it must be emphasized that the implication does not go the other way: the doctrine that there are singular propositions is consistent with a view according to which proper names are never purely designative.[16]

---

13 See *The Principles of Mathematics* (Cambridge: Cambridge University Press 1903; 2nd edn., London: Allen and Unwin 1937), esp. Appendix A; and *The Collected Papers of Bertrand Russell*, IV, *Foundations of Logic: 1903-05*, edited by Alasdair Urquhart, with the assistance of Albert C. Lewis (London and New York: Routledge 1994), Part III.

14 See her 'Modalities and Intensional Languages,' *Synthese* **13** (1961) 303-30, reprinted in *Modalities* (New York/Oxford: Oxford University Press 1993), 5-23.

15 'How to Russell a Frege-Church,' *Journal of Philosophy* **78** (1975) 716-29. Reprinted in Michael J. Loux, ed., *The Possible and the Actual* (Ithaca and London: Cornell University Press 1979) 210-24. The passage is at 217 of Loux.

16 In 'On Denoting,' *Mind* **14** (1905) 479-93, Russell gave up the doctrine that proper names are purely designative, but continued to hold that there are singular propositions. Even after his abandonment of propositions, which occurred not much later, *true* singular propositions in effect remained in his ontology, in the guise of certain 'facts,' or 'complexes.'

We thus have four doctrines: that proper names are rigid designators; that proper names are purely designative; that proper names are obstinate designators; that there are singular propositions. Neither the first nor the fourth implies any of the others; in the presence of a little metaphysics, the second implies the first, and in any case the fourth; the third implies the first, but neither of the other two. Of the four I think the doctrine that there are singular propositions is philosophically the most fundamental, and it is the one with which I shall be concerned in the remainder of this paper.

II

Suppose I say, speaking with reference to the object in my hand, "This piece of chalk is white." In so doing I say of or about the object in my hand that it is white; I predicate of it that it is white. But I also describe the object in my hand as a piece of chalk, and so it is at least plausible that the proposition I assert will not be true unless the object with reference to which I speak is in fact a piece of chalk.[17] So there appear to be two ways in which the proposition I assert may fail to be true: it will fail to be true if the object to which I refer is not white, and it will fail to be true if the object to which I refer is not a piece of chalk. It is just this that makes intelligible the familiar sort of dialogue in which, e.g., I say, "This piece of chalk is white," you say, "It's not a piece of chalk," and I respond, "Well, anyhow, it's white."[18] Here I assert of the object, whatever it really is, that it is white; I assert the singular proposition with respect to the thing in my hand that it is white. And this appears to be

---

17 It might be said that the words 'piece of chalk' serve merely to aid in the identification of the object of reference and hence that the proposition asserted requires for its truth only that the object of reference, whether or not it is a piece of chalk, be white. I am inclined to disagree, on the ground that what is said cannot correctly be said to be unqualifiedly true unless the object referred to is a piece of chalk. But I doubt that much hangs on the point.

18 Compare A.N. Whitehead, *The Concept of Nature* (Cambridge: Cambridge University Press 1920), Chapter II.

what I would have asserted had I simply said, indicating the thing in my hand, "This is white." In so doing, I would not have described the object; I would not have referred to it as the so-and-so; I would have asserted a proposition that requires for its truth only that the thing to which I referred be white. Perhaps it will be objected that the demonstrative 'this' as it figures in the imagined utterance is short for 'the object in my hand.' But surely it is not: what I would have said does not imply that I have a hand, let alone that, in this context, the referent of "this" is in it.

A certain form of expression common among philosophers is legitimate only if there are singular propositions. We may be asked to consider the proposition with respect to Shakespeare that *he* wrote *Hamlet*. On the assumption that proper names are purely designative, the proposition we are asked to consider is the proposition that Shakespeare wrote *Hamlet*. But in any case we are invited to consider a certain singular proposition, a proposition that might in the right sort of context be asserted by uttering the words 'He wrote *Hamlet*' and that Shakespeare himself might have asserted by uttering the words 'I wrote *Hamlet*.'[19]

An easy extension of this form of expression involves the use of variables. We may be asked to consider the proposition with respect to an arbitrary object x that it is (say) red-all-over. That proposition, we may be told, is incompatible with the proposition with respect to the same object x that it is green-all-over. ('Let x be any object. Then the proposition that x is red-all-over entails the proposition that x is not green-all-over.') The assumption is that for each object x, or least for each x within a certain range or category of objects, there is a unique

---

19 The form of expression discussed here is sufficiently hard to avoid that even enemies of singular propositions sometimes fall into its use. Frege, hardly a friend of singular propositions, lapses on a couple of occasions. Thus: "It is not necessary that the person who feels cold should himself give utterance to *the thought that he feels cold*. Another person can do this by using a name to designate the one who feels cold." (*Posthumous Writings*, trans. Peter Long and Roger White, with the assistance of Raymond Hargreaves [Oxford: Blackwell 1979], 134-5. My emphasis.) And: "Now everyone is presented to himself in a special and primitive way, in which he is presented to no one else. So, when Dr. Lauven has *the thought that he was wounded* ...." (B. McGuinness, ed., *Collected Papers*, trans. M. Black, *et al.* [Oxford: Blackwell 1984], 359. My emphasis.)

proposition which requires for its truth simply that x, whatever it is, be red-all-over. If there are no singular propositions, the assumption is unwarranted.

And with this extension, there also become available certain of the things Russell calls "propositional functions."[20] For instance, the propositional function x *is white* is the function that assigns to an object x the proposition that x is white: the proposition that x is white is the value of the propositional function x *is white* for the object x as argument. The universal quantification of such a propositional function is true if and only if all values of the function are true, and the existential quantification of such a function is true just in case at least one value of the function is true. Universal and existential quantifiers, at least in these limited roles, become functions of functions.

III

I have not argued that proper names are purely designative, and hence I have left open the question whether, for example, the sentence 'Clinton is a politician' expresses a singular proposition. But whether or not it is expressed by the sentence 'Clinton is a politician,' there is (so it seems to me) the singular proposition with respect to Clinton that he is a politician. Call that proposition C. A question of some interest is this: if Clinton had not existed, what would have been the truth value of C? It is sometimes held that the question has a false presupposition, namely, that even had Clinton not existed, there would have been such a proposition as C.[21] Now, I am inclined to agree that had Clinton not existed there would have been no such proposition as C; but I am also inclined to think that the question does *not* pre-

---

20 Russell did not use 'propositional function' consistently, even within the confines of a single book. I follow the use described at 508-10 of *The Principles of Mathematics*, though of course there are others in that book.

21 I *think* it is fair to attribute this view to Moore. See his Casimir Lewy, ed., *Lectures on Philosophy*, (London: Allen & Unwin 1966), 129-31.

suppose that there would have been such a proposition as C even if he had not existed.[22] But this needs explanation.

By way of an analogy, consider this question: if the Arabic numeral system had never been devised, what would have been the truth value of the sentence '2 + 3 = 5'? Some will say that had the Arabic numeral system never been devised, there would have been no such sentence as '2 + 3 = 5.' Maybe that's what should be said. But the Arabic numeral system *was* devised, and hence we *have* the sentence '2 + 3 = 5'; we can therefore ask what the truth value of that sentence is with respect to a counterfactual situation in which people do not use Arabic numerals but use, say, Roman numerals instead. The question is a sensible one even though the sentence is not itself part of the counterfactual situation. To employ the jargon of possible worlds, the question is as to the truth value of the sentence '2 + 3 = 5' at a possible world, or at a certain class of possible worlds; and it is significant even if those are possible worlds in which the sentence does not exist.

The point carries over to the proposition C. We *have* that proposition, and we may therefore inquire about its truth value with respect to a counterfactual situation in which it does not exist. If there is any remaining doubt about this, I think it can be dispelled in the following way. Our question is: if Clinton had not existed, what would have been the truth value of C? But that question comes to this: if Clinton had not existed, would he have been a politician? (Note the use of "he." I do not here assume that proper names are purely designative.) That question evidently does not presuppose that in the contemplated counterfactual situation, there would be such a proposition as C.

But once the question is thus reformulated we are apt to be faced with another objection to its legitimacy: we can sensibly ask, with respect to Clinton, whether he would have been a politician in one or another counterfactual situation only if the counterfactual situation is one in which he exists. It will be said that just as there is no question, with respect to the Socialist governor of Massachusetts in July 1997, whether he is bald, so there is no question, with respect to Clinton, whether he

---

22 On this point I have benefited from discussions with Aviv Hoffman, though he is firmly opposed to the position toward which I am inclined.

would have been a politician had he not existed. In terms of possible worlds: we can legitimately ask, concerning an object that exists in a possible world, whether in that world it is a politician; but we cannot ask such a question of an object that does not exist in that world.

We can agree that there is no question, with respect to the present Socialist governor of Massachusetts, whether he is bald. And of course there is no such thing as the singular proposition, with respect to the present Socialist governor of Massachusetts, that he is bald. But Clinton exists! We have him, just as we have the proposition C. And hence there is no failure of presupposition in asking, with respect to him, whether he would have been a politician had he not existed.

Indeed, once the question is put this way, the answer to it seems plain: if Clinton had not existed, *he* would not have been a politician. And from this it follows that if Clinton had not existed, C, the singular proposition with respect to him that he is a politician, would have been false.

This seems right. But the conclusion may have been reached too quickly. The question raised was this: supposing Clinton not to have existed, what would the truth value of C have been? The question concerns the truth value of C at a certain counterfactual situation, or class of such situations. But which situation, or class of situations? Well, we are inclined to say, any situation in which Clinton does not exist. But what this answer comes to will depend on what the semantic function of 'Clinton' is. If that name is short for some definite description, then a situation in which Clinton does not exist can be understood to be a situation in which nothing answers to the description. If, for example, 'Clinton' is short for 'the president of the U.S. in 1997,' then the supposition that Clinton does not exist is the supposition that there is no such thing as the president of the U.S. in 1997. So if in asking what the truth value of C would have been had Clinton not existed I was using 'Clinton' as short for 'the president of the U.S. in 1997,' then it might well seem that I gave the wrong answer: evidently C might have been true even though there had been no such thing as the president of the U.S. in 1997. Perhaps it is unlikely that 'Clinton' should have the sense of 'the president of the U.S. in 1997.' Still, I have not ruled out of court the view that the name is short for some definite description. Hence it might well seem that I have not shown that C would have been false had Clinton not existed.

The argument may thus seem to require that 'Clinton' be purely designative. I think it does not. But it does need restatement; the counterfactual situation, or class of such situations, with respect to which the truth value of C is to be assessed must be more carefully specified. It will not do to say simply that the situations in question are those in which Clinton does not exist. They are rather to be specified as those counterfactual situations in which a certain singular proposition is false — namely, the proposition with respect to Clinton that he exists. Here I use the name 'Clinton,' but it does not matter whether I use it purely designatively or as a disguised definite description; for the singular proposition in question *can* be specified as the proposition with respect to the president of the U.S. in 1997 that he exists. Let E be that proposition. My question is then just this: if E had been false, what would have been the truth value of C? And my answer is that if E had been false, C would have been false.

But it is necessary to face another objection. Some philosophers will say that there really is no such proposition as E. I have in mind philosophers who have no objection to singular propositions in general but who see, or think they see, a special barrier to there being such a proposition as E. If there is such a proposition as E, it is presumably contingent; but how is it possible, these philosophers ask, for E to be false? Falsity of E would mean nonexistence of its subject, and hence nonexistence of the proposition itself.

We have in effect already seen how to reply. We can agree that if there is such a proposition as E it is contingent. We can also agree that any situation with respect to which E is false is a situation in which E does not exist; that is, any possible world at which E is false is a possible world in which there is no such proposition as E. But to conclude that E could not be false is to assume that a proposition has a truth value only with respect to those situations in which it exists. And the assumption must be rejected. We have E, just as we have C. And we can evaluate it, as we can C, with respect to counterfactual situations in which it does not exist.

Sentences used to assert E are indeed peculiar. Thus the sentence 'I exist,' which I suppose Clinton might use to assert E, has the peculiarity that an assertive utterance of it is bound to be an assertion of a true proposition: no one can assertively utter the sentence, in its standard sense, and thereby say something false. But it does not follow that the proposition asserted is one that cannot be false. An assertive utterance of the sentence 'I cannot pronounce the name of the great state of Mississippi' is bound to be false. But it hardly follows that the proposition asserted is impossible.

I have in effect asserted the contingency of E. But on what ground? I have nothing better to say than that it seems to me undeniable that Clinton — that is, the president of the U.S. in 1997 — is an object x such that x might not have existed. *He* might not have existed, just as you and I might not have existed. We are all of us contingent beings. It follows from this together with what I argued earlier that C is contingent. Of course, we are doubtless prepared to argue for the contingency of C on other grounds: it is metaphysically possible that Clinton should have been a professional golfer rather than a politician. Contingency of E nevertheless suffices. But if I am right that C would have been false had E been false, then surely the same is true of, for example, the singular proposition with respect to Clinton that he is a human being. That proposition is also contingent. Contingency of the proposition is of course compatible with Clinton's being essentially a human being, for that is a matter of its being impossible that he should *exist* and yet not be a human being.

IV

The argument just given for the contingency of C and of the singular proposition with respect to Clinton that he is a human being, comes down to this: since those propositions are singular propositions with respect to Clinton, they entail E, which is itself a contingent truth; hence they are false at worlds at which E is false. If the argument is a good one, it ought to apply across the board to singular propositions with respect to Clinton; indeed, it ought to apply to singular propositions with respect to any contingent existent. I think it does. But there is a problem.

Just as we can specify C by saying that it is the proposition with respect to Clinton that he is a politician, so we can specify another singular proposition with respect to Clinton by saying that it is the proposition with respect to him that he is not a politician. And it is natural to take this second proposition to be the negation of C, a proposition which is true at a possible world w just in case C is false at w. But if C is false at worlds at which E is false, and if this second proposition is the negation of C, then it will be a singular proposition which is true at those worlds, contrary to my contention that singular propositions with respect to Clinton are false at worlds in which he does not exist.

What must be said, I think is that the proposition with respect to Clinton that he is not a politician, though it is a singular proposition with respect to Clinton, is not the negation of C.[23] Assuming for purposes of exposition that 'Clinton' is purely designative, we may say that the proposition with respect to Clinton that he is not a politician is the proposition:

(1)   Clinton is a non-politician,

whereas the negation of C is the proposition:

(2)   Not: Clinton is a politician.

There is no possible world at which both C and (1) are true; but there are worlds at which both are false, namely those at which E is false. At any possible world, however, C and (2) have opposite truth values. Hence we must not suppose that according to (2) it is true of Clinton that he is not a politician; for then there would be worlds — namely, those in which Clinton does not exist — in which C and (2) would agree in truth-value. So from (2) it does not follow by Existential Generalization that there is something of which it is true that it is not a politician; for EG permits inferences only from its being true of an object x that it is such-and-such to there being something of which it is true that it is such-and-such.

We must distinguish in the same way the singular proposition:

(3)   Clinton is nonexistent

---

23 Compare G.E. Moore, Casimir Lewy, ed., *Commonplace Book* (London: Allen and Unwin 1962), 262.

from the non-singular negation of E:

(4)   Not: Clinton exists.

(Here again I assume that 'Clinton' is purely designative.) Since E is contingent, so is (4). But (3) is impossible.

V

Of the things there are, some might not have actually existed. It is tempting to say, similarly, that of the things there might have been, only some actually exist. That would be misleading, however, for it might be understood to imply that there *are* things that don't actually exist. It is better to say that there might have existed things other than any there actually are. But even this can be misunderstood.

In order for there to have been things other than any there actually are, it is not enough that there be a true proposition expressible in a sentence of the form:

> Though there is no such thing as _____, there might have been

or of the form:

> Though there are no such things as _____s, there might have been.

There are no such things as blue tulips, but I suppose there might have been. But it is not clear that this requires that there have been something other than anything there actually is. If it is not essential to everything there is that it is not a blue tulip, then, although nothing there is *is* a blue tulip, something there is *might have been* a blue tulip.

If on the other hand it is essential to everything there is that it not be a such-and-such and if it is possible that there should have been a such-and-such, then it is possible that there should have been something other than anything there actually is. Now it is (or seems to me to be, anyhow) essential to everything there is that it is not a sister of mine; yet it seems to me possible that I should have had a sister; and so it seems to me that it is possible that there should have been something other than anything there actually is.

Some of the things there are might not have existed, and there might have existed things other than any of the things there actually are. A duality is suggested, but there is an important point of difference. The first doctrine can be illustrated, not simply by citing kinds of things that do exist but might not have, but by mentioning specific examples: Nixon, Boggs, Clinton, and the rest of us. But the second doctrine cannot in that way be illustrated: there are no examples of things that might have existed but don't.

Had some of the things that exist not existed, certain of the singular propositions that exist would not have existed. Is it true, similarly, that had there been things other than any there actually are, there would have existed singular propositions other than any there are? I think it is. If, for instance, I had had a sister, there would have been something other than anything there is, for nothing there is could have been a sister of mine; but then there would have been singular propositions with respect to any such person — singular propositions which, as things are, simply do not exist.

CANADIAN JOURNAL OF PHILOSOPHY
Supplementary Volume 23

Is de re *Belief Reducible to* de dicto?[1]

NATHAN SALMON
University of California, Santa Barbara

I

Yes and no. It depends on the meaning of the question. Traditionally, those on the affirmative side — predominantly neo-Fregeans — hold that Ralph's believing about Ortcutt, *de re*, that he is a spy is identical with, or otherwise reducible to, Ralph's believing some proposition or other of the form *The such-and-such is a spy*, for some concept *the such-and-such* that is thoroughly conceptual or qualitative (or perhaps thoroughly qualitative but for the involvement of constituents of Ralph's consciousness or of other mental particulars), and that uniquely *determines*, or is uniquely a *concept of*, Ortcutt (in Alonzo Church's sense of 'determines' and 'concept of').[2] Concerns over Ralph's believing that whoever is shortest among spies is a spy while not suspecting anyone in particular have led some neo-Fregeans (not all) to qualify their affirmative response by requiring that the concept *the such-and-such* and its object bear some connection that is epistemologically more substantial than that between *the shortest spy* and the shortest spy. For example,

---

1 I am grateful to the Santa Barbarians Discussion Group for its comments on some of the arguments presented here. Anthony Brueckner and Francis Dauer made particularly helpful observations.

2 See for example Daniel Dennett, 'Beyond Belief,' in A. Woodfield, ed., *Thought and Object* (Oxford University Press 1982), 1-95 (e.g., at 84); John Searle, 'Are There Irreducibly *De Re* Beliefs,' in *Intentionality* (Cambridge University Press 1983), ch. 8, § 2, 208-17.

in his classic 'Quantifying In,' David Kaplan required that the concept be (among other things) *vivid* in a certain sense.[3] If the question is whether a *de re* belief attribution like

(1)   Ralph believes of Ortcutt that he is a spy,

logically entails in English, and is logically entailed by, the claim that for some thoroughly conceptual or qualitative concept *such-and-such* that uniquely determines Ortcutt in an epistemologically special manner, Ralph believes that the such-and-such is a spy, I believe the answer is unequivocally 'No.' (Kaplan also no longer endorses this theory.) If the question is instead whether it is in the nature of human cognition, rather than by logic, that (1) is true iff for some epistemologically special, thoroughly qualitative concept *such-and such* of Ortcutt, Ralph believes that the such-and-such is a spy, the answer is still 'No.' If there is a Twin Earth in the great beyond, and my *Dopplegänger* there believes his wife to be beautiful, I nevertheless have no *de re* judgment concerning her pulchritude (how could I?), even though he and I share all the same thoroughly qualitative beliefs of the form *The such-and-such is beautiful*, and neither of us possesses any thoroughly qualitative concept that uniquely determines his wife.[4]

There is a significantly weaker sense in which *de re* belief may correctly be said to be reducible to *de dicto*. It is that Ralph's belief about Ortcutt (a *res*) that he is a spy is identical with, or otherwise reducible to, Ralph's belief of some proposition (a *dictum*) to the effect that Ortcutt is a spy — though not necessarily a proposition of the form *The such-and-such is a spy* where *such-and-such* is a special, thoroughly qualita-

---

3   In D. Davidson and J. Hintikka, eds., *Words and Objections: Essays on the Work of W. V. Quine* (Dordrecht: D. Reidel 1969), 178-214; reprinted in L. Linsky, ed., *Reference and Modality* (Oxford University Press 1972), 112-44. All page references herein are to the latter printing.

4   The Twin Earth thought experiment is due to Hilary Putnam. See his 'Meaning and Reference,' *Journal of Philosophy* **70** (1973) 699-711. For a similar argument, see Tyler Burge, 'Individualism and the Mental,' in P. French, T. Uehling, and H. Wettstein, eds., *Midwest Studies in Philosophy IV: Studies in Metaphysics* (Minneapolis: University of Minnesota Press 1979), 73-121.

tive concept of Ortcutt. This weaker thesis is fairly modest as far as reducibility claims go. Nevertheless, it too has been challenged. Indeed, philosophers who make one or another of the more full-blooded reducibility claims typically reject my claim that *de re* belief is analyzable into belief of a proposition, as I intend the analysis.

The classic case against reducibility of *de re* belief to *de dicto* was made in Quine's 'Quantifiers and Propositional Attitudes.'[5] He described a scenario, which I shall call 'Act I,' in which Ralph has witnessed a man, his face hidden from view by a brown hat, engaged in clandestine activity that prompted Ralph to conclude that he was a foreign spy. What Ralph does not realize is that the man wearing the hat is Ortcutt, whom Ralph remembers having seen once at the beach and whom Ralph regards as a patriotic pillar of the community, hence no spy. Ralph has conflicting views concerning Ortcutt, separately believing and disbelieving him to be a spy. On the basis of Act I, Quine argued that true *de re* belief attributions like (1) and

(2)   Ralph believes of the man seen at the beach that he is a spy,

stand in need of regimentation. Clearly (2) should not be viewed as imputing to Ralph a *de dicto* belief that the man seen at the beach is a spy. Using 'B_{dd}' as a symbol for belief of a proposition, the sentence

(3)   Ralph B_{dd} that the man seen at the beach is a spy,

says something very different from (2), indeed something that is false with respect to Quine's example.[6] A crucial feature of a *de re* construc-

---

5   *Journal of Philosophy* **53** (1957) 177-87; reprinted in Quine's *The Ways of Paradox* (New York: Random House 1967), 183-94; also in L. Linsky, ed., *Reference and Modality* (Oxford University Press 1971), 101-11, and elsewhere. All page references herein are to the Linsky printing. See also Tyler Burge, 'Kaplan, Quine, and Suspended Belief,' *Philosophical Studies* **31** (1977) 197-203, and 'Belief *De Re*,' *Journal of Philosophy* **74** (1977) 338-62.

6   Kaplan symbolizes (3) as 'Ralph **B** ˊthe man seen at the beach is a spyˋ'. While I have altered his symbol for *de dicto* belief I am preserving elements of his syntax, which is aptly suited to clarifying the issues under discussion. (See especially note 22 below.)

tion like (2), distinguishing it sharply from (3), is that the occurrence of 'the man seen at the beach' is open to substitution of 'the man in the brown hat.' It is tempting to provide (2) a quasi-formalization in:

(4) $(\exists x)[x =$ the man seen at the beach & Ralph $\mathbf{B_{dd}}$ that x is a spy],

thus removing 'the man seen at the beach' from the scope of 'Ralph believes that.' This is equivalent to something familiar to readers of Russell:

(4′) $(\exists x)[(y)(y$ is a man seen at the beach $\leftrightarrow x = y)$ & Ralph $\mathbf{B_{dd}}$ that x is a spy].

Either way, it would seem therefore that (2) is true if and only if the component open sentence,

(5)   Ralph $\mathbf{B_{dd}}$ that x is a spy,

is true under the assignment to the variable 'x' of the individual who uniquely satisfies 'y is a man seen at the beach,' i.e. of Ortcutt. The meaning of '$\mathbf{B_{dd}}$' is such that a sentence of the form $\ulcorner \alpha\, \mathbf{B_{dd}}$ that $\phi \urcorner$ is true if and only if the referent of the subject term α believes the proposition expressed by ϕ (the proposition referred to by the argument $\ulcorner$ that $\phi \urcorner$). But, Quine reasoned, this yields a truth condition for (2) that is essentially incomplete. Whether it is fulfilled depends not only on *what* the value of the variable in (5) is but also on *how* that value was assigned, since Ralph believes that the man in the brown hat is a spy but does not believe that the man at the beach is. If the variable receives its value by means of the particular description 'the man seen at the beach' rather than 'the man in the brown hat' — as it seems to have done — then under that assignment, performed that way, (2) should simply recapitulate (3), and consequently should be false rather than true.

Quine concluded that (2) should not be seen as attributing *de dicto* belief at all. Instead Quine counseled that (4) and (4′) be scrapped, and that (2) be seen as ascribing to Ralph a different relation — that of *de re* ('relational') belief — to the beach man and the property of being a spy:

(6)   Ralph $\mathbf{B_{dr}}$ (the man seen at the beach, to be a spy).

In Quine's words, (6) "is to be viewed not as dyadic belief between Ralph and the proposition *that* Ortcutt has [the attribute of being a spy], but rather as an irreducibly triadic relation among the three things" (*op. cit.*, p. 106). The proposal thus echoes Russell's "multiple-relation" theory of belief.[7] Also true with respect to Act I is the following:

(7)   Ralph $\mathbf{B_{dr}}$ (the man seen at the beach, ~[to be a spy]).

Quine emphasized that the joint truth of (6) and (7) does not indicate an inconsistency on Ralph's part.

I have argued against Quine that any sweeping proposal to parse 'Ralph believes of α that $\phi_{he/she/it}$' into a ternary-relational assertion is doomed.[8] My objection focused on specific instances involving a complicated substituend for ϕ (specifically, a belief ascription). This leaves open the question of whether a less ambitious proposal might fare better, at least when restricted to gentler ϕ like 'He is a spy.' Is there anything problematic about regimenting (2) and its ilk, rewriting it in the style of (6) as 'Ralph believes the man seen at the beach to be a spy'?

There is. Quine conjectured that (6) should be seen as a logical consequence of (3).[9] Kaplan labelled the inference pattern 'exportation,' and argued against it through his example of the shortest spy. Quine recanted, and later recanted his recant.[10] Still, it would appear that the

---

7   See 'On the Nature of Truth and Falsehood,' in Russell's *Philosophical Essays* (New York: Simon and Schuster 1968), 147-59; *Our Knowledge of the External World* (New York: New American Library 1956), 52-3; D. Pears, ed., *The Philosophy of Logical Atomism* (La Salle: Open Court 1985), 79-93.
     Quine writes (6) as 'Ralph believes z(z is a spy) of the man seen at the beach', Kaplan as 'Ralph **Bel** ('x is a spy', the man seen at the beach)'.

8   'Relational Belief,' in P. Leonardi and M. Santambrogio, eds., *On Quine: New Essays* (Cambridge University Press 1995), 206-28

9   'Quantifiers and Propositional Attitudes,' 106

10 The recant is made in 'Replies,' in D. Davidson and G. Harman, eds., *Words and Objections*, 337-8, 341-2; the recant of the recant in 'Intensions Revisited,' in P. French, T. Uehling, and H. Wettstein, eds., *Contemporary Perspectives in the Philosophy of Language* (Minneapolis: University of Minnesota Press 1979), 268-74, at 272-3, reprinted in Quine's *Theories and Things* (Harvard University Press 1981), 113-23, at 119-21.

predicates for *de dicto* and *de re* belief are not logically independent. Whatever the final decision with regard to exportation, the logical validity of the following inference is difficult to resist:

(*I*)   Every proposition Ralph believes, Kevin disbelieves.
Ralph believes the man seen at the beach to be a spy.
Therefore, Kevin believes the man seen at the beach not to be a spy.

But if the first premise is symbolized by means of 'B_{dd}' and the second by means of 'B_{dr}' then a middle term is missing and the validity remains unexplained.

II

In 'Quantifying In,' Kaplan proposed a full-blooded reducibility thesis for modality as well as belief and other propositional attitudes. He proposed first (p. 130) that

N_{dr} (the number of planets, to be odd),

i.e., 'The number of planets is such that it is necessary for it to be odd,' be analyzed into:

$$(\exists\alpha)[\Delta_N(\alpha, \text{the number of planets}) \ \& \ N_{dd}\ulcorner\alpha \text{ is odd}\urcorner].$$

The variable 'α' may be taken as a first approximation as ranging over singular terms, but should ultimately be regarded as ranging over thoroughly conceptual or qualitative individual concepts, with the quasi-quotation marks accordingly interpreted either standardly or as

---

I must note that exportation cannot be generally valid for all propositional attributions. Otherwise, from the empirical premise that there are in fact exactly nine planets, and the philosophical observation that there might instead have been an even number of (or more specifically, eight or ten) planets, one could validly infer that nine might have been even (or eight or ten).

quasi-sense-quotation marks.[11] The first conjunct '$\Delta_N(\alpha$, the number of planets)' says that α necessarily determines the object that *actually* numbers the planets — in effect, that α rigidly designates that number, in the sense of Kripke. Analogously, Kaplan proposed (p. 138) that (6) be analyzed thus:

(K6) $(\exists\alpha)[\mathbf{R}(\alpha$, the man seen at the beach, Ralph) & Ralph $\mathbf{B_{dd}}$ $^\ulcorner\alpha$ is a spy$^\urcorner]$.

The first conjunct says that α provides a *de re* connection for Ralph to the man seen at the beach. In Kaplan's terminology, α 'represents' the man seen at the beach for Ralph. Kaplan provides an analysis for his epistemologically special notion of representation, whereby '$\mathbf{R}(\alpha$, the man seen at the beach, Ralph)' entails, but is strictly stronger than, '$\Delta(\alpha$, the man seen at the beach)' (i.e., α determines the man seen at the beach). It has not been established, however, that this further step is properly a matter of philosophical logic — rather than, for example, of philosophical psychology.[12] Beyond the mentioned entailment, the exact analysis of Kaplan's '$\mathbf{R}$' will not concern me here.

---

11 An *individual concept* is a concept for (i.e. a concept whose function is to determine) an individual, and may thus serve as the semantic content of singular term.

12 Evidently on Kaplan's account, the following sentence is alleged to be an analytic truth:
> If Ralph believes the man seen at the beach to be a spy, then there is a vivid individual concept α that determines, and is for Ralph a name of, the man seen at the beach such that Ralph believes $^\ulcorner\alpha$ is a spy$^\urcorner$.

Similarly for its converse. I believe, on the contrary, that neither the conditional nor its converse is analytic. Even if the conditional were both necessary and *a priori*, the inference from antecedent to consequent, or vice versa, does not feel to me like one that is licensed strictly as a matter of the principles governing correct reasoning and the meanings of 'believe,' 'vivid,' 'name of,' etc. As a matter of fact, the Twin Earth considerations mentioned in the first paragraph of this article demonstrate that the conditional need not even be true. By contrast, the mutual inference between (4) (or (2)) and (6) does feel to me to be licensed by pure logic. Cf. my remarks concerning the modal-propositional-logical system *T* as compared with stronger systems, in 'The Logic of What Might Have Been,' *The Philosophical Review* **98** (1989) 3-34.

Kaplan's ingenious reductive analysis of *de re* propositional attribution might be interpreted as a proposal for dealing with any propositional attribution that involves an open sentence. One might regard an open 'that'-clause, like 'that x is a spy,' as having no meaning in isolation, but as contributing indirectly to the meanings of sentences in which it occurs. A contextual definition for 'that x is a spy' is provided as follows: First, analyses are provided for atomic formulae $\ulcorner \Pi^n(\beta_1, \beta_2, ..., $ that x is a spy, $..., \beta_{n-1})\urcorner$ containing the 'that'-clause among its argument expressions. The most common cases are: those where $n = 1$ and Π^1 is a predicate for a *de dicto* modality, i.e. a modal predicate of propositions ('necessarily true,' 'probably true,' etc.), and those where $n = 2$ and Π^2 is a predicate for a *de dicto* propositional attitude ('believes,' 'doubts,' 'hopes,' 'fears,' 'wishes,' etc.). In the latter case,

$$\beta \; \Pi_{dd} \text{ that } x \text{ is a spy}$$

is analyzed as:

$$(\exists\alpha)[R(\alpha, x, \beta) \; \& \; \beta \; \Pi_{dd} \ulcorner \alpha \text{ is a spy}\urcorner].$$

Plugging this contextual definition of 'that x is a spy' into (4) yields (*K6*), or rather, something classically equivalent to it. More complicated constructions involving the analysandum are then subject to scope ambiguities exactly analogous to those found in Russell's Theory of Descriptions. The negation $\ulcorner{\sim}(\beta \; \Pi_{dd} \text{ that } x \text{ is a spy})\urcorner$, for example, may be analyzed as involving a 'primary occurrence' of the 'that'-clause, or alternatively as involving a 'secondary occurrence,' where the latter corresponds to the genuine negation of the original, un-negated analysandum:

$$(\exists\alpha)[R(\alpha, x, \beta) \; \& \; {\sim}(\beta \; \Pi_{dd} \ulcorner \alpha \text{ is a spy}\urcorner)]$$
$${\sim}(\exists\alpha)[R(\alpha, x, \beta) \; \& \; \beta \; \Pi_{dd} \ulcorner \alpha \text{ is a spy}\urcorner].^{13}$$

---

13 Cf. my 'A Millian Heir Rejects the Wages of *Sinn*,' in C. A. Anderson and J. Owens, eds., *Propositional Attitudes: The Role of Content in Logic, Language, and Mind* (Stanford: CSLI 1990), 215-47, at 239-40. Kaplan does not explicitly regard (*K6*) as a consequence of a contextual definition for open `that'-clauses; I suggest

One virtue of Kaplan's analysis is that it may reduce the inference (*I*) to a valid argument of first-order logic. Declining any analysis of *de re* belief into *de dicto* leaves few alternatives. One may take 'B_{dd}' and 'B_{dr}' as primitives, for example, and propose Carnapian 'meaning postulates' for them that would enable one to derive (*I*). Perhaps one may save the inference instead through an analysis of the former predicate in terms of the latter.[14] Or one may reject inferences like (*I*) as invalid.

Kaplan argued on somewhat different grounds that leaving the *de re* form unanalyzed into the *de dicto* is inadequate (pp. 140-3). His argument invokes a later development in Quine's example:

> In Quine's story, [(7) holds]. But we can continue the story to a later time at which Ralph's suspicions regarding even the man at the beach have begun to grow. Not that Ralph now proclaims that respected citizen to be a spy, but Ralph now suspends judgment as to the man's spyhood. At this time (7) is false (pp. 141-2).

In Act II, Ralph has not changed his mind concerning whether the man in the brown hat is a spy. Thus (1), (2), and (6) are all still true. While (3) is still false — Ralph still does not believe that the man seen at the beach is a spy — Ralph no longer believes that the man seen at the beach is not a spy.

The important feature of Act II is that Ralph's suspension of judgment is not only *de dicto* but *de re*. Ralph's attitudes towards Ortcutt

---

this merely as a possibly enlightening interpretation of his program. He proposes (K6) specifically as an analysis of (6), rather than of (4), which Quine had found improper. Kaplan does, however, suggest (114 *n*3) that instead of repudiating (4) altogether, it might be taken as analyzed by (6). Quine later came around to this same view, in 'Intensions Revisited,' 268, 274 *n*9.

14 Quine appears to prefer this option Cf. 'Quantifiers and Propositional Attitudes,' section II. He there takes `$B_{dr}$' to be *multi-grade*, i.e. "letting it figure as an *n*-place predicate for each $n > 1$" ('Intensions Revisited,' 268). This allows one to say that Ralph believes of the man in the brown hat and the man at the beach that the former is taller than the latter by writing `Ralph B_{dr} (the man in the brown hat, the man at the beach, $\lambda xy[x$ is taller than $y]$)'. The *de dicto* predicate `$B_{dd}$' may then be taken to be the limiting case of `B_{dr}' where $n = 2$. But how exactly does this give us (*I*)?

still conflict, but not in the straightforward manner of believing him to be a spy while also believing him not to be a spy. Concerning Ortcutt, Ralph believes him to be a spy while also actively suspending judgment. Using 'SJ' as a predicate for suspension of judgment, both of the following are true in Act II:

> Ralph B_{dd} that the man in the brown hat is a spy
> Ralph SJ_{dd} that the man seen at the beach is a spy.

The consequences of the latter regarding belief are given by the following conjunction, which provides a kind of analysis of at the least the core meaning:

> ~[Ralph B_{dd} that the man seen at the beach is a spy] & ~[Ralph B_{dd} that ~(the man seen at the beach is a spy)].

Indeed, the truth of this conjunction with respect to Act II may simply be taken as stipulated.[15] Also true, partly in virtue of the foregoing, are the following:

(6)   Ralph B_{dr} (the man seen at the beach, to be a spy)
(8)   Ralph SJ_{dr} (the man seen at the beach, to be a spy).

Without analyzing *de re* belief in terms of *de dicto*, rendering (8) in terms of withheld belief poses a special difficulty. One is tempted to write:

> ~[Ralph B_{dr} (the man seen at the beach, to be a spy)] & ~[Ralph B_{dr} (the man seen at the beach, ~[to be a spy])].

But the first conjunct flies in the face of the continued truth of (6) in Act II. Not to mention that the second conjunct (which is the negation of

---

15 I criticize this analysis (which is Kaplan's, not mine) of suspension of judgment as being too strong, in my 'Being of Two Minds: Belief with Doubt,' *Noûs* **29** (1995) 1-20. There is no doubt in this case, however, that the conjunction is indeed true with respect to Act II.

(7)) is unjustified. We have no guarantee that Ralph is not acquainted with Ortcutt in some third way. The problem is to express the withheld belief of Ralph's new doxastic situation indicated by (8) consistently with (6).

The difficulty, according to Kaplan, is that the left conjunct above — the apparent negation of (6) — is ambiguous. He writes:

> Cases of the foregoing kind, which agree with Quine's intuitions, argue an inadequacy in his regimentation of language. For in the same sense in which (7) and (6) do not express an inconsistency on Ralph's part, neither should (6) and ⌜~(6)⌝ express an inconsistency on ours. Indeed it seems natural to claim that ⌜~(6)⌝ is a consequence of (7). But the temptation to look upon (6) and ⌜~(6)⌝ as contradictory is extremely difficult to resist. The problem is that since Quine's 'B_{dr}' suppresses mention of the specific name [or concept] being exported, he cannot distinguish between
>
> $$(\exists\alpha)[R(\alpha, \text{the seen man at the beach, Ralph}) \ \& \ \sim(\text{Ralph } B_{dd} \ulcorner\alpha \text{ is a spy}\urcorner)]$$
>
> and
>
> $$\sim(\exists\alpha)[R(\alpha, \text{the man seen at the beach, Ralph}) \ \& \ \text{Ralph } B_{dd} \ulcorner\alpha \text{ is a spy}\urcorner].$$
>
> If ⌜~(6)⌝ is read as [the former], there is no inconsistency with (7); in fact on this interpretation ⌜~(6)⌝ is a consequence of (7) (at least on the assumption that Ralph does not have contradictory beliefs). But if ⌜~(6)⌝ is read as [the latter] (Quine's intention, I suppose) it is inconsistent with (6) and independent of (7).
>
> So long as Ralph can believe of one person that he is two, as in Quine's story, we should be loath to make either [reading of ⌜~(6)⌝] inexpressible.[16]

Analyzing *de re* suspension of judgment in terms of *de dicto* in the style of (*K6*) yields the following Kaplanesque analysis of (8):

$$(\exists\alpha)[R(\alpha, \text{the man seen at the beach, Ralph}) \ \& \ \text{Ralph } SJ_{dd} \ulcorner\alpha \text{ is a spy}\urcorner].$$

The principal consequences of this regarding belief are summed up by:

---

16 *Ibid*, 141. Here as elsewhere I have slightly altered the text for the purpose of matching numbered expressions with the numbers used in the present paper.

(K8) $(\exists\alpha)[R(\alpha,$ the man seen at the beach, Ralph) & $\sim$(Ralph $\mathbf{B_{dd}}$ $^{\ulcorner}\alpha$ is a spy$^{\urcorner}$) & $\sim$(Ralph $\mathbf{B_{dd}}$ $^{\ulcorner}\sim(\alpha$ is a spy)$^{\urcorner}$)].

This represents Kaplan's way of laying bare the withholding of belief expressed in (8). It is perfectly compatible with (K6). Both may be true so long as the two α's are different, as are *the man in the brown hat* and *the man seen at the beach*.

The ambiguity that Kaplan sees in $^{\ulcorner}\sim(6)^{\urcorner}$ is precisely the Russellian primary-occurrence/secondary-occurrence ambiguity that arises in $^{\ulcorner}\sim(5)^{\urcorner}$ on the contextual-definition interpretation of his project. The important point is not whether the reader (or the current writer) agrees that the alleged primary-occurrence reading is legitimate. Kaplan's principal point is that if $^{\ulcorner}\sim(6)^{\urcorner}$ is interpreted so that it is the genuine negation of (6), then without analyzing *de re* suspension of judgment ultimately in terms of *de dicto* belief the withheld belief in (8) becomes inexpressible.

III

Tyler Burge has responded to Kaplan's argument, claiming (in effect) that Quine can analyze (8) as follows:

$(\exists\alpha)[$Ralph $\mathbf{B_{dr}}$ (the man seen at the beach, $^{\ulcorner}(\lambda z)(z = \alpha)^{\urcorner})$ & Ralph $\mathbf{SJ_{dd}}$ $^{\ulcorner}\alpha$ is a spy$^{\urcorner}]$.

The consequences of this for belief may then be summarized by:

(B8) $(\exists\alpha)[$Ralph $\mathbf{B_{dr}}$ (the man seen at the beach, $^{\ulcorner}(\lambda z)(z = \alpha)^{\urcorner})$ & $\sim$(Ralph $\mathbf{B_{dd}}$ $^{\ulcorner}\alpha$ is a spy$^{\urcorner}$) & $\sim$(Ralph $\mathbf{B_{dd}}$ $^{\ulcorner}\sim(\alpha$ is a spy)$^{\urcorner}$)].[17]

That is, there is some individual concept *the such-and-such* whereby Ralph believes the man seen at the beach to be the such-and-such, but

---

17 In 'Kaplan, Quine, and Suspended Belief,' 198. I have expanded on Burge's actual proposal, keeping to both its letter and spirit, in order to secure the full force of suspension of judgment as opposed to mere failure to believe.

Ralph believes neither that the such-and-such is a spy nor that the such-and-such is not a spy. This existential claim is made true by the very concept, *the man seen at the beach*. Comparison of (B8) with (K8) reveals that, in effect, Burge rewrites Kaplan's representation clause '$\mathbf{R}(\alpha$, the man seen at the beach, Ralph)' in terms of *de re* belief. For Kaplan, this puts the cart before the horse; he invokes representation precisely to analyze *de re* belief in terms of *de dicto*. But reduction of *de re* to *de dicto* is precisely what Burge rejects. Burge offers (B8) as a Quinean analysis of *de re* suspension of judgment in terms of both *de dicto* and *de re* belief, with *de re* treated as primitive, or at least as unanalyzable in terms of *de dicto*.[18]

Ironically, the idea of replacing '$\mathbf{R}(\alpha$, the man seen at the beach, Ralph)' with 'Ralph $\mathbf{B_{dr}}$ (the man seen at the beach, $\ulcorner(\lambda z)(z = \alpha)\urcorner)$' is originally due to Kaplan. He had suggested replacing (K6) with

(B6) $(\exists\alpha)$[Ralph $\mathbf{B_{dr}}$ (the man seen at the beach, $\ulcorner(\lambda z)[z = \alpha]\urcorner$) & Ralph $\mathbf{B_{dd}}\ulcorner\alpha$ is a spy$\urcorner$].

Acknowledging that this is not equivalent to the supplanted notion, at least when (B6) is taken as analyzed by means of $\mathbf{R}$-representation, Kaplan went on to say, "Still this new notion of representation, when used in place of our current $\mathbf{R}$ in an analysis of the form of [(K6)], leads to the same relational sense of belief."[19]

---

18 Whereas Burge aims to refute Kaplan's argument for reducibility, he does not himself endorse the proposal he makes on Quine's behalf, and instead says that the conjunction of (6) with (8) may be formulated along the lines of something like:

Ralph believes the man seen at the beach to be *this man* and a spy, and Ralph neither believes the man seen at the beach to be *that man* and a spy nor believes the man seen at the beach to be *that man* and not a spy,

as spoken with three references to Ortcutt, in his guises as *this man* (in the brown hat) and as *that man* (seen at the beach). This proposal seriously distorts the very *de re* locutions it employs. Indeed, it contains a contradiction, its first conjunct expressing about Ortcutt exactly what the second conjunct denies.

19 'Quantifying In,' 139 *n*30. Quine proposes (in 'Intensions Revisited,' at 272-73) taking $\ulcorner(\exists x)$[Ralph $\mathbf{B_{dr}}$ $(x, \ulcorner(\lambda z)(z = \alpha)\urcorner)]\urcorner$ — e.g., 'There is someone whom Ralph takes to be the shortest spy' — as the further premise required to validate the

If Kaplan was correct about this, then he inadvertently showed the way to refutation of his argument against Quine. But he was not correct; the new notion does not strictly 'lead to the same sense' as the old. Analyzing (*B*6) in the style of Kaplan, one obtains (something equivalent to):

(*B*6*K*) $(\exists\beta)(\exists\alpha)[R(\alpha, \text{the man seen at the beach, Ralph}) \& \text{Ralph } \mathbf{B_{dd}} {}^\ulcorner\alpha = \beta{}^\urcorner \& \text{Ralph } \mathbf{B_{dd}} {}^\ulcorner\beta \text{ is a spy}{}^\urcorner]$.

This does not strictly entail (*K*6). Likewise, analyzing (*B*8) *à la* Kaplan in terms of '**R**', one obtains:

(*B*8*K*) $(\exists\beta)(\exists\alpha)[R(\alpha, \text{the man seen at the beach, Ralph}) \& \text{Ralph } \mathbf{B_{dd}} {}^\ulcorner\alpha = \beta{}^\urcorner \& \sim(\text{Ralph } \mathbf{B_{dd}} {}^\ulcorner\beta \text{ is a spy}{}^\urcorner) \& \sim(\text{Ralph } \mathbf{B_{dd}} {}^\ulcorner\sim(\beta \text{ is a spy}){}^\urcorner)]$,

which does not entail (*K*8). From Kaplan's perspective, the new notions are weaker than the old ones.

Why, then, does Kaplan say that the new notion of representation "leads to the same relational sense"? As Burge notes (p. 199), (*K*8) is derivable from (*B*8*K*) using the additional premise:

(9) $(\alpha)(\beta)[\text{Ralph } \mathbf{B_{dd}} {}^\ulcorner\alpha = \beta{}^\urcorner \rightarrow (\text{Ralph } \mathbf{B_{dd}} {}^\ulcorner\alpha \text{ is a spy}{}^\urcorner \leftrightarrow \text{Ralph } \mathbf{B_{dd}} {}^\ulcorner\beta \text{ is a spy}{}^\urcorner) \& (\text{Ralph } \mathbf{B_{dd}} {}^\ulcorner\sim(\alpha \text{ is a spy}){}^\urcorner \leftrightarrow \text{Ralph } \mathbf{B_{dd}} {}^\ulcorner\sim(\beta \text{ is a spy}){}^\urcorner)]$.

---

exportation inference from ${}^\ulcorner$Ralph $\mathbf{B_{dd}}$ that α is a spy${}^\urcorner$ to ${}^\ulcorner$Ralph $\mathbf{B_{dr}}$ $(\alpha,$ to be a spy$)^\urcorner$. See note 10 above. Influenced by Jaakko Hintikka, Quine incorrectly glosses this proposed premise as ${}^\ulcorner$Ralph has an opinion as to who α is$\urcorner$. Even this stronger premise, however, is not up to the task; suppose, for example, that Ralph is of the erroneous opinion that the shortest spy is none other than Ortcutt. See Igal Kvart, 'Quine and Modalities De Re: A Way Out?' *Journal of Philosophy* **79** (June 1982), 295-328, at 298-302; and my 'How to Measure the Standard Metre,' *Proceedings of the Aristotelian Society* (New Series) 88 (1987/1988) 193-217, at 205-6, 213-4. Quine's intent may be better captured by taking the additional premise to be instead ${}^\ulcorner$Ralph $\mathbf{B_{dr}}$ $(\alpha, {}^\ulcorner(\lambda z)(z = \alpha)^\urcorner)^\urcorner$ — e.g., 'Ralph believes the shortest spy to be the shortest spy.' This move, in turn, suggests an analysis of (6) *à la* Kaplan/ Burge into (*B*6) (perhaps as part of a general analysis of attributions of *de re* beliefs other than identity beliefs). The alternative premise Kvart proposes, by comparison, suggests instead an analysis more along the lines of Kaplan's original (*K*6).

This additional premise also suffices to obtain ($K6$) from ($B6K$). No matter. If Kaplan leaned on some premise like (9) — and it is unclear whether he did — Burge clearly does not. Instead, he objects that "if Ralph is Everyman, (9) cannot be guaranteed" (p. 199). Burge does not specify the sort of circumstance he has in mind in which (9) fails, but there is no need for him to do so. Even the most thorough of logicians (let alone Everyman) does not draw all logically valid inferences from all his/her beliefs. Otherwise there would be no theorems of mathematics left to prove. Nothing as sweeping as (9) is even close to being true.

How, then, can Burge rely on the replacement strategy? He is not strictly committed, as Kaplan was, to analyzing ($B6$) into ($B6K$) and ($B8$) into ($B8K$). Nevertheless, he contends (evidently with Kaplan) that ($B8K$) successfully captures ($K8$), so that one attracted to Kaplan's analysis cannot object to ($B8$) on the ground that it does not render (8) equally as well as ($K8$) does. Burge cites the following considerations in support of this contention:

> Now an obvious candidate for fulfilling the role of β [in ($B8K$)] is α itself. If we approve the candidate, and assume that Ralph believes $\ulcorner \alpha = \alpha \urcorner$, then ($B8K$) and ($K8$) indeed become strictly equivalent. ... The claim that everyone believes the self-identity statement for each 'representing' singular expression in his repertoire is fairly plausible. Even more plausible — and equally adequate in yielding equivalence between ($B8K$) and ($K8$) — is the Frege-like view that everyone believes *some* identity statement for each representing singular expression in his repertoire (p. 199).

This argument is multiply flawed. To begin with, contrary to Burge the mentioned "Frege-like view" is woefully inadequate to the task of yielding an implication of either ($K8$) by ($B8K$) or vice versa. It is unclear what Burge means by the obscure phrase 'approve a candidate for fulfilling the role of β.' Both ($K8$) and ($B8K$) follow from the assumption that Ralph believes $\ulcorner \alpha = \alpha \urcorner$ while believing neither $\ulcorner \alpha$ is a spy$\urcorner$ nor $\ulcorner \sim(\alpha$ is a spy$)\urcorner$, for some concept α that represents Ortcutt — such as perhaps the concept, *the man Ortcutt, whom I saw that time at the beach.* In this sense, one may derive ($B8K$) from the premise that Ralph suspends judgment concerning whether the man at the beach is a spy and the further premise that Ralph believes that the man at the beach is the man at the beach, by casting *the man at the beach* in the roles of both α and β in ($B8K$) (more precisely, by two judicious applications of Existential Generalization on an appropriately expanded variant of

($K8$)). But when going in the other direction, attempting to derive ($K8$) from ($B8K$), the latter is given and may be true in virtue of a pair of distinct concepts α and β. The roles of α and β have already been cast; the task is to establish that Ralph lacks further relevant beliefs. Not only the "Frege-like view," but even the stronger claim that Ralph believes the particular identity $\ulcorner \alpha = \alpha \urcorner$ whenever α is representing is inadequate to yield ($K8$) from ($B8K$) without the intervention of something like (9). In particular, the mere assumption that Ralph believes $\ulcorner \alpha = \alpha \urcorner$ in no way permits the replacement of ($B8K$) by the special case where α and β are the same.

To establish this, I submit Act III: A more decisive Ralph has become convinced that the man in the brown hat and the man at the beach are working in tandem. As regards Ortcutt, Ralph no longer suspends judgment whether he is a spy. On the contrary, Ralph believes him a spy twice over, as it were. Further, Ralph also happens to believe $\ulcorner \alpha = \alpha \urcorner$ for every individual concept α in his repertoire. In particular, Ralph believes that the man seen at the beach is the man seen at the beach. When queried, 'Which one, if any, is the most trusted man in town?' Ralph points to Ortcutt. As it turns out, Ralph is wrong about this; Wyman is more trusted than Ortcutt. When asked whether whoever is more trusted than every other man in town is a foreign spy, Ralph hesitates momentarily and wonders, ever so briefly, before inferring (much to his dismay) that the most trusted man is indeed a spy. Until he is through hesitating and finally makes the substitution — however brief the period of hesitation may be — Ralph suspends judgment whether the most trusted man in town is a spy, even while believing both that Ortcutt is most trusted and that he is a spy. (Burge presumably will not object to this hypothesis, given his rejection of (9). The hypothesis is in any case unobjectionable.)

Ralph's suspension of judgment whether the most trusted man is a spy cannot of itself constitute *de re* suspension of judgment about Ortcutt. Indeed, it does not even involve reference to Ortcutt. Since *the most trusted man in town* is a concept of (determines) Wyman and not Ortcutt, it cannot represent Ortcutt for Ralph in the requisite manner. With respect to Act III, ($K8$) remains false despite the truth of ($B8K$). Burge's response to Kaplan thus fails.

The significance of Act III extends beyond the fact that it yields a counter-model to Burge's contention that ($K8$) and ($B8K$) are alike in truth value if Ralph believes $\ulcorner \alpha = \alpha \urcorner$ for each of his representing concepts α. (*K8*) and (*B8K*) are Kaplan's analyses, respectively, of (8) and of (*B8*), the latter being Burge's proposal for capturing (8) without analyzing *de re* belief in terms of *de dicto*. But the general point does not specifically concern Kaplan's particular manner of analyzing *de re* into *de dicto*. Act III also directly refutes Burge's account of *de re* suspension of judgment. The principal difference between Act II and Act III is that in the former there is *de re* suspension of judgment concerning Ortcutt on the part of Ralph and in the latter there is not. Sentence (8) differentiates between the two acts, being true with respect to one and false (its negation true) with respect to the other. But (*B8*) is true with respect to both acts. Since it can be true even when (8) is false, Burge's attempt at capturing (8) through (*B8*) fails.

Strengthening Burge's clause 'Ralph $\mathbf{B_{dr}}$ (the man seen at the beach, $\ulcorner (\lambda z)(z = \alpha)\urcorner)$' to assert that Ralph has correct *de re* belief (or *de re* knowledge) does not solve the problem. Even if Ralph were correct in thinking that Ortcutt was the most trusted man, he may still hesitate before inferring that the most trusted man is a spy, thus satisfying the new formulation without thereby engaging in *de re* suspended judgment — unless one who believes that the shortest spy is a spy thereby engages in *de re* belief.[20]

IV

Burge's primary concern is to reject Kaplan's full-blooded reducibility. He objects that "if one uses 'denote' strictly, it is implausible that in all

---

20 Cf. my *Frege's Puzzle* (Atascadero, CA: Ridgeview 1986, 1991), at 171-2. An alternative scenario is also possible in which Ralph believes (on the basis of general suspicions) that the most trusted man in any town is a spy, and knows Ortcutt to be the most trusted man in town, while not yet concluding about Ortcutt that he in particular must be a spy. Such a case refutes the analysis suggested in note 19 above. Intuitively, one who believes that whoever is most trusted among men in town is a spy does not *ipso facto* believe of the most trusted man, *de re*, that he is a spy. (Notice that the description 'the most trusted man in town,' like 'the shortest spy,' qualifies neither as *vivid*, nor as a *name of* its referent, in Kaplan's quasi-technical senses.)

cases of *de re* belief, one of the believer's beliefs contains a thought symbol or individual concept that denotes the *res*" ('Belief *De Re*,' p. 351). By "thought symbol or individual concept," Burge means a thoroughly conceptual or qualitative concept. The "strict use of 'denote'" Burge intends is essentially Church's use of 'determines' for the binary relation (which is not context-relative) between a concept and its object.

On this point Burge and I are in complete agreement. The Twin-Earth considerations raised in the first paragraph are sufficient to demonstrate the point. But this point does not weaken Kaplan's argument, which is aimed at establishing that *de re* belief is reducible to *de dicto*. Even if the argument succeeds, it does nothing to establish Kaplan's particular, full-blooded way of carrying out the reduction. On the contrary, as I shall argue in the next section, with a certain modification the same argument can be redirected against Kaplan's reduction.

My own version of modest reducibility is this: that *de re* belief about an object *x* is nothing more or less than belief of the corresponding *singular proposition* (singular *dictum*) — a proposition that is about *x* by including *x* directly as a constituent, instead of a conceptual or intensional representation of *x*. Ironically, the principal argument in favor of this form of modest reducibility begins, and proceeds, nearly the same as Quine's argument against reducibility. It is this: The logical form of a *de re* attribution like (1) is better revealed by rewriting it as:

About Ortcutt, Ralph believes that he is a spy.

This is true in English if and only if its component open sentence,

(5')   Ralph believes that he is a spy,

(or 'Ralph B_{dd} that he is a spy') is true as spoken with reference to Ortcutt. That is, (1) is true if and only if (5') is true under the assignment of Ortcutt to the pronoun 'he.' Indeed, the pronoun functions in (5') exactly as the free variable does in (5). It is precisely this that disturbs Quine about (1). The variable/pronoun stands in a position in which what matters is not what is referred to but how it is referred to. By pure English semantics alone, (1) is true if and only if Ralph believes the proposition expressed by 'He is a spy' under the assignment of Ortcutt to 'he.' This is also the proposition expressed by the open sentence '*x* is a spy' under the assignment of Ortcutt to '*x*.' Quine could not make sense of this because of a severe limit he implicitly imposed — following Frege, and to a lesser extent, Russell — on the range of propositions potentially believed by Ralph, no one of which by Quine's reckoning has yet been singled out. Granted, the proposition expressed by 'He is a spy' under the assignment of Ortcutt to 'he' is neither that the man seen at the beach is a spy nor that the man in the brown hat is a spy. It is a third proposition, I say, independent of these others and dismissed by Frege, Russell, and Quine as no possible object of belief by Ralph. Following Russell, we may say that the variable/pronoun in (5)/(5′) functions as a 'logically proper name' of its assigned referent. The open sentence expresses a singular proposition about Ortcutt, the proposition that *he* is a spy.[21]

Accordingly, I have suggested that (2), and hence also (6), should be analyzed in terms of propositional belief not by (*K6*) but instead by means of (something trivially equivalent to):

(S6) (λx)[Ralph $\mathbf{B_{dd}}$ that x is a spy](the man seen at the beach).

This may be read, 'The man seen at the beach is such that Ralph believes that he is a spy.' (S6) is classically equivalent to (4). Whereas (4) provides for a logical form that in some respects mirrors that of (*K6*), the underlying idea is very different. It is that (2) ascribes to Ralph belief of a singular proposition about the man seen at the beach. *De re* belief is *de dicto* belief of a singular *dictum* about the *res*.[22]

---

21 Cf. *Frege's Puzzle*, 2-7. See also my 'How to Become a Millian Heir,' *Noûs* 23 (1989) 211-20; and 'A Millian Heir Rejects the Wages of *Sinn*,' 223-7.

22 'Relational Belief,' 216. The analysis is broadly Russellian in spirit. However, Russell himself embraced an epistemology that prevented him from accepting the analysis (and which may be part of the original motivation for his multiple-relation theory of *de re* belief). Quine also rejects it. Indeed, this is what led Quine to propose replacing (2) with something along the lines of (6). His objections, however, are dubious. See Kaplan, 'Opacity,' in L. E. Hahn and P. A. Schilpp, eds., *The Philosophy of W. V. Quine* (La Salle: Open Court 1986), 229-89; and my 'Relational Belief.'

    Identifying the singular proposition about Ortcutt that he is a spy with the

In addition, I have suggested that a propositional-belief attribution like (3) be analyzed as follows by means of the existential generalization of a ternary relation, **BEL**, which holds among a believer, a proposition, and something like a *proposition guise* or *way of taking* the proposition when the believer agrees to the proposition taking it that way:

$(\exists x)$[Ralph **BEL** (that the man seen at the beach is a spy, x)].[23]

Putting these two proposals together, I analyze (6) as:

(S6′) $(\lambda x)[(\exists y)$(Ralph **BEL** [that x is a spy, y])](the man seen at the beach).

That is, the man seen at the beach is such that Ralph agrees to the proposition that he is a spy, taking it in at least one way in which he grasps it. Like Kaplan's rival analysis, this analysis also accommodates inference (*I*).

Analyzing (*B*6) in the manner I propose, at the first stage one obtains:

(B6S) $(\exists \beta)[(\lambda x)$[Ralph $\mathbf{B_{dd}}\ulcorner x = \beta\urcorner$](the man seen at the beach) & Ralph $\mathbf{B_{dd}}\ulcorner \beta$ is a spy$\urcorner$].

Just as (*B*6K) does not strictly yield (*K*6), (*B*6S) is weaker than (*S*6). An additional premise like (9) (except with its bound variable 'α' interpreted as ranging over singular-term-contents, construed as including individuals as well as individual concepts) is required in order to derive (*S*6) from (*B*6S).[24]

---

corresponding ordered pair, the proposed analysis of (6) might be revealingly reformulated as:

Ralph $\mathbf{B_{dr}}$ (the man seen at the beach, to be a spy) $=_{def}$ Ralph $\mathbf{B_{dd}}$ <the man seen at the beach, to be a spy>.

23 More exactly, my view is that the dyadic predicate '$\mathbf{B_{dd}}$' is definable as: $(\lambda xp)[(\exists y)(x$ **BEL** [p, y])].

24 Alternatively, something like Kaplan's full-blooded reducibility thesis might be invoked as a third premise in addition to (9), thus removing (*B*6S) still further

V

I analyze (8) thus:

(S8) $(\lambda x)[(\exists y)$[Ralph grasps the proposition that x is a spy by means of y & ~(Ralph **BEL** [that x is a spy, y]) & ~(Ralph **BEL** [that ~$(x$ is a spy), y])]](the man seen at the beach).

There are numerous similarities between (K6) and (S6'), as well as between (K8) and (S8). In particular, the analyses claim to uncover a hidden existential quantifier, which may joust with a negation sign for dominant position. This *existentialism* (to coin a term) is brought out in cases of *de re* suspended judgment, in which the negation is inserted after the existential quantifier. Despite his decidedly differing philosophical outlook, Burge's (B8) also capitalizes on Kaplan's discovery of the existential quantifier internal to *de re* suspended judgment. Like (K8), (S8) is true with respect to Act II but false with respect to Act III. Hence (B8), which is true with respect to Act III, is not equivalent to (S8), nor is (S8) derivable from (B8) together with the premise that Ralph believes $\ulcorner \alpha = \alpha \urcorner$ for every individual concept α that he grasps.

These similarities obscure the important differences that remain between Kaplan's analysis and mine. Foremost, where my existential quantifier ranges over proposition guises, or ways of taking propositions, Kaplan's ranges over thoroughly conceptual or qualitative individual concepts (or over singular terms expressing such concepts). It is essentially this feature of Kaplan's analysis that both Burge and I (and Kaplan today) find objectionable. (See note 12 above.) Kaplan located the hidden existential quantifier in the use of open 'that'-clauses, like 'that he is a spy' and 'that x is a spy,' which have no meaning in isolation even under the assignment of a value to its free pronoun/variable. In effect, Kaplan found existentialism in the very nature of *de re*

---

from (S6). Alternatively, the 'α' may be replaced by an objectual variable. Analogously, Kaplan may have intended a version of (9) in which 'α' ranges only over 'representing' names, in his sense, while 'β' is not similarly restricted. Burge's objection that the relevant version of (9) is not guaranteed is appropriate regardless.

propositional attribution. By contrast, I locate it in the particular phenomenon of belief. By my account, there is no logical reason to expect an analogous existentialism to occur in connection with all propositional attributions—including for example in 'Ralph proved that' or 'It is necessary that.'[25] Indeed, if there is a primary-occurrence/secondary-occurrence ambiguity in $\ulcorner\sim(5)\urcorner$ under the assignment of the man at the beach as value for the variable 'x', there is no like ambiguity in 'It is not necessary that there be n planets' under the assignment of the number of planets to the variable 'n' (nor in '$\sim[N_{dr}$ (the number of planets, to number the planets)]').

On the other side of the coin, on my account there is also no logical reason why the competition for dominance between the existential quantifier and negation should not occur also with *de dicto* belief. In fact it does. Kripke's famous puzzle about belief includes such a case.[26] Before presenting the puzzle Kripke emphasizes that it concerns *de dicto* belief rather than *de re*. He says:

> the *de dicto* or "small scope" reading ... is the *only* reading, for belief contexts ... that will concern us ... *de re* beliefs — as in 'Jones believes, *of* Cicero (or: *of* his favorite Latin author), that he was bald' — do *not* concern us in this paper. Such contexts, if they make sense, are by definition subject to a substitutivity principle for both names and descriptions. Rather we are concerned with the *de dicto* locution expressed explicitly in such formulations as, 'Jones believes that: Cicero was bald' (or: 'Jones believes that: the man who denounced Catiline was bald'). The material after the colon expresses the *content* of Jones's belief. Other, more explicit formulations are: 'Jones believes the proposition—that—Cicero—was—bald,' or even in the 'formal' mode, 'The sentence 'Cicero was bald' gives the content of a belief of Jones' (pp. 105-6).

In Kripke's original example, a Frenchman, Pierre, comes to believe on the basis of cleverly crafted travel brochures that London is pretty — or as he would put it, that '*Londres est jolie*.' Later he is hijacked to an unattractive part of London, and after learning the native language through assimilation (not through an ESL class or a French-English

25 Cf. 'A Millian Heir Rejects the Wages of *Sinn*,' especially 234-47.

26 Saul Kripke, 'A Puzzle about Belief,' in N. Salmon and S. Soames, eds., *Propositions and Attitudes* (Oxford University Press 1988), 102-48.

dictionary), he comes to believe that London is not pretty, without re-alizing that the cities he knows by the names 'London' and '*Londres*' are one and the same. Even now that he is disposed, on reflection, to assent sincerely to 'London is not pretty,' Pierre continues to assent sincerely and reflectively also to '*Londres est jolie.*' Kripke constructs a puzzle by pressing the question: Does Pierre believe that London is pretty? The question is not whether Pierre believes *of* London, *de re*, that it is pretty. That issue is easily settled. Like Ralph with respect to Ortcutt and his possible hidden agenda in Act I, Pierre both believes London to be pretty and disbelieves London to be pretty. But as Kripke has emphasized, his question is not this. Using our notation, we may say that Kripke is concerned not with

Pierre B_{dr} (London, to be pretty),

which (along with 'Pierre B_{dr} [London, ~(to be pretty)]') is undoubt-edly true with respect to the example, but with

(10) Pierre B_{dd} that London is pretty.

Kripke forcefully argues that any possible response to the question of whether (10) is true is beset with serious conceptual difficulties.

Kripke argues further that it is imprudent to draw any conclusions, positive or negative, with respect to the question. Nevertheless per-haps most commentators — including myself — are persuaded that (10), as well as

(11) Pierre B_{dd} that ~(London is pretty),

are indeed true with respect to Kripke's example. In short, I and others charge Pierre not merely with inconsistency, but with believing a con-tradiction. One lesson of Kripke's puzzle is that not all contradictory beliefs subject the believer to justifiable censure.[27]

---

27 I respond to Kripke's puzzle, and to his objections to the solution I propose, in *Frege's Puzzle*, 129-32; and in 'Illogical Belief,' in J. Tomberlin, ed., *Philosophical Perspectives, 3: Philosophy of Mind and Action Theory* (Atascadero, Ca.: Ridgeview 1989), 243-85.

Finding this conclusion unwarranted, Kripke considers a modified case for which such a conclusion is ruled out by hypothesis:

> Suppose Pierre's neighbors think that since they rarely venture outside their own ugly section, they have no right to any opinion as to the pulchritude of the whole city. Suppose Pierre shares their attitude. Then, judging by his failure to respond affirmatively to 'London is pretty,' we may judge, from Pierre's behavior as an *English* speaker, that he lacks the belief that London is pretty: never mind whether he disbelieves it, as before, or whether, as in the modified story, he insists that he has no firm opinion on the matter.
>
> Now ... we can derive a contradiction, not merely in Pierre's judgments, but in our own. For on the basis of his behavior as an English speaker, we concluded that he does *not* believe that London is pretty (that is, that it is not the case that he believes that London is pretty). But on the basis of his behavior as a *French* speaker, we must conclude that he *does* believe that London is pretty. This is a contradiction (pp. 122-3).

As with Ralph in Act II, Pierre now both believes London to be pretty and suspends judgment. Despite the *déjà vu* of this second act, the transition from one act to the next in Kripke's drama raises at least one very significant issue not raised in Kaplan's continuation of Quine's tale. As Kripke has laid out the problem, it is not to reconcile Pierre's *de re* belief about London with his *de re* suspension of judgment. Kaplan has indicated one way to do this. The new problem is that Pierre seems for all the world to have a *de dicto* belief that London is pretty, on the one hand, but equally seems for all the world to harbor *de dicto* suspended judgment. With respect to Kripke's new act, it would appear that (10) is true together not with (11) (which is clearly false) but with:

(12)   Pierre SJ_{dd} that London is pretty.

(Compare (6) and (8) above.) Kaplan's treatment of suspension of judgment expresses the withheld belief in (12) by:

(K12)   ~[Pierre B_{dd} that London is pretty] & ~[Pierre B_{dd} that ~(London is pretty)].

But as Kripke emphasizes, this directly contradicts (10).

As I see it, Kripke's puzzle is a problem of reconciliation. (Kripke sees it somewhat differently.) In this version of the puzzle, the problem is this: How can Pierre's belief that London is pretty be reconciled with his suspended judgment? In this respect, it is like the reconciliation problem in Kaplan's Act II. The difference is that Kaplan's problem concerned *de re* belief where Kripke's concerns *de dicto*. Although the two reconciliation problems are variants of one another, Kaplan's solution to the *de re* version does not extend in any straightforward manner to the *de dicto*. For Kaplan's analysis of (8) into (K8) does not yield a straightforward analogue for (12); and indeed, his account of suspended judgment leads directly from (12) to (K12), whose differences with (10) are irreconcilable. What is wanted is a uniform solution to both the *de re* and the *de dicto* versions of the general reconciliation problem.

Kripke also notes (in connection with his Paderewski example) that the general problem does not in the end turn on issues concerning translation between languages. Nor does the general problem turn on a peculiarity of proper names. The same problem arises in connection with some general terms. Elsewhere I have proposed the strange case of Sasha, who believes that the condiment called 'ketchup' is supposed to be used with certain sandwiches, while the condiment called 'catsup,' which he wrongly takes to be distinct from ketchup, is supposed to be used instead with scrambled eggs. Suppose Sasha is persuaded that ketchup tastes good on hamburgers but claims to have no opinion concerning whether catsup does. Or again consider the confused native Santa Barbaran who sincerely declares, 'When I was in England I tasted a terrific sauce made from toe-**mah**-toes. I wonder whether toe-**mae**-toes could be made into as good a sauce.' Whether Kaplan's strategy for dealing with *de re* suspension of judgment is successful or not, it has no obvious extension to this case of *de dicto* suspended judgment. The almost exact analogy between the problems posed by suspension of judgment in the *de re* and *de dicto* cases strongly suggests that a correct solution to any should apply to each.[28]

---

28 'A Millian Heir Rejects the Wages of *Sinn*,' 220-2. It is difficult to see how one can maintain that the belief that tomatoes make a good sauce is not a belief of a certain proposition (but instead a relation to various entities) without committing oneself to the conclusion that no belief is of a proposition.

Pierre's suspended judgment does not pose the same problem for my account that it does for Kaplan's. I propose analyzing (10) and (12) into the following:

(S10) $(\exists x)$[Pierre **BEL** (that London is pretty, x)]

(S12) $(\exists y)$[Pierre grasps that London is pretty by means of y & ~(Pierre **BEL** [that London is pretty, y]) & ~(Pierre **BEL** [that ~(London is pretty), y])].

No contradiction follows from (S10) and (S12). The desired reconciliation is achieved. What does follow is that the x and the y are distinct proposition guises. In the example these are given to Pierre by the distinct sentences 'London est jolie' and 'London is pretty,' respectively.

The reconciliation is made possible through the limited commitments of (S12) as compared to those of (K12). Following the originator of the reconciliation problem, one might argue as follows:

> Cases of the foregoing kind, which agree with Kaplan's intuitions, argue an inadequacy in his regimentation of language. For in the same sense in which (10) and (11) do not express a censurable inconsistency on Pierre's part, neither should (10) and (12) express an inconsistency on ours. But the temptation to look upon (10) and (K12) as contradictory is extremely difficult to resist. So long as Ralph or Pierre can believe of one person or city that it is two, as in Quine's, Kaplan's, and Kripke's stories, we should be loath to make either (S8) or (S12) inexpressible.

If examples like Kaplan's involving belief combined with suspension of judgment argue that *de re* belief is reducible to *de dicto*, they equally argue that the existentialism in terms of which the reduction proceeds is not peculiar to the *de re* notion, but internal to the *de dicto* notion. Recognition of this fact paves the way for modest reducibility in lieu of the more full-blooded variety. Through reconciliation comes insight.[29]

---

29 Cf. *Frege's Puzzle*, 92-128.

CANADIAN JOURNAL OF PHILOSOPHY
Supplementary Volume 23

On Some Untamed Anaphora[1]

GEORGE M. WILSON
Johns Hopkins University

I

A sentence of the form

(1)   Either Jones or Smith entered the room, and he saw the Maltese Falcon,

has some notable properties due largely to the sprightly behavior of the pronoun in its second conjunct. For instance, that pronoun can not be a pronoun of laziness for the disjunctive noun phrase, 'Jones or Smith,' since (1) patently does not express the thought that

(1')   Either Jones or Smith entered the room, and either Jones or Smith saw the Maltese Falcon.

(1'), but not (1), would be true if Jones entered the room but didn't see the Maltese Falcon, and Smith saw the Maltese Falcon but never entered the room. Rather, (1) is equivalent to the disjunction of conjunctions

---

1 Some of the basic ideas in this paper are presented in a section of my paper 'Reference, Generality, and Anaphora,' to appear in a volume in honor of Keith Donnellan, edited by Paolo Leonardi. However, the version in the present paper extensively emends and extends those ideas, and I believe that the presentation is significantly clearer. It certainly contains a more detailed investigation of some of the phenomena in question.

(1″)   Either Jones entered the room, and he (Jones) saw the Maltese Falcon, OR Smith entered the room, and he (Smith) saw the Maltese Falcon.

This casts doubt, through failure of generalization, upon the idea that the pronoun in the simpler sentence

Jones entered the room, and he saw the Maltese Falcon

is a pronoun of laziness for the name 'Jones.' The problem is to explain how it comes about that (1) has the content of (1″).

The issues are immediately seen to be more complicated when we notice that the conditional statement

(2)   If either Jones or Smith entered the room, then he saw the Maltese Falcon

is intuitively equivalent, not (in analogy with (1)) to the disjunction

(2′)   If Jones entered the room, then he (Jones) saw the Maltese Falcon, OR, if Smith entered the room, then he (Smith) saw the Maltese Falcon,

but to the conjunction

(2″)   If Jones entered the room, then he (Jones) saw the Maltese Falcon, AND, if Smith entered the room, then he (Smith) saw the Maltese Falcon.

Why should the context of a conditional convert, so to speak, an 'or' into an 'and'? The phenomena these examples illustrate are interesting in themselves, and they deserve more careful elaboration and analysis.

However, as the discussion unfolds, I will argue that the problems posed by these pronouns with disjunctive nominal antecedents are closely linked to well-known questions about the proper treatment of unbound anaphora, especially the unbound anaphora in two types of case which have attracted extensive attention in the literature on the subject. In fact, I believe that if we can give a viable account of the semantic mechanisms that are at work in examples (1) and (2), we will be well on our way toward a novel theory of the semantic mechanisms that operate in the more famous cases as well.

Here are the two noted, or notorious, types of case I have in mind. It was Gareth Evans who emphasized and illuminated the fact that, in sentences of the form

(A)   [Only one F] Φ'd, and he (she, it) Ψ'd,

the pronoun is *not* most naturally understood as a variable bound by the antecedent quantifier phrase 'Only one F.'[2] Thus, the statement

(3)   Only one man entered the room, and he saw the Maltese Falcon

is not normally understood to mean

(3')   Only one man both entered the room and saw the Maltese Falcon,

although that is the reading that (3) would bear if 'he' was literally bound by the expression 'Only one man.' Nevertheless, it *is* plain that the pronoun is somehow interpreted in the light of its quantifier phrase antecedent, and the problem once more is to explain the nature of the semantic dependence in question.

Stephen Neale, adapting a proposal of Evans's, suggests that the pronoun 'goes proxy for' a definite description which is suitably recoverable from the first conjunct in instances of (A).[3] A pronoun which receives its interpretation in this fashion is, in their terminology, an 'E-type' pronoun. For Neale, (3) has the content of

---

2 Gareth Evans, 'Pronouns, Quantifiers, and Relative Clauses (I),' *Collected Papers* (New York: Oxford University Press 1985), 114-5. Evans uses the example "Just one man drank champagne, and he was ill."

3 Stephen Neale, *Descriptions* (Cambridge, MA: MIT Press 1990). See especially chapters 5 and 6.

(3″)   Only one man entered the room, and the man who entered the room saw the Maltese Falcon.

Given the further assumption that the recovered description is Russellian, (3″) captures the truth conditions of (3) correctly.

The second type of case we will consider (in section IV) has been even more widely discussed. These are sentences, involving so-called 'donkey anaphora,' which have the general form of

(B) $[Q + NP$ who (which) Φ'd an $F]$ Ψ'd him (her, it),

where the pronoun is anaphorically dependent on the indefinite description within the relative clause of the quantifier phrase. The instance of (B) most frequently cited is

(4)   Every farmer who owned a donkey beat it.

On at least its most salient reading, (4) says

(4′)   Every farmer who owned a donkey beat each donkey that he owned.

However, this reading is difficult to reconcile with plausible theses about the meaning and structure of (4), especially concerning the logical character of indefinite descriptions in such a context. In particular, suppose that the indefinite description, 'a donkey,' which is the antecedent of the pronoun in (4), occurs there, as it does in many other settings, as an existential quantifier. If so, it cannot occur as a quantifier phrase that takes wide scope in relation to 'every farmer,' since that parsing simply does not yield the intuitive content of (4). But, if the indefinite description is an existential quantifier whose scope is confined to the relative clause within the grammatical subject of the sentence, then the pronoun that appears as the object of the verb is not bound by that quantifier, and we so far have no account at all of the patent interpretative relation between the description/pronoun pair.

Alternatively, we might suppose that the indefinite description is, in this context, a universal quantifier phrase. This proposal will assign to (4) the right truth conditions, i.e. the truth conditions rendered by (4′). And yet, it is instructive to contrast (4) with

(5)   At least one farmer who owned a donkey beat it.

This, it seems to me, is equivalent to

(5′)   At least one farmer who owned a donkey beat at least one donkey that he owned.

(We will return to the question of the truth conditions of (5) in sections III and IV.) If this observation is sound, then the indefinite description in (5) is not a universal quantifier, with or without wide scope, and hence the indefinite description, in (4) and in (5), would have to have different contents. The notion that the logical force of an indefinite description can vary in this manner is not appealing, and, if we were even tempted to accept it, then we would want a well-motivated account of how and why the variation occurs.

Actually, the contrast between (4) and (5) is not as sharp, in one central respect, as these remarks suggest. In the environment of (5), the interpretation of 'a donkey' as an existential quantifier phrase, binding the pronoun 'it,' produces the truth conditions we properly expect. Nevertheless, in (5), as in (4), the indefinite description does not stand in the syntactic relation of *c*-command to the pronoun with which it is linked.[4] Indeed, this is true in every instance of (B) above. Moreover, it is a widely accepted thesis in the theory of natural language quantification (a thesis I will not question) that a quantifier phrase cannot literally bind a pronoun which it does not *c*-command. So, the pronoun in (5) is just as much an instance of 'unbound anaphora' as the pronoun

---

4 A node A of a phrase structure tree *c-commands* a node B iff (i) A does not dominate B, (ii) B does not dominate A, and (iii) the first branching node that dominates A also dominates B. So, if S is a sentence containing an anaphor and its antecedent, the antecedent *c*-commands the anaphor iff the node of the phrase structure tree for S that dominates the antecedent *c*-commands the node that dominates the anaphor. (There are alternative conceptions of *c*-command, but their differences would not affect our discussion.) See, for example, Liliane Haegman, *Introduction to Government and Binding* (Oxford: Basil Blackwell 1991), 198.

in (4), and it is, as it were, merely an accident that we get the right truth conditions for (5) when we treat the pronoun as a variable bound by the associated indefinite description (qua existential quantifier).

Early versions of Discourse Representation Theory (DRT) explained the crucial difference between (4) and (5) by rejecting the view that indefinite descriptions are existential quantifiers at all.[5] 'Classical' DRT held that indefinite descriptions, in effect, introduce a variable at the position they hold in the sentential context and that the occurrences of variables so introduced are bound by the quantifier phrases '[Q + NP]' which head the relative clauses containing the problematic indefinite descriptions. Hence, (4) is (roughly)

[Every farmer x, every donkey y] if x owns y, then x beats y,

and (5) is

[At least one farmer x, at least one donkey y] x owns y & x beats y.

These formulations, in my opinion, are accurate at least about the respective truth conditions. But, whatever the merits of this proposal for dealing with (B)-type sentences, its application to type (A) sentences is, at best, unclear. As we observed above, it was Evans's point that 'Only one man' in (1) does not bind the pronoun to which it is interpretatively tied, and it will not improve matters to take the pronoun there to be implicitly bound, in virtue of a default condition of Existential Closure, by an ordinary existential quantification over men.[6]

---

5 In speaking of 'classical' DRT, I am following the (admittedly loose) usage in Gennaro Chierchia, *Dynamics of Meaning: Anaphora, Presupposition, and the Theory of Grammar* (Chicago: University of Chicago Press 1995). The paradigms of the work he is referring to with this label are found in H. Kamp, 'A Theory of Truth and Discourse Representation' in J. Groenendijk, T. Janssen, and M. Stokhof, eds. *Formal Methods in the Study of Language* (Amsterdam: Mathematical Centre 1981), 277-322, and I. Heim. *The Semantics of Definite and Indefinite Noun Phrases* (Ph.D. dissertation, the University of Massachusetts, Amherst, 1982). The dissertation was published in 1989 by Garland Press, New York.

6 In classical DRT, a rule of Existential Closure was widely adopted that assigned existential force to indefinites (and other variables) that are not otherwise bound by a quantifier in the discourse.

By contrast, Neale's theory of E-type pronouns, which works so well for statements of form (A), is less successful when applied to instances of (B). I have, in effect, indicated above that Neale's theory will require the pronoun in (4) to 'go proxy for' the 'description' 'each donkey he owns,' and the very same pronoun in (5) will have to 'go proxy for' yet another 'description,' i.e. 'at least one donkey he owns.' Surely, we do not have much of an explanation of the fluctuating semantical behavior that these pronouns exhibit unless and until the determinants of the fluctuations are themselves explained. These concerns will be developed more carefully and at greater length later in the paper. At any rate, it is my claim that neither classical DRT nor the theory of E-type pronouns fare well in accounting for cases of *both* types (A) and (B). In the course of the discussion, we will develop reasons for thinking that it is possible to give an intuitive and more systematic account of this range of recalcitrant examples and various of their structural kin.

II

It is universally recognized that a pronoun may be used in such a way that it 'picks up' its referent from a singular term to which it is appropriately connected in a sentence or discourse, and that this kind of internal co-reference occurs even though the pronoun is not *c*-commanded by its antecedent. An example is

(6)   Every lawyer <u>Bob</u> hired told <u>him</u> not to testify,

and an even simpler case, repeated from section I, is

(7)   <u>Jones</u> entered the room, and <u>he</u> saw the Maltese Falcon.

Here and henceforward I will use underlining to signal the fact that it is part of the linguistic meaning of the sentence, when so employed, that the indicated pronoun is to be construed as inheriting its referent from the antecedent singular term.[7] Of course, these same sentences

---

7   For a discussion and defense of this kind of conception, see, for instance, Robert Fiengo and Robert May, *Indices and Identity* (Cambridge, MA: MIT Press 1994),

could also be used in such a way that the pronouns they contain do not invoke this sort of obligatory co-reference. For example, the pronouns might be used demonstratively, and, their referents, thus independently established, might or might not be Bob in (6) or Jones in (7). However, I will assume throughout that these and similar examples have a meaning in English which, when it is expressed in a particular utterance, entails that the pronoun and its antecedent, if they refer at all, have the same referent. The assumption is somewhat controversial, but I do not have the space to defend it here, although it will gain some degree of support by functioning successfully in the analyses that follow.[8] In addition, it is a large and difficult problem to delineate the conditions, grammatical and otherwise, that have to be satisfied in order for this kind of obligatory co-reference to come into play. I have nothing to contribute to that question, but it is chiefly important, for the purposes at hand, to stress what I noted earlier: obligatory co-reference is by no means restricted to constructions in which one term *c*-commands the other.

Example (1), given at the outset of the paper, reminds us that a slightly more complicated variant of (7) is possible. We have

(1)   <u>Either Jones or Smith</u> entered the room, and <u>he</u> saw the Maltese Falcon,

---

especially chapter 1. Also, I should note that my simple notation of underlining becomes immediately inadequate as soon as one considers any example involving two or more such anaphoric connections. More adequate and more commonly employed is some system of indexing the noun phrases and anaphors, as they appear in the relevant chains. An extensive discussion of the theory of indices is presented in Fiengo and May, and their discussion brings out the conceptual and other complexities that are implicated in a full theory of this topic. I have used underlining only because it seemed much easier to read and follow, given the examples studied in this paper.

8 For example, Tanya Reinhart in *Anaphora and Semantic Interpretation* (London: Croon Heim 1983) rejects relations of obligatory co-reference induced by the linguistic meanings of the relevant sentences or discourse fragments. She attempts to give a 'pragmatic' account of the character of the antecedent-anaphor linkages that I am here viewing as semantically induced.

This, of course, is a cousin of

> <u>Both Jones and Smith</u> entered the room, and <u>they</u> saw the Maltese Falcon,

although, by and large, in this paper I will bypass the special complications engendered by plural pronouns. As I have already stated, the truth conditions of the conjunction in (1) are clear enough. (1) is equivalent to

(1″)   Either <u>Jones</u> entered the room, and <u>he</u> saw the Maltese Falcon, OR <u>Smith</u> entered the room, and <u>he</u> saw the Maltese Falcon,

where, in each conjunct, the name and pronoun are semantically required, in the manner just mentioned, to have the same referent. Our question is: by what means does this distinctive propositional structure arise?

A simple hypothesis is the following. First, we suppose that, in (1), the complex conjunctive predicate 'x entered the room and x saw the Maltese Falcon' has been ascribed disjointly to either Jones or Smith. In other words, (1) has the logical form of

> (λx) (x entered the room and x saw the Maltese Falcon) Jones or Smith.

Moreover, in light of the general equivalence between

> Pred (*NP1* or *NP2*)

and

> Pred (*NP1*) or Pred (*NP2*),

we arrive at the rendering of (1) in terms of (1″).

As simple and attractive as this hypothesis may be, I am inclined to reject it because it does not apply to a case of one degree greater complexity. Consider

(8)   Only Jones or Smith entered the room, and he saw the Maltese Falcon.

Following Evans and others, I assume that 'Only A,' where 'A' is proper name or other singular term, is itself a quantifier phrase having the meaning of 'A and no one (nothing) other than A.'[9] I will presuppose throughout the discussion that natural language quantifier phrases can and should be represented as *restricted quantifiers*.[10] In particular, we can represent 'Only A' as a restricted quantifier by '[Only x: $x = A$],' and, similarly, 'Only A or B' can be represented as '[Only x: $x = A$ or $x = B$].' Now, I take it that (8) *is* equivalent to

> Only Jones entered the room, and he (Jones) saw the Maltese Falcon, OR only Smith entered the room, and he (Smith) saw the Maltese Falcon.

But, this is not the result we get by applying to (8) the analysis in the previous paragraph. Completing the conjunctive predicate with the quantifier phrase in question yields

> [Only x: $x =$ Jones or $x =$ Smith] (x entered the room and x saw the Maltese Falcon).

This says that

> Only Jones or Smith both entered the room and saw the Maltese Falcon,

a proposition which could be true even if many others besides Jones and Smith entered the room as long as those others did not see the Maltese Falcon. In the same way, the simpler sentence

(9)   Only Jones entered the room, and he (Jones) saw the Maltese Falcon

---

9 Evans, 96

10 For a very clear explication of restricted quantifiers, see Neale, 38-47.

does not mean the same as '[Only x: x = Jones] (x entered the room and x saw the Maltese Falcon).'

However, it is not at all implausible that (9) should be construed as

(9') [Only x: x = Jones] (x entered the room) and <u>he</u> saw the Maltese Falcon,

where the scope of the quantifier phrase runs through the first conjunct, and where the referent of the pronoun is established through inheritance in virtue of its non-c-command connection with the antecedent name. There is nothing syntactically more curious or semantically harder to interpret in (9') than there is in, say, sentence (7).

The distinction I am stressing here is the following. Suppose we have a construction of the form

$[Q...A...]$ —— he (she, it) ——,

where 'A' is a singular term, and the pronoun somehow derives its interpretation from the functioning of 'A' within the quantifier phrase. If the quantifier phrase c-commands the pronoun, then the pronoun may genuinely be a variable which the quantification binds, but if the relation of c-command does not hold, then the pronoun is, as a matter of meaning, co-referential with the singular term which the quantifier phrase imbeds. The intuitive ambiguity of

(10) Mary's mother loves her husband

should be understood along these lines. On one interpretation, (10) means

(10') [The x: x is mother of Mary] x loves x's husband,

and the pronoun in (10) *is* a variable c-commanded and bound by the definite description. But, (10) can also say

(10") [The x: x is mother of <u>Mary</u>] x loves <u>her</u> (Mary's) husband,

in which the pronoun picks up its referent through the intended link to the name 'Mary.'

In a famous example, due originally to Geach, I believe that we find another instance of the same phenomenon.[11] The sentence

> Only Satan pities himself

may have the structure of

> [Only x: x = Satan] x pities x,

but it may also be structured as

> [Only x: x = <u>Satan</u>] x pities <u>him</u>self.

The sentence, on its second parsing, is formed from the two place predicate 'x pities y' by letting the quantifier phrase occupy the 'x'-position and by filling the 'y'-position with a pronoun that is semantically required to inherit its referent from the occurrence of the name 'Satan.'[12] Of course, both structures yield the same truth conditions, although their semantical differences show up in various subtle ways.

Returning to (8), the following approach seems natural. Since we can form the quantifier phrase '[Only x: x = A]' and combine this with a predicate '$\Phi\alpha$' to form the closed sentence '[Only x: x = A] Φx,' we can take another step and abstract the more complex one-place predicate '[Only x: x = α] Φx' (i.e. 'Only α Φ'd'). We stipulate that 'α'is to be a dummy variable holding the positions in the simple or complex predicate where appropriate arguments are to be supplied. An object o satisfies this complex predicate just in case o is Φ and nothing other than o is Φ. Finally, we can continue one step further to form the conjunctive predicate '[Only x: x = α] Φx and $\Psi\alpha$.' An instance of this is

(11)   [Only x: x = α] (x entered the room) and α saw the Maltese Falcon,

---

11 Peter Geach, *Reference and Generality* (Ithaca: Cornell University Press 1962), 128

12 Essentially the same diagnosis is given by Scott Soames, 'Direct Reference, Propositional Attitudes, and Semantic Content,' *Philosophical Topics* **15** (1987) 47-87.

or, what comes to the same thing (for present concerns)

(11') [Only x: $x = \underline{\alpha}$] (x entered the room) and <u>he</u> saw the Maltese Falcon,

in which the second occurrence of 'α' in (11) has been replaced by an anaphorically dependent pronoun in (11'). We get the right truth conditions for (8) if we suppose that (8) is true iff either Jones or Smith satisfy (11), i.e., (11').

Although I think that this hypothesis is substantially on the right track, as it stands, it seems to me to fail to tell the full story of (8) accurately. For one thing, the proposal assigns truth conditions to the whole conjunction in (8) but does not discriminate truth conditions for either of its constituent conjuncts. And yet, the sentences that appear here as conjuncts may also occur, chained in a similar way, as discreet constructions in a larger discourse, sometimes separated by other utterances that constitute a part of that discourse. Thus, we might have

(8) (a) Only <u>Jones or Smith</u> entered the room ... blah blah blah...
  (b) <u>He</u> saw the Maltese Falcon,

and, instead of (1),

(1) (a) Either <u>Jones or Smith</u> entered the room ... blah blah blah...
  (b) <u>He</u> saw the Maltese Falcon.

Further, we have an intuitive sense of what proposition each of the conjuncts in both (1) and (8) expresses, and we can assess the truth values of (1a) and (1b) or of (8a) and (8b) independently, at least within certain limits. (1a) and (8a) simply express the obvious disjunctive propositions, e.g., 'Only Jones entered the room, or only Smith entered the room.' On the other hand, (1b) and (8b), given their anaphoric connection to the relevant disjunctions, mean, in effect,

In at least one of these cases, <u>he</u> saw the Maltese Falcon.

The cases in question for (1b) are, of course: the case in which Jones entered the room and the case in which Smith entered the room. For

(8b), the cases that are invoked are: the case in which *only* Jones entered the room and the case in which *only* Smith entered the room, and, in both examples, the pertinent cases have been 'introduced' into discourse by (1a) and (8a) respectively. The 'cases' here (and in the following discussion) are propositions — for (1a) and (8a), they are the propositions expressed by the sentential disjuncts that are contracted in the overt forms with the disjunctive subject terms.[13] In an obvious sense, the cases, in these examples, are the propositional *instances* of the implicit sentential disjunctions in (1a) and (8a).

The initial disjunction, (1a) or (8a), serves a kind of double function in these discourses. It expresses, as usual, the expected propositional disjunction, but it also introduces, through each of its disjuncts, the possible cases with reference to which (1b) or (8b) are case by case interpreted. That is, a type of case is specified, in each instance, by the open sentence that results from the omission of the disjunctive nominal argument in the first conjunct, and a particular case of that type is given by the ascription of that condition to one or another of the referents designated in the subject phrase. In assigning a truth value to (1b) or (8b), we assess, first of all, the truth or falsity of 'In the case in which Jones (or: only Jones) entered the room, he saw the Maltese Falcon,' and the truth or falsity of 'In the case in which Smith (or: only Smith) entered the room, he saw the Maltese Falcon,' understanding the occurrence of the pronoun, in such a setting, to refer to the individual specified for the case at hand. Second, the proposition expressed by (1b) or by (8b), given its contextual involvement with (1a) or (8a), is true just in case the disjunction of the pertinent first stage propositions is true. But, this is to claim that the proposition expressed by (1b) is tantamount to

> Either Jones entered the room, and he saw the Maltese Falcon, OR Smith entered the room, and he saw the Maltese Falcon,

---

13 Obviously, the concept of 'a case' employed here and in the rest of the paper would require much more careful discussion. In particular, if one moves beyond the relatively simple examples I examine, the structure of a case can become quite complicated, but I do not believe that those complications change the basic picture I am attempting to draw.

and that the proposition expressed by (8b) is

> Either only <u>Jones</u> entered the room, and <u>he</u> saw the Maltese Falcon, OR only <u>Smith</u> entered the room, and <u>he</u> saw the Maltese Falcon.

These are the results that we have anticipated. The analysis has the consequence that the propositions expressed by (1b) or (8b) are equivalent to the propositions expressed by the full conjunctions in (1) or (8) respectively, but that upshot is explained by the fact that the disjunctions in (1a) and in (8a) are performing the sort of double function described above.

There is nothing unique or particularly surprising about the interpretative mechanism that is operating in these constructions. In fact, the same phenomenon naturally arises whenever we have an anaphor which is analogously connected to a disjunctive antecedent. Consider, for example,

(12) Nick bought <u>either a Mercedes or a Bentley</u>, (and) Pete bought <u>one</u> as well.

Although other readings of (12) may be possible, the most obvious reading is

(12′) Either Nick bought <u>a Mercedes</u>, and Pete bought <u>one</u> as well, OR Nick bought <u>a Bentley</u>, and Pete bought <u>one</u> as well.

That is, the second conjunct of (12) says that, in one specified case or the other, Pete bought 'one' as well, where the proper interpretation of 'one' depends upon which 'alternative' is taken to be on stage. Similar reflections apply to

> Bob <u>either punched or kicked Norm in the stomach</u>, and <u>so did</u> Bill.

I believe that we can give more direct and telling support for the claim that the second full sentence in '<u>Either A or B</u> Φ′d, and <u>he</u> Ψ′d' or '<u>Only A or B</u> Φ′d, and <u>he</u> Ψ′d' expresses its own propositional content in these discourse environments and, moreover, for the more specific claim that the propositions expressed are of the character I have delineated above. Imagine that it is affirmed that

(13)   (a) Jane believes that <u>either Jones or Smith</u> entered the room, and (b) Jane is worried that <u>he</u> saw the Maltese Falcon.

There is a strong inclination to suppose that the content clause in (13b) succeeds in expressing a more or less determinate proposition which gives the object of Jane's worry, although plainly aspects of the linguistic context have been exploited to make it possible for (13b) to do so. It is true that we can envisage various uses of sentence (13), but, everything else being equal, it seems to me that (13b) is most naturally interpreted as informing us that Jane is worried that the person who entered the room — Jones or Smith, as the case may be — saw the Maltese Falcon. Or, in the formulation proposed before, Jane is said to be worried that (either <u>Jones</u> entered the room, and <u>he</u> saw the Maltese Falcon, OR <u>Smith</u> entered the room, and <u>he</u> saw the Maltese Falcon). Therefore, it is reasonable to conclude that this is the proposition which is expressed by the content clause of (13b), and, hence, that this same proposition is expressed by the same sentence in similar and simpler discourses — for example, when it occurs without a prefixed operator, as in (8b).

Recent philosophy of language has increasingly underscored the importance of context in determining which proposition is expressed by a literal utterance of a sentence with a fixed linguistic meaning, and philosophers have been forced to upgrade the complexity of the contributions that context can make to the literal expression of a particular proposition. The study of demonstratives and indexicals has alerted us to the complicated ways in which context helps to determine a particular referent for tokens of a context-sensitive referential term. But, the more recent attention to the phenomenon of 'impliciture' calls to our attention how often an utterance, whose literal meaning is determinate and all of whose component singular terms have established referents, fails, without a further contribution from the speech act context, to express a truth-assessable proposition.[14] Thus,

---

14   For an excellent discussion of the concept of 'impliciture' and its applications, see Kent Bach, 'Conversational Impliciture,' *Mind and Language* 2 (1987) 124-62.

The rope is strong <u>enough</u>,
Mildred <u>thereby</u> convicted Herb of a terrible crime,

and

Consequently, Fred became very rich,

are grammatically complete sentences, but unless the pertinent discourses and/or the presuppositions that the discourses engender somehow indicate the required supplementing contents, no thoughts will have been propounded.

Both impliciture and contextual reference determination appear to be hand in hand at work in the examples we have been investigating. In (1b) and (8b), the statements contain an anaphoric pronoun which demands that a value or values be retrievable, in some manner, from (1a) and (8a), but, these propositional antecedents present a pair of potential values both of which are equally salient and seem equally relevant to the propositions that the dependent sentences should express. The proposal now before us is (i) that (1b) and (8b) are, as it were, sequentially construed as evaluated in relation to each of the cases described in their antecedent disjunctions, (ii) that the pronouns in (1b) and (8b) are assigned values which they inherit on a case by case basis, and (iii), that (1b) and (8b) express the logical sum of all of the case-restricted propositions thus obtained.

III

We are now in a good position to examine, as promised, examples in which the pronominal antecedent is a quantifier phrase. In particular, let us begin by comparing (1) with its quantified counterpart

(14) (a) <u>A man</u> entered the room, and (b) <u>he</u> saw the Maltese Falcon.

In light of the fact that the pronoun is not c-commanded by the quantifier phrase, this should have the form of

[<u>An x: x is a man</u>] (x entered the room) and <u>he</u> saw the Maltese Falcon,

127

where the scope of the quantifier phrase is restricted to (14a) and, accordingly, does not bind the pronoun in (14b). Given the familiar trade-off between existential generalizations and suitably exhaustive disjunctions of their instances, we would expect that the account proposed for (1) should generalize into a similar account of (14).

It is plain, however, that (14a), unlike (1a), does not directly represent any individual cases in terms of which (14b) might be construed. (14a) says merely that at least one man entered the room, but, in saying this, it does effectively specify a *type* of individual case: a case (i.e., a Russellian singular proposition) in which 'entering the room' is ascribed to some particular man. What we would expect from our discussion of (1) is that (14b) is understood, in context, as adverting to this type of case and having the content, in analogy with (8b), of

In at least one such case, he saw the Maltese Falcon.

Here, as in example (8), the cases in question are the propositions that constitute propositional *instances* of (14a). But (14a) is an existential generalization over men. Therefore, the range of instances (or: cases) for (14b) includes any singular proposition of the form 'α is a man who entered the room,' when some particular man has been assigned to 'α'as its referent. In a rough but intuitive sense, the cases over which the implicit quantification ranges are simply the minimal individual cases in which it is or would be true that a man (some man or other) entered the room, i.e., the cases in which the man m_1 entered the room, man m_2 entered the room, and so on, throughout the domain of men. Thus, (14b) says, partly in virtue of its exploitation of its contextual connection with (14a), that there is a man who entered the room and saw the Maltese Falcon.[15] For this example, the suggested analysis as-

---

15 In the second part of her dissertation (cited in *n.* 5), Irene Heim introduced a kind of 'file change' semantics that has been developed by various writers and that continues to be influential. Although I will not explore the similarities and differences here, her 'files' and my 'cases' are introduced to play a similar role, i.e., to register content that has been introduced earlier in a discourse and stored among the presuppositions of the discourse — content that may then be exploited in helping to determine the truth conditions of utterances that occur in the

signs to (14) the same truth conditions as does an account that takes the initial quantifier phrase, 'A man,' in (14a) to have wide scope over the whole conjunction. But, that concurrence of results is only an artifact of the specific example chosen.

We obtain a more distinctive result if

(3)   (a) <u>Only one man</u> entered the room, and (b) <u>he</u> saw the Maltese Falcon.

is treated, in the same fashion, as a quantified analogue of (8a) + (8b). (3) has the form of

[<u>Only one x: x is a man</u>] (x entered the room) and <u>he</u> saw the Maltese Falcon.

Following the model of our treatment of (14b) (and, for that matter, generalizing our approach to (8)), (3b) has the content of

In at least one such case, <u>he</u> saw the Maltese Falcon,

although, for (3), the individual cases to which the quantification over cases alludes are, naturally, the individual propositional instances of 'Only one man entered the room.' But, what *are* the instances of such a proposition?

Well, notice, first, that (3a) is potentially ambiguous. Just as 'only A' meant 'A and nothing other than A,' the phrase 'only one F' may have a corresponding 'unrestrictive reading' in which it means 'some (one) F and nothing else.' On an 'unrestrictive' reading, (3a) says that no one entered the room except one man. However, 'only one man' also has a 'restrictive' meaning whose content is 'some (one) F and no other F.' Read restrictively, (3a) conveys that one man and no other *man* entered the room, and thereby allows for the possibility that some women also entered. Hence, the predicate 'F,' in 'only one F,' commonly does more

---

subsequent discourse. See also the discussion of this and related questions in Chierchia's *Dynamics of Meaning*.

than merely indicate the domain of the quantifier: it may relativize the uniqueness condition implicit in the 'only one' quantifier phrase to the class of Fs. What is more, it is the second of these readings that is surely the most natural.

Therefore, if (3a) has its unrestrictive reading, an individual instance of it is expressed by a sentence of the form 'Only α entered the room,' (i.e., '[Only $x: x = α$] x entered the room)') whenever 'α'designates a particular man. Interpreted restrictively, an instance of (3a) will be formulated instead by 'Only α is a man who entered the room' (i.e., '[Only $x: x = α$] x is a man who entered the room'). Relative to the unrestrictive reading of (3a), (3b) expresses the proposition

> For some man m (in the case in which only m entered the room) he saw the Maltese Falcon,

and, relative to the more likely restrictive reading, (3b) has the content

> For some man m (in the case in which only m is a man who entered the room) he saw the Maltese Falcon.

It is a merit of this account that it recognizes the correlated ambiguity in (3a) and (3b) and offers a simple explanation of it. It should be remarked that the restrictive reading of (3a), on this account, assigns to an associated instance of (3b) the truth conditions that Russell's theory of descriptions ascribes to

(15)   The man who entered the room saw the Maltese Falcon.

Hence, our proposed analysis has the further merit of agreeing with Neale about the truth conditions of the anaphorically dependent statements, but the picture our account devises of how these truth conditions come to be assigned to (3b), in its discourse context, is significantly different from his.

Just as we can frame a quantifier phrase by attaching 'only' to a definite singular term, we can also form quantifier phrases by prefixing 'only' to a certain range of expressions that are themselves quantifier phrases. The expression 'one F,' is, of course, an example, but we also have, e.g., 'a few Fs,' 'several Fs,' 'some Fs,' and 'n Fs,' where 'n'

names a number. Although I have tried to steer clear of the complications presented by the third person plural pronouns, it is worth mentioning that our account of (3) promises to generalize to all or most meaningful instances of '[Only Q + NP] Φ and they Ψ.' Let us take as a sample,

(16) (a) Only two men entered the room, and b) they saw the Maltese Falcon.

In order to illustrate how the basic pattern emerges in this discourse sequence, it will help another time to look at a more complicated analogue of (8):

(17) (a) Only Smith and Brown or Jones and Knight entered the room, and (b) they saw the Maltese Falcon.

Predictably, this means

(17′) Only Smith and Brown entered the room, and they saw the Maltese Falcon, OR Jones and Knight entered the room, and they saw the Maltese Falcon.

The first occurrence of 'they' in (17′) clearly refers conjointly to Smith and Brown, the second to Jones and Knight, and both occurrences inherit their referents from the antecedent conjunction of names with which they are linked in the sentence or discourse. Further, we note that '[Only A and B] Φ′d, and they Ψ′d' is true just in case A and B Φ′d, nothing other than A and B Φ′d, and both A and B Ψ′d.

Similar to (1b) and (8b), (17b) should say

In at least one such case, they saw the Maltese Falcon,

and the range of cases to which the prefixed quantifier adverts should be all the propositional instances of 'Only two men entered the room.' In fact, (17a) also has a restrictive and non-restrictive reading, but we will focus here only on the more natural restrictive reading. An instance of (17a), then, will be generated whenever the open sentence 'Only α and β are men who entered the room,' is ascribed to an arbitrary pair of men, m_1 and m_2. This means, for instance, that (17b), interpreted restrictively, is true iff

> For some two men, m_1 and m_2, (in the case in which only $\underline{m}_1$ and $\underline{m}_2$ are men who entered the room) they saw the Maltese Falcon.

More simply, this says, as it should, that two men, and no more than two men, entered the room, and both saw the Maltese Falcon. Other instances of '[Only Q + Np] Φ'd, and they Ψ'd' can be handled along essentially the same lines.

At this juncture, I want to defend briefly a contested claim that I have made about the second conjunct in

(14)   (a) A man entered the room, and (b) he saw the Maltese Falcon.

We remarked earlier that, for Neale, the pronoun in (14b) 'goes proxy for' a Russellian definite description, 'the man who entered the room,' and (14b) is held to have the truth conditions that this thesis entails. I have contended, on the other hand, that the uniqueness condition that Neale's account imposes on (14b) is mistaken and so have agreed with 'classical DRT' on this point. For me then, (14b) stands in contrast with the second conjunct in

(8a)   Only one man entered the room, and (b) he saw the Maltese Falcon,

in which the uniqueness condition *is*, in fact, expressed. Similarly, Neale maintains that

(5)   At least one farmer who owns a donkey beats it

demands that the donkey owning farmers have just one donkey, and that claim, I maintain, is also false, for reasons shortly to be given.

Proposition (14) is a good example to bring out the implausibility of Neale's thesis. Suppose that I assert (14), solely on evidence of disturbance to the room and the fact that no one could enter without seeing the Maltese Falcon. Surely, my assertion still counts as true even if it turns out that more than one man entered the room and saw the Maltese Falcon. Neale is very much aware of this problem, and he adumbrates several ways of trying to meet the difficulty, e.g., by relativizing the reconstructed description to relevant times or to different events of entering.[16] I do not want to examine the various possible emendations in detail, but I can give a reason for doubting that any of them will succeed.

Let us imagine that someone asserts that

> Judy will see <u>a straight line on the screen</u>, and <u>it</u> will be black.

Suppose also that, at the time of the seeing, what Judy perceives on the screen is a black cross, formed by the intersection of vertical and horizontal straight lines, both of them black. Here, as in the case of (14), it seems to me that the statement is true, and, on the face of the matter, its truth depends upon a single event of Judy's seeing the black cross, i.e., seeing both of the lines together. It might be insisted that, even in the imagined circumstances, there was a seeing of the horizontal line distinct from the seeing of the vertical line, but, in my opinion, the insistence would only be driven by a desire to save the semantic theory. No plausible relativization to times or events will do the job that Neale has in mind for them. Similarly, the proposition

> At least one viewer who saw <u>a straight line on the screen</u> noticed that <u>it</u> was black

is not falsified even if every viewer saw the two straight lines as inextricably crossed on the screen, noticing that both were black. This tells against Neale's closely related thesis about the truth conditions of (5).

The limited issue here casts broader doubt on Neale's general approach to the relevant unbound anaphora. Compare (5) and (14) with

(18) (a) <u>Each man</u> entered the room, and (b) <u>he</u> saw the Maltese Falcon.

---

16 Neale, 241-51

We now have *three* different discourse settings in which the form of words, 'He saw the Maltese Falcon,' have three different interpretations, depending upon the quantifier phrase to which an occurrence of the pronoun is linked. One would like to have an explanation of why the different interpretations are determined, in this specific fashion, by the character of the antecedent quantifier phrase. According to Neale's theory, the pronouns in these environments stand in for appropriate descriptions, and, the framework of the theory distinguishes descriptions of *two* kinds: Russellian definite descriptions and 'numberless' or 'number neutral' descriptions (e.g., 'whichever man entered the room').[17] The number neutral descriptions are deployed to explain the intuitive truth conditions of (18b) and other related examples, and it is quite true that phrases of the form 'the F which G' often allow for a kind of number neutral interpretation. However, if I am right about the truth conditions of (8b), then a theory of the sort Neale develops is forced to postulate a third sort of description — a 'description' having the meaning of 'at least one F which is G.' As the 'descriptions' proliferate, the attractiveness of the 'recovered description' approach begins to wane. Indeed, the sentence

(19)   At most one man will enter the room, and he will see the Maltese Falcon

threatens to conjure up still one more species of 'description,' and it is hardly clear where all of this will end. None of these considerations impugn a weaker thesis — the thesis that all of these anaphoric pronouns 'go proxy for' a suitable *quantifier phrase*. But even the weaker thesis leaves us in need of a systematic account of why the pronouns in (8), (14), (18), and (19) are differentially interpreted by their antecedent quantifiers as they are. Perhaps the discussion in this paper can be taken as the beginnings of such an account.

---

17 Neale, 234-5

IV

I mentioned at the outset of the paper that pronouns with disjunctive nominals as their non-*c*-command antecedents behave in a distinctive fashion in the context of conditionals. I pointed out that

(2)   If <u>either Jones or Smith</u> entered the room, then <u>he</u> saw the Maltese Falcon

does not have the truth conditions of

(2′)   If <u>Jones</u> entered the room, then <u>he</u> saw the Maltese Falcon, OR if <u>Smith</u> entered the room, then <u>he</u> saw the Maltese Falcon,

as we might have first thought from our discussion of (1). Rather, brief reflection reveals that (2) is actually equivalent to

(2″)   If <u>Jones</u> entered the room, then <u>he</u> saw the Maltese Falcon, AND if <u>Smith</u> entered the room, then <u>he</u> saw the Maltese Falcon.

And now, one would like to know where the conjunction in (2″) comes from? It is not that 'either-or' in (2) acquires, in this grammatical neighborhood, the sense of 'and.' If so, (2) would say

If <u>Jones and Smith</u> entered the room, then <u>he</u> (or rather: <u>they</u>, one of <u>them</u>, etc.) saw the Maltese Falcon,

and, of course, it does not. The puzzle is not unlike the one described in connection with

(4)   Every farmer who owned <u>a donkey</u> beat <u>it</u>,

in which it appears that an existential quantifier, i.e., the indefinite description in the relative clause, must mysteriously adopt the sense of a universal quantifier.

The equivalence of (2) and (2′) may well remind us of the fact that instances of

If (*P* or *Q*) then *R*

are equivalent to corresponding instances of

(If *P* then *Q*) and (if *Q* then *R*)

in truth functional propositional logic and, indeed, in most of the more familiar propositional logics. This equivalence is important here, I believe, but we have to take some care about its explanatory role. (2) and (2′) are only superficially of the forms set out above. The 'consequent' of (2) contains an anaphor making some kind of back reference to both items mentioned in the disjunctive nominal within the conditional's antecedent, and, the pronouns in the consequents in (2″) are each assigned different referents through different lines of anaphoric inheritance.

Nevertheless, it is my impression that it is somehow constitutive of the way in which we standardly understand conditionals with disjunctive antecedents that, in working out what they say, we process them as the logical product of the simpler conditionals in question. Or, in any event, we do so when the surface consequent contains an anaphor that picks up values from both of the implicit disjuncts. We see the same pattern in conditionals with anaphors interpretatively dependent on disjunctive antecedents of related sorts. For example,

(20)   If Nick bought <u>either a Mercedes or a Bentley</u>, then Smith bought <u>one</u> as well

has the content of

(20′)   If Nick bought <u>a Mercedes</u>, then Smith bought <u>one</u> as well, AND if Nick bought <u>a Bentley</u>, then Smith bought <u>one</u> as well.

In (2) and (20) and in other like examples, the propositional disjuncts in the antecedents feed an appropriate value to the anaphor, and the original conditional, in such examples, is true iff all the resulting value-loaded conditionals are themselves true.

Here is what seems to be going on in (2). The disjuncts implicit in the antecedent introduce us once more to the two familiar cases featuring the entrances of Jones and Smith, but, in the conditional, these two cases are introduced, so to speak, as branching *suppositions*. In relation to the supposition that Jones entered the room, the pronoun in the consequent takes Jones as its value, and the consequent itself proposes that, *under the supposition of that case*, Jones saw the Maltese Falcon. In relation to the alternative supposition, the pronoun designates Smith, and we are to evaluate whether, *under the alternative supposition*, Smith saw the Falcon.[18] The conditional as whole is true just in case the consequent, as interpreted by either case, comes out true *under either supposition*. In other words, (2) has the intuitive force of

> In each of these cases, if it obtains, then <u>he</u> saw the Maltese Falcon.

The prefixed quantifier phrase, in this suggested paraphrase, refers to the two cases (or: instances) mentioned in the conditional's antecedent, and thereby picks out the two subordinate conditionals whose conjunction is actually at issue. (2), therefore, is true iff the open sentence 'If α entered the room, then <u>he</u> saw the Maltese Falcon' is itself true both when 'α' designates Jones and when it designates Smith.

It is well recognized that a conditional like

(21)   If <u>a man</u> entered the room, then <u>he</u> saw the Maltese Falcon

has, on its preferred reading, the force of a universal quantification over men. Thus, it raises a puzzle about indefinite descriptions in the antecedents of conditionals similar to the puzzle about indefinite descriptions in 'donkey sentences' like (4). But now, given our discussion

---

18 These remarks are meant to do no more than give a suggestive picture of the role of the disjuncts in the antecedents of the conditionals under study. Clearly, the relevant notion of 'a supposition' and of 'truth under a supposition' would require extensive treatment. (Although I believe that my remarks are compatible with a number of possible approaches to these matters.) This would force us to enter, seriously and at length, into the daunting territory of the theory of conditionals and the enormous literature it has generated.

of (2), we have every reason to find the preferred reading at least predictable. When we discussed (8a) ('A man entered the room,' as it occurs in the context of (8)), I said that the sentence served two functions in that setting. It expressed the proposition that at least one man entered the room, and it specified the type of case required for the proper interpretation of (8b), i.e., the cases expressed by each of its propositional instances. The required cases there were the minimal individual cases, concerning particular men, sufficient for its obtaining that at least one man entered the room. I think we should say much the same thing about (21). In the light of our account of (2), (21) will mean that

In each such case, if it obtains, then <u>he</u> saw the Maltese Falcon,

where the pronoun inherits its referent, case by case, from each of the propositional instances of 'A man entered the room.' In this setting, these instances are treated as suppositions under which the truth values of the corresponding consequents are to be evaluated. Therefore, (21) is true if the conditional

If $\underline{\alpha}$ entered the room, then <u>he</u> saw the Maltese Falcon

is true, as desired, under every assignment of a man to 'α.'

From this perspective, there is no reason to deny that indefinite descriptions in conditionals like (21) have the sense of existential quantifiers. What we should say, I am proposing, is that the sentential antecedents that contain such descriptions have a special, although unsurprising, function which they serve in the conditionals under scrutiny. Moreover, that function is not essentially different from the 'case-identifying' function that the same sentences have when they occur 'conjunctively' in a sequence of assertions. In my opinion, any theory that seeks to explain the behavior of the pronoun in (21) by adopting a non- standard account of the logical contribution of indefinite descriptions has mis-diagnosed the situation, and this point is demonstrated by the fact that the nominal disjunction in (2) raises essentially the same problems of interpretation as does the indefinite description in (21). These examples, given their common structure, should be dealt with together, and that is what I have tried to do by working from the latter examples back to the former.

Finally, what can we say about the infamous sentence (4) ('Every farmer who owns <u>a donkey</u> beats <u>it</u>')? Things would fall in place immediately *if* we could simply assume that it has the underlying logical form of

(4″)   [Every x: x is a farmer] (if x owns <u>a donkey</u>, then x beats <u>it</u>).

(4″) is a universal generalization of a conditional having otherwise the same internal structure as (21). If the assumption were adopted, nothing further would need to be said to provide us with an analysis of (4). Despite the widespread popularity, promoted by beginning logic courses, of translations of 'Every F is a G' into universally generalized conditionals, the rendering of (4) in terms of (4″) is not well supported by serious syntactical or semantical considerations. For instance, compare (4) with (5) ('At least one farmer who owns a donkey beats it'). By parity of reasoning, this presumably would have the underlying logical form of

[At least one x: x is a farmer] (x owns <u>a donkey</u> and x beats <u>it</u>).

However, it is doubtful that cogent consideration will explicate and justify the quite different treatment of the relative clauses employed in the two examples. Are we to suppose that the relative pronoun is ambiguous, having a 'conditional' sense in one instance (in (4)) and a 'conjunctive' sense in the other (in (5))? Or, alternatively, do we assume that there is a level of grammatical deep structure in which universal quantifier phrases in relative clauses are subordinated to 'if-then' constructions, while existential quantifier phrases in relative clauses govern associated conjunctions of predicates? The first idea is unmotivated and unattractive, and nothing in contemporary syntax encourages the second. Unfortunately, I have no better idea to offer in their place, and I do not know of anything to warrant us in treating (4) as a generalized form of a conditional with a structure of the type in (21). I say that this is unfortunate because I think that the problematic universal quantifications in (4) and (21) *should* have some common explanation that calls upon 'conditionalization' as the crucial factor. It is just that I do not know how the common factor should itself be explicated. Thus, in the absence of a theory of relative clauses — and of relative pronouns in particular — that helps us with this question, I am forced to leave the matter unresolved.

In this paper, my basic claim has been that obligatory co-reference between a pronoun and its singular term antecedent is only an instance, albeit a very important instance, of a more general phenomenon. I have attempted to bring this out by investigating in some detail a sort of intermediate case, i.e., some examples in which the antecedent of the anaphor is a disjunction of singular terms. These intermediate cases serve as a kind of bridge to examples which have been more exhaustively studied by others, and, I believe, the former cast light on the latter. Once we get the intermediate cases right, it is easy enough to see how their analysis might be extended to apply to various sentences and discourse fragments containing pronouns that analogously depend for their interpretation upon quantifier phrases that do not bind them.[19]

---

19 I have profited, in thinking about these materials, from suggestions from Kent Bach, Paolo Leonardi, Peter Ludlow, and Ernesto Napoli. I am especially indebted to Jeff King for extensive comments on an earlier version and to many discussions, over the years, with Mark Wilson.

CANADIAN JOURNAL OF PHILOSOPHY
Supplementary Volume 23

"Kilimanjaro"[1]

VANN McGEE
Massachusetts Institute of Technology

This is not an overly ambitious paper. What I would like to do is to take a thesis that most people would regard as wildly implausible, and convince you that it is, in fact, false. What's worse, the argument I shall give is by no means airtight, though I hope it's reasonably convincing. The thesis has to do with the fuzzy boundaries of terms that refer to familiar middle-sized objects, terms like 'Kilimanjaro' and 'the tallest mountain in Africa.' It is intuitively clear (though not beyond doubt — see Timothy Williamson's book *Vagueness*[2]) that Kilimanjaro has a fuzzy boundary, so that there are some clods of earth at the base of the mountain for which there isn't anything, either in our practices in using the word 'Kilimanjaro' or in the facts of geography, that determines an answer to the question whether the clod is a part of Kilimanjaro.

The intuitively most natural explanation of this phenomenon is linguistic. The way we use the word 'Kilimanjaro' is such that molecules in the interior of the mountain are determined to satisfy 'is a part of Kilimanjaro,' and molecules well outside the mountain are determined to satisfy 'is not a part of Kilimanjaro.' But this classification is not exhaustive. There are molecules near the edge of the mountain that competent users of the language would refuse to declare either 'a part of

---

1 Much of the line of reasoning presented here was developed during long conversations I enjoyed with Brian McLaughlin, discussions which resulted in a joint paper, 'Distinctions Without a Difference,' *Southern Journal of Philosophy*, **33**, supplement (1995) 203-51. I would also like to thank Catherine Elgin and Ralph Wedgwood for helpful discussions.

2 London and New York: Routledge 1994

Kilimanjaro' or 'not a part of Kilimanjaro,' under even the best of epistemic circumstances. Now the fact that ordinary speakers refuse to classify a thing is no proof that there isn't a right way to classify it, nor is the fact that ordinary speakers have predominantly, or even invariably, classified a thing a certain way an infallible guide to its correct classification. One wouldn't want to answer the question 'Is a panda a bear?' by taking an opinion survey. But a mountain doesn't have a hidden essence or any other decisive qualities that are concealed from the speaking public's view. There doesn't appear to be anything, either in the nature of Kilimanjaro or in our use of 'Kilimanjaro,' that would settle the question whether the edge molecules are a part of Kilimanjaro.

The most natural explanation for the indeterminacy is that there are two sorts of terms, vague and precise (though damn few of the latter), and the reason questions of the form 'Is such and such a molecule a part of Kilimanjaro?' lack determinate answers is that 'Kilimanjaro' is a vague term.

The alternative explanation is that there are two sorts of objects, vague and precise, and the reason for the indeterminacy is that Kilimanjaro is a vague object. While doubtlessly there are vague terms — terms such that there are objects about which it is indeterminate whether the term applies to them — 'Kilimanjaro' is not a such a term.[3] Our practices in using the word 'Kilimanjaro' link the word inerrantly with uniquely determined object. It's just that the object chosen is a vague object.[4]

---

3 Even if you think that all vagueness is either linguistic or mental in origin, you can still make sense of the claim that Kilimanjaro is a vague object, by understanding 'vague object' in a derivative sense: A vague object is one that is, considering the purposes that are likely to arise in practice, especially apt to be named by a vague term. This derivative sense is not what we shall have in mind when we discuss the thesis that Kilimanjaro is a vague object. Instead, the thesis will be that the vagueness of Kilimanjaro is part of what the mountain is, independent of human language and thought.

4 In principle, one might hold that 'Kilimanjaro' suffers from both kinds of indeterminacy: It is a vague term whose reference is indeterminate among a number of vague objects. It is doubtful that anyone will find such a Baroque position attractive, however, since the principal motive for postulating vague objects is to avoid (as much a possible) the difficulties that come with vague singular terms.

On first hearing, the alternative strikes one as zany, and, on closer examination, it sounds even worse. There is a theory of fuzzy objects, which assigns numerical values to points in space, assigning 1 to the points that are definitely within Kilimanjaro, 0 to points that are definitely outside it, and intermediate values to points on the border.[5] To assign such a fuzzy object to the word 'Kilimanjaro,' our usage would have to determine a precise inner boundary, a precise outer boundary, and a precise numerical function connecting them. Fuzzy objects, so conceived, would be even harder to latch onto than precise objects, so that our reasons for thinking that our usage does not connect 'Kilimanjaro' with a precisely determined precise object operate even more powerfully as reasons to think that our usage does not attach 'Kilimanjaro' to a precisely determined vague object. Thus any account that treats proper names as firmly affixed to fuzzy objects will require a way of understanding fuzzy objects that is altogether different from anything currently in view.

In view of these difficulties, why would anyone be tempted by vague objects? The reason is that, without them, it's hard to see how a theory of reference, as it's ordinarily conceived, can get off the ground. We can, if we want, develop the theory of reference and satisfaction as an exercise in pure mathematics, treating "Provided Kilimanjaro exists, 'Kilimanjaro' refers to Kilimanjaro" as something that's true in virtue of the meaning of the word 'refers.' That's unproblematic. But if we want to use the notions of reference and satisfaction as the basis of a serious attempt to understand how human beings use language, we need to propose that there is something speakers of the language do, say, or think that connects the word 'Kilimanjaro' with its referent. But, unless there are vague objects, there isn't any such thing as *the* referent of the word 'Kilimanjaro.' There are many things that have equally good claim to being the referent of 'Kilimanjaro' — the many geographical entities that we could get by drawing a precise boundary about the mountain's spatiotemporal perimeter in a manner consistent with our usage of the word. But the laws of semantics, as we customarily

---

5 See Lofti Zadeh, 'Fuzzy Logic and Approximate Reasoning,' *Synthese* 30 (1975) 407-28.

understand them, resolutely require that, if the word 'Kilimanjaro' refers at all, it refers to one and only one thing. There isn't anything speakers of English do, say, or think that singles out one and only one thing as the referent of 'Kilimanjaro.' Consequently, if we think of the reference relation as describing, in a substantive way, the thoughts and practices of speakers of the language, we are forced to conclude that 'Kilimanjaro' doesn't refer.

The same goes for the names of persons. This will be so even if you think (as I certainly do not) that there's an indissoluble spiritual monad at the core of a human's being, provided you also think that a person has a physical part as well. Let Sporty be some little molecule at the periphery of Maya Angelou's body. Then the mereological sum

Maya Angelou + Sporty

and the mereological difference

Maya Angelou - Sporty

are distinct, yet they have equally good claim to being what speakers of English refer to as 'Maya Angelou.' We can avoid this outcome only if we succumb to the extreme view that a person is an indivisible spiritual substance with no physical parts whatever.

We shall get this outcome whatever our theory of proper names. If we have a causal theory of names, according to which the word 'Kilimanjaro' refers to the thing that causes our use of the word, we find that there are many slightly differing geographical entities that have indistinguishable causal roles. If instead we have a 'cluster of descriptions' view, according to which there is a list of attributes we associate with the word 'Kilimanjaro,' and the word refers, if at all, to the one and only one item that satisfies a predominance of the items on the list, we find that the descriptions are vague in a way that prevents the identification of a unique thing that satisfies a predominance of them. Suppose that one of the descriptions on our list is 'mountain at latitude 3.07° S., longitude 37.35° E.' A glance at an aerial photograph will convince us that there is one and only one mountain at that location, but there is nothing we do, say, or think that fixes the mountain's precise boundary. Thinking of the many ways we might mark the mountain's precise boundary convinces us that there are many equally good candidates for the unique object that satisfies 'mountain at 3.07° S., 37.35° E.,' all of which are equally good candidates for the referent of 'Kilimanjaro.'

We have the same worry with definite descriptions. Philosophers have fretted a great deal over the fact that phrases like 'the lowest mountain in Africa' lack a determinate referent, on account of the mushiness of the boundary between mountains and hills. But, if we only have precise objects to work with, it looks like we have insuperable difficulties trying to fix a referent for 'the tallest mountain in Africa.'

Without vague objects, few if any singular terms are going to have determinate referents. What's more, we have the same difficulty for a great many general terms. If the geographic facts are at all as we understand them, there can be only one entity at 3.07° S., 37.35° E. that satisfies the term 'mountain,' yet there are innumerable entities at 3.07° S., 37.35° E. that have equally good claims to being mountains. It looks as if there's nothing at 3.07° S., 37.35° E. of which it's determined that it satisfies 'mountain.' The problem is the same at any other geographic location, so it doesn't appear that there's anything of which it's determined that it satisfies 'mountain' at all. The same goes for almost any other count noun.

People have thought of the problem of vagueness as the problem of how to deal with border cases of adjectives and of mass nouns. There are many things that are determinately red, many other things that are determinately not red, and a few mischief makers in between. This is an interesting problem, but it's a problem we can learn to live with, since typically the borderline cases are relatively few, and in those situations in which the borderline cases are either so numerous or so important as to cause us practical difficulties, we can alleviate the problem simply by reformulating our questions in a more precise language. With singular terms and count nouns, however, the situation is altogether more disturbing. There isn't, anywhere in the world, anything of which it's determined that it satisfies 'mountain.' Forget about thinning hair. Nothing is determined to satisfy 'bald man,' because nothing is determined to satisfy 'man.'

Quine worked very hard to convince us that there isn't any object x such that the practices of speakers of English determine that x is one of the things they refer to when they use the word 'rabbit.'[6] Now rabbits are pretty well distinguished from their surrounding environment, but they are not demarcated with utter precision; hence, unless we have an ontology that includes vague objects, we get the same conclusion much more easily. Speakers all agree to the sentence 'There is exactly one rabbit in the hutch,' so, unless we want to ascribe to them wholesale error, we have to allow that there is at most one thing in the hutch that is a referent of 'rabbit.' But there is nothing in their practices that prefers either Cottontail + Spunky or, Cottontail - Spunky as the referent (where Spunky is a molecule on Cottontail's perimeter), so there is nothing in the hutch of which it is determined that it is in the extension of 'rabbit.'.

The structure of the argument here is different from that of Chapter 2 of *Word and Object*. There it was argued that, even after you've determined the truth values of all the sentences, you still haven't determined the reference relation. Here the source of the inscrutability is that there are certain sentences, things like 'Spunky is a part of Cottontail,' that lack a determinate truth value. But though the arguments are different, the conclusions are much the same.

If you are already convinced (as I'm inclined to be) by Quine's argument, the realization that vagueness gives you yet another reason to suppose that reference is inscrutable will not greatly alarm you. But many people have thought that they could block Quine's argument one way or another. To get determinacy of reference, they need to block the argument from vagueness as well, and the postulation of precise terms referring to vague objects seems like the most promising approach to try.

The philosophical stakes are high here. Not only our usual ways of talking about language but also our ordinary ways of thinking about thought are under attack. On our ordinary understanding, for it to be the case, in the *de re* sense, that Marco Polo believed of Kilimanjaro that it is the highest mountain in Africa, there has to be some combination

---

6 *Word and Object* (Cambridge, MA: MIT Press 1960), ch. 2, and 'Ontological Relativity' in *Ontological Relativity and Other Essays* (New York: Columbia University Press 1969), 26-68

of causal and mental factors that picks out one and only one entity as the object his belief is about. If what we have is a cloud of entities, and what Marco believes is that somewhere in the cloud there is a mountain that is higher than any other mountain in Africa, then his belief isn't a *de re* belief about Kilimanjaro. In order for us to have *de re* beliefs, at least on our usual understanding of them, our thoughts and practices have to pick out one particular thing as the object the belief is about. But unless we postulate vague objects, our thoughts and practices never succeed in picking out one particular physical object, so we don't have any *de re* beliefs about physical objects. Without vague objects, we must relinquish our usual ways of understanding the relations between thoughts and their objects, along with our accustomed ways of regarding the connections between words and their referents.

The postulation of vague objects is one way of getting an affirmative answer to the question, 'Is there vagueness in the world, as well as vagueness in language?' Another potential source of 'vagueness in the world' is quantum indeterminacy, but that's not a topic we shall discuss here. This is, as I say, not an ambitious paper.

The classical treatise on vague objects is an article by Gareth Evans entitled 'Can There Be Vague Objects?'[7] It's a one-page article that bears all the signs of having been written late one night and mailed off to *Analysis* the next morning. The main sign of hasty writing is his use of the symbol 'Δ,' which he sometimes reads as 'It is determined that' and sometimes as 'It is determined whether.' It is easy enough to straighten matters out, however, using '$\square$' for the former and 'Δ' for the latter. Note well that, in the present context, '$\square$' does not mean 'It is necessary that.' The two symbols are interdefinable, either by

$$\Delta\phi =_{Def} (\square\phi \vee \square\sim\phi),$$

or by

$$\square\phi =_{Def} (\Delta\phi \wedge \phi).$$

There are also the dual notions '∇' ('It is indeterminate whether') and '$\lozenge$,' defined by:

---

7 *Analysis* **38** (1978) 208

$$\nabla\phi =_{\text{Def}} \sim\!\Delta\phi,$$

and

$$\lozenge\phi =_{\text{Def}} \sim\!\square\!\sim\!\phi.$$

What Evans purports to give is an argument that there are no vague objects, but what is in fact written down is a fallacious argument that there are no indefinite identity statements.[8] So, to get anything useful out of the paper, we shall have to read it with more than usual sympathy; but I think the effort is worthwhile.

Here is the argument:[9] Suppose, for *reductio ad absurdum*, that we have this:

$$\nabla a=b.$$

---

8 Nathan Salmon (*Reference and Essence* (Princeton: Princeton University Press 1981), 243-45) uses the same formal argument (discovered independently of Evans) as a demonstration of the conclusion that identity is not a vague relation. There is a misstep in Salmon's argument. Having assumed '$a = b$' as a premiss for *reductio ad absurdum*, Salmon characterizes '$a = b$' as "an *assumption* — something we are taking to be determinately the case for the sake of argument" (244n). But assuming a statement for the sake of a *reductio* or conditional proof is not at all the same as assuming that that statement is determinately true. Indeed, if assumptions we made for the sake of conditional proofs could be presumed to be determinately true, we could prove outright that no statement is indeterminate in truth value, as follows:

1. ⎰ ϕ	(assumption)
2. ⎱ $\ulcorner\phi\urcorner$ is determinately true	(assumptions are determinately true)
3. ($\phi \to \ulcorner\phi\urcorner$ is determinately true)	(conditional proof)
4. ⎰ $\sim\!\phi$	(assumption)
5. ⎱ $\ulcorner\sim\!\phi\urcorner$ is determinately true	(assumptions are determinately true)
6. ($\sim\!\phi \to \ulcorner\sim\!\phi\urcorner$ is determinately true)	(conditional proof)
7. Either $\ulcorner\phi\urcorner$ or $\ulcorner\sim\!\phi\urcorner$ is determinately true	(from 3 and 6 by truth-functional logic)

9 A useful and careful investigation of the logic of Evans's argument can be found in Richard Heck's 'That There Might Be Vague Objects (So Far As Concerns Logic),' which is part of his 1991 MIT Ph.D. thesis.

Because '$a=a$' is a law of logic, it is determinately true; hence:

$$\sim \nabla a = a.$$

But the law of identity gives us this:

$$(a=b \rightarrow (\nabla a = a \leftrightarrow \nabla a = b)).$$

Whence, by truth-functional logic:

$$\sim(a=b),$$

"contradicting," Evans says, "the assumption with which we began, that the identity statement '$a=b$' is of indeterminate truth value."

But where is the contradiction? There is a pragmatic inconsistency in putting forward an assertion of the form ⌜ϕ, but it is indeterminate whether ϕ⌝, just as there is a pragmatic inconsistency in asserting ⌜ϕ, but I don't believe that ϕ⌝. But I would be misguided in inferring from the pragmatic inconsistency of ⌜ϕ, but I don't believe that ϕ⌝ that I believe every true sentence, and I would be similarly misguided if I thought myself entitled to deny every sentence of the form ⌜ϕ, but it is indeterminate whether ϕ⌝ on the basis of the fact that no such sentence is ever assertible. Indeed, if any sentence of the form ⌜$\nabla\phi$⌝ is assertible, then the disjunction

$$((\phi \wedge \nabla\phi) \vee (\sim\phi \wedge \nabla\sim\phi))$$

is assertible, since the latter follows from the former by classical logic. The disjunction is assertible, even though neither disjunct is.

What the pragmatic indeterminacy does show is that no sentence of the form ⌜$\nabla a = b$⌝ can be known to be true. The reason no such sentence can be known to be true is that no sentence of the form ⌜$\nabla a = b$⌝ can be determinately true. That is, we have:

$$\sim \Box \nabla a = b.$$

To see this, notice that Evans's argument gives us the conditional:

$(\nabla a=b \rightarrow \sim(a=b))$.

Putting a '$\square$' in front and distributing, we get:

$(\square\nabla a=b \rightarrow \square\sim(a=b))$.

But, obviously,

$(\square\sim(a=b) \rightarrow \sim\nabla a=b)$,

whence:

$(\square\nabla a=b \rightarrow \sim\nabla a=b)$.

But also, by axiom schema (T):

$(\square\nabla a=b \rightarrow \nabla a=b)$,

whence the conclusion follows.

   If there is no higher-order vagueness, so that if something is determinately true, it is determinate that it's determinately true, while if something is not determinately true, it's determinate that it's not determinately true — in symbols,

$(\square\phi \rightarrow \square\square\phi)$
$(\sim\square\phi \rightarrow \square\sim\square\phi)$

— then the modal logic of 'determinately' is **S5**, in which case, as Evans notes,

$\sim\nabla a=b$

is an outright theorem, gotten thus:

$(a=b \rightarrow \square a=b)$	(shown above)
$(\lozenge\sim(a=b) \rightarrow \sim(a=b))$	(contraposition)
$(\square\lozenge\sim(a=b) \rightarrow \square\sim(a=b))$	(putting a '$\square$' in front and driving it through)

$(\sim(a{=}b) \rightarrow \Box \Diamond \sim(a{=}b))$ (schema (B), a theorem schema of S5)

$(\Box \sim(a{=}b) \rightarrow \sim\nabla(a{=}b))$ (definitions of 'Δ' and '∇')

$(\sim(a{=}b) \rightarrow \sim\nabla(a{=}b))$ (truth functionally from the preceding three lines)

$(a{=}b \rightarrow \sim\nabla a{=}b)$ (from the first line, by definition of 'Δ' and '∇')

$\sim\nabla a{=}b$ (from the preceding two lines)

But there is not the slightest reason to suppose that there is no higher-order vagueness.

Now that we know what the argument shows formally, we may ask what it shows philosophically. What Evans says is this:

> It is sometimes said that the world itself might *be* vague. Rather than vagueness being a deficiency in our mode of describing the world, it would then be a necessary feature of any true description of it. It is also said that amongst the statements which may not have a determinate truth value on account of their vagueness are identity statements. Combining these two views we would arrive at the idea that the world might contain certain objects about which it is a *fact* that they have fuzzy boundaries. But is this idea coherent?

That's all he says, before launching into the proof. So we're pretty well left on our own in figuring out the formal argument's significance.

Let us begin with a very simple but not very convincing argument that there is some object that is uniquely picked out as the referent of 'Kilimanjaro.' The sentence

$(\exists x)\Box\ x = \text{Kilimanjaro}$

tells us that there is, in reality, a thing that is picked out, uniquely and determinately, as Kilimanjaro. The sentence:

Kilimanjaro = Kilimanjaro

is a theorem of logic, hence determinately true:

$\Box$ Kilimanjaro = Kilimanjaro.

$(\exists x)\Box\ x = \text{Kilimanjaro}$

follows by existential generalization.

We should be chary of this argument, inasmuch as an exactly parallel argument leads us to the conclusion that 'the world's shortest tall person' has a determinate reference. What's dubious about the argument is its employment of existential generalization within the context of the 'determinately' operator.[10] The development of modal logic has forced us to be a little more discriminating in dealing with questions about referential opacity, so that we no longer presume that operators can be partitioned tidily into those within the scope of which existential generalization is or is not valid. Instead, we anticipate that the legitimacy of the inference from $\ulcorner Fa \urcorner$ to $\ulcorner (\exists x)Fx \urcorner$ may well depend on a as well as on F. The question we want to answer is whether the inference from $\ulcorner$Kilimanjaro is an $F \urcorner$ to $\ulcorner$For some x, x is an $F \urcorner$ is invalidated by the presence in F of the word 'determinately'?

Just to make sense of the attachment of the word 'determinately' to an open sentence containing free variables is a bit of a stretch, since we primarily think of determinacy as an attribute of sentences. A sentence is determinately true, determinately false, or unsettled. We need to go beyond this familiar usage if we want to say of an object that it either determinately satisfies, determinately fails to satisfy, or is indeterminate with respect to an open sentence with one free variable. Of course, we get to use the word 'determinately' however we want to. It's an English word, but it's being employed in a technical way. We want our technical usage to be such as to enable us better to understand why a sentence that is indeterminate in truth value has that status. A sentence that has the form $\ulcorner Fa \urcorner$ might be indeterminate either because of the vagueness of a, the vagueness of F, or a combination of both. But if F is perfectly sharp, so that every object satisfies $\ulcorner \Delta Fx \urcorner$, the indeterminacy of $\ulcorner Fa \urcorner$ can only be due to the indeterminacy of a; that is, we can only have $\ulcorner ((\forall x)\Delta Fx \land \nabla Fa) \urcorner$ if a lacks a precisely determined referent.

For each open sentence, we would like a threefold classification (in general, a *vague* threefold classification). There is an *extension*, consisting of those things that are determined to satisfy the open sentence and an *anti-*

---

10 Another worry about existential generalization comes from the fact that, in natural languages, there are denotationless proper names. This worry is less serious, since it can be soothed by adopting the premiss, 'Kilimanjaro exists,' then proceeding in free logic.

extension, consisting of those things of which it is determined that they fail to satisfy the open sentence. These two sets cannot overlap, but they need not be exhaustive. There can be a third category, consisting of things for which it is undetermined whether they satisfy the open sentence.

It's useful to introduce a logical device called *supervaluations* at this point.[11] Fixing our attention on situations in which we have a precisely fixed, nonempty universe of discourse U — this means setting aside vagueness that arises because of indefiniteness with respect to the domain of quantification — define a *U-model* to be a function that assigns a member of U to each individual constant and a set of n-tuples from U to each n-place predicate, subject to the constraint that $\{<u,u>: u \in U\}$ is assigned to '='. A *variable assignment* is a function that assigns a member of U to each variable, and what it is for a variable assignment to satisfy an open sentence in a model is defined in the usual way. σ satisfies $\ulcorner Fa \urcorner$ in $\mathfrak{A}$ if and only if $\mathfrak{A}(a) \in \mathfrak{A}(F)$. σ satisfies $\ulcorner Fx \urcorner$ in $\mathfrak{A}$ if and only if $\sigma(x) \in \mathfrak{A}(F)$. σ satisfies $\ulcorner (\phi \vee \psi) \urcorner$ in $\mathfrak{A}$ if and only if σ satisfies ϕ or ψ or both in $\mathfrak{A}$. σ satisfies $\ulcorner \sim\phi \urcorner$ in $\mathfrak{A}$ if and only if σ doesn't satisfy ϕ in $\mathfrak{A}$. σ satisfies $\ulcorner (\exists x)\phi \urcorner$ in $\mathfrak{A}$ if and only if there is an x-variant of σ that satisfies ϕ in $\mathfrak{A}$, where an x-variant of σ is a variable assignment that agrees with σ except possibly at x. σ satisfies $\ulcorner (\forall x)\phi \urcorner$ in $\mathfrak{A}$ if and only if every x-variant of σ satisfies ϕ in $\mathfrak{A}$. Thus our definition of *satisfaction in a model* is classical and bivalent. Within each model, every individual constant denotes one and only one individual, and each variable assignment either satisfies a formula or satisfies the negation of the formula. The definition of *truth in a model* is likewise classical and bivalent. A sentence (formula with no free variables) is *true* in $\mathfrak{A}$ if and only if every variable assignment satisfies the sentence in $\mathfrak{A}$, and a sentence is *false* in $\mathfrak{A}$ if and only if it's satisfied by no variable assignment in $\mathfrak{A}$. It's a theorem that every sentence is either true in $\mathfrak{A}$ or false in $\mathfrak{A}$.

These models are models of the first-order predicate calculus, and the phenomenon we're really interested in is vagueness in natural lan-

---

11 Supervaluations were invented by Bas van Fraassen, 'Singular Terms, Truth Value Gaps, and Free Logic,' *Journal of Philosophy* **63** (1966) 464-95. Their application to problems of vagueness is due to Kit Fine, 'Vagueness, Truth, and Logic,' *Synthese* **30** (1975) 265-300. Their application to Evans's specific argument about vague identity statements is due to David Lewis, 'Vague Identity: Evans Misunderstood,' *Analysis* **48** (1988) 128-30.

guages. The rationale is that there are various fragments of English that can be tolerably well represented by formalizing them in the predicate calculus, and these fragments, while vastly simpler than English, are nonetheless expressively rich enough so that the problems we are trying to solve strike us full force. The methodology is to attack simpler problems first.

The models we use are sharp. Within a model, every individual constant is assigned a unique individual and every formula is assigned an extension that is the complement of the antiextension. Our thoughts and practices do not, however, pick our a unique referent for each singular term, nor do they pick out an exhaustive classification for each open sentence. The explanation is that our thoughts and practices do not pick out a unique model as the actual model. They pick out a class of models. The fundamental hypothesis of supervaluation theory is that the semantics of a vague language can be described by singling out an appropriate class of models, thus:

> *Supervaluation Hypothesis* (first version): There is a class $\mathcal{K}$ of U-models such that a variable assignment σ determinately satisfies a formula ϕ if and only if σ satisfies ϕ in every member of $\mathcal{K}$.

An equivalent formulation of the hypothesis makes use of the following definition:

> *Definition.* A U-model $\mathfrak{A}$ is *acceptable* if and only if, for any variable assignment σ and open sentence ϕ, if σ determinately satisfies ϕ, then σ satisfies ϕ in $\mathfrak{A}$.

> *Supervaluation Hypothesis* (second version):[12] A variable assignment σ determinately satisfies an open sentence ϕ if and only if σ satisfies ϕ in every acceptable U-model.

If $\mathfrak{A}$ is an acceptable model, then every sentence that is determinately

---

12 In van Fraassen's original terminology, for each acceptable U-model $\mathfrak{A}$, the function that assigns to each sentence its truth value in $\mathfrak{A}$ is called a *classical valuation*, while the function that assigns the value *true* to those sentences true in every acceptable U-model is called a *supervaluation*.

true is true in $\mathfrak{A}$. There is no converse requirement that every sentence that is true in $\mathfrak{A}$ be determinately true. We only require a one-way correspondence between semantic features of the vague language and semantic features of the acceptable models. I want to emphasize this, in order to avoid a certain misunderstanding.[13] It may be plausibly argued that there are certain terms in the language for which it is essential to the meaning of the term that the term be vague. We employ the acceptable models in an attempt to represent the semantic features of the terms, but because the acceptable models are precise, there will be essential features of the meanings of the terms that the acceptable models fail to respect. But if the acceptable models disregard essential semantic properties of the language they are supposed to represent, it's hard to see how they can be any help at all in understanding the semantics of that language.

The answer is that the acceptable models are required to respect some semantic features of the language they describe, but they aren't required to respect every semantic feature of the language. This is because we require only one direction of fit between the language we're trying to represent and the acceptable models; namely, if $\mathfrak{A}$ is an acceptable model, then if a sentence is determinately true, it's required to be true in $\mathfrak{A}$, but not *vice versa*. Thus there are some semantic features of the language you can see just by looking at $\mathfrak{A}$, but there are other semantic features you can only see when you look at the totality of all the acceptable models. (There will be yet other features of the language that you won't see until you look at acceptable models of the (vague) metalanguage, notably, higher-order vagueness; but that needn't concern us here.)

For the special case in which the universe of discourse is countable, we can give another formulation of the Supervaluation Hypothesis, discovered by Henkin and Orey in quite a different context:[14]

---

13 If I read them correctly, Jerry Fodor and Ernest Lepore ('What Cannot Be Evaluated Cannot Be Evaluated, and It Cannot Be Supervalued Either,' *Journal of Philosophy* 93 (1996) 516-35) and Timothy Williamson (*op. cit.*, §5.7) have succumbed to this misunderstanding.

14 See C. C. Chang and H. J. Keisler, *Model Theory*, 3rd ed. (Amsterdam: North-Holland 1990), §2.2.

> *Supervaluation Hypothesis* (third version): Assuming that *U* and the language are both countable, the Supervaluation Hypothesis holds if and only if the following three conditions obtain:
> The set of formulas determinately satisfied by a given variable assignment is closed under logical-consequence.
> If two variable assignments assign the same values to all variables that appear free in ϕ, then if one of them determinately satisfies ϕ, the other does too.
> If every *x*-variant of σ determinately satisfies ϕ, then σ determinately satisfies $\ulcorner(\forall x)\phi\urcorner$.

If *U* is uncountable, then the Supervaluation Hypothesis implies the three conditions, but not conversely. No one has yet been able to say what further logical closure conditions need to obtain, in addition to the three listed here, in order to guarantee the Supervaluation Hypothesis for uncountable domains.

The Supervaluation Hypothesis has a rather bad reputation, and the reason for this has been the excessive enthusiasm of its proponents, much more than the hostility of its enemies. It has been thought that the model theory provides a deep explanation of the way we use vague language; specifically, it has been thought to explain the fact that we are able to use classical logic even in the face of semantic indeterminacy. But that can't be right. Model theory is just mathematics, and as such, it can't explain anything about language use. The model theory is useful because it describes certain logical features of the way vague terms are employed. In particular, the Supervaluation Hypothesis is useful because it enables the model-theoretic description of the logical possibilities for vague languages to ride piggyback on the familiar model theory of precise languages. But the Supervaluation Hypothesis presumes the classification of variable assignments into those that determinately satisfy an open sentence, those that determinately fail to satisfy it, and those that are unsettled. It doesn't explain the classification.

The Supervaluation Hypothesis enables us to apply the model theory of modal logic to the study of the 'determinately' operator, since we can treat the acceptable *U*-models like possible worlds. As long as we are not interested in nested '□'s, we can give the satisfaction condition for $\ulcorner\Box\phi\urcorner$ (read 'determinately ϕ') as follows:

σ satisfies ⌐□φ⌐ in 𝔄 if and only if σ satisfies φ in every acceptable *U*-model.

(Extending this definition to encompass nested '□'s would give us a logic of 'determinately' that satisfies the axioms of **S5**, thus denying the phenomenon of higher-order vagueness. To get a plausible treatment of nested '□'s, we would have to complicate our story, perhaps by introducing an accessibility relation on the acceptable *U*-models.)

Once we have the Supervaluation Hypothesis, it's easy to say what it is for a singular term to be precise. It's for the term to denote the same thing in every acceptable model. Borrowing a term from modal logic, a precise singular term is a *rigid designator*. Similarly, a general term is precise just in case it has the same extension in every acceptable model. If *a* is a rigid designator, 𝔄 an acceptable model, and σ a variable assignment with σ(*x*) = 𝔄(*a*), then σ satisfies ⌐φ(*x*)⌐ in 𝔄 if and only if σ satisfies ⌐φ(*a*)⌐ in 𝔄, even if φ contains 'determinately.' If *a* and *b* are both rigid designators, then, whether or not φ contains 'determinately,' the identity axiom

$$(a=b \rightarrow (\phi(a) \leftrightarrow \phi(b)))$$

will be true in every acceptable model.

There are two plausible options for the status of 'Kilimanjaro' and Kilimanjaro: Either 'Kilimanjaro' is a precise term denoting a vague object, or 'Kilimanjaro' is a vague term and Kilimanjaro a precise object.

To say that 'Kilimanjaro' is a precise term means that the thoughts and practices of speakers of the language, either directly or by means of causal connections with their environment, pick out one and only one object as the referent of 'Kilimanjaro.' This object is the referent of 'Kilimanjaro' in every acceptable model. On this account, the semantics of the term 'Kilimanjaro' is unproblematically classical; the activities of speakers fix a unique object as the referent of the term. What's problematic is the metaphysics: Kilimanjaro is a vague object, and vague objects are deeply mysterious.

On the alternative account, there are only precise objects. For the present, let's suppose precise physical objects to be mereological sums of elementary particles. Then Kilimanjaro, being a physical object, is a mereological sum of elementary particles. But there isn't any mereological sum of elementary particles that our thoughts and practices pick out, direct or indirectly, as the referent of 'Kilimanjaro.' Instead, we have a large collection of mereological sums of elementary particles that our activities pick out as equally good candidates for what the name refers to. In each acceptable model, the word 'Kilimanjaro' denotes exactly one of these optimal candidates, but the candidate chosen varies from model to model.

On the alternative account, it is not the task of semantics to say what determines the referent of a singular term, since, with few or no exceptions, a singular term will not have a determinate referent. A singular term will have a whole class of candidate referents, and it is the task of semantics to say what connects a term with its candidate class. General terms will likewise have candidate referents, and these will be unexpectedly numerous. Thus, while there is only one mountain at 3.07° S., 37.35° E., there are a great many candidate-mountains at that location. For each acceptable model $\mathfrak{A}$, exactly one of the candidate-mountains at 3.07° S., 37.35° E., will be in the extension in $\mathfrak{A}$ of 'mountain'; that's because 'There is exactly one mountain at 3.07° S., 37.35° E.' is determinately true. The truth in every acceptable model of such principles as 'There is a mountain in the immediate vicinity of every candidate-mountain' and 'No two mountains overlap very much' will help get the right number of mountains at each location.

There are linkages among the candidate-referents for different terms. 'Kilimanjaro' will have many candidate-referents and 'mountain' will have many more. Within any particular acceptable model, exactly one of the former will be the referent of 'Kilimanjaro,' and only a few of the latter will be referents of 'mountain.' The selection of candidates must be coordinated, so that the referent in $\mathfrak{A}$ of 'Kilimanjaro' will be among the referents in $\mathfrak{A}$ of 'mountain'; that way, 'Kilimanjaro is a mountain' will be determinately true. The task of semantics, on the alternative conception, is to describe the various classes of candidate-referents and the linkages between them; in other word, to say what makes a model acceptable.[15] An immensely complex task, but no one ever suggested that human language was simple.

---

15 Details aside, this was the program announced by Hartry Field in 'Quine and the Correspondence Theory,' *Philosophical Review* **83** (1974) 200-28.

The Evans argument purports to show that the precise term/vague object alternative cannot be sustained, by showing that 'Kilimanjaro' is not a rigid designator. Its strategy is straightforward: From the indeterminate truth value of 'Sparky is a part of Kilimanjaro,' we cannot conclude anything about the rigidity of 'Kilimanjaro,' for the source of the indeterminacy might be 'Sparky' or 'Kilimanjaro' or 'is a part of.' However, if we can find a *rigid* general term F such that ⌜F(Kilimanjaro)⌝ is indeterminate, the cause of the indeterminacy can only be 'Kilimanjaro.'

Let us assume, for the moment, that a land mass is fully specified by determining what its constituent molecules are. That is, for any collection of molecules, there is uniquely determined at most one land mass that has those molecules as its parts. Let us also assume that for any given molecule, our language provides a description in the language that is true of that molecule and no other. This is so because molecules are spatially discrete, so that, to uniquely pick out a molecule, it is enough to find a region that contains that molecule and no others. (There is fuzziness about what counts as a molecule, and there are problems about the exact specification of spatial locations, but let's not worry about those now.) We also assume that there isn't any land mass that contains part but not all of a given molecule.

Given these assumptions, every land mass can be precisely specified by stating what its constituent molecules are. Thus there is a (very long) list $a_1, a_2, ..., a_N$ of precise names such that every land mass in Tanzania is sure to be named somewhere on the list. The list is all-inclusive because it includes every combination of Tanzanian molecules, and because every land mass is determined by its constituent molecules. Because 'Tanzania' and 'land mass' are both fuzzy, there will be doubtful cases of 'land mass in Tanzania,' and the only way to be sure that our list includes every land mass in Tanzania will be to put all such doubtful items on the list. If this means that our list contains extra items that aren't land masses in Tanzania, this will do no harm; we only insist that the list include every land mass in Tanzania.

The following statements are determinately true:

$$(\forall x)(x \text{ is a land mass in Tanzania} \rightarrow \bigvee_{i \leq N} x = a_i).$$

There is no philosophy going on here, just combinatorics. A land mass is determined by determining what molecules it contains, and $a_1, a_2, \ldots,$ a_N enumerate all the available combinations of molecules. Since

> Kilimanjaro is a land mass in Tanzania,

we derive:

$$\bigvee_{i \leq N} \text{Kilimanjaro} = a_i.$$

Evans's argument gives us:

$$(\forall x)(\forall y)(x = y \rightarrow \Box\, x = y).$$

Since each of the a_i's is precise, they are rigid designators, hence suitable for universal instantiation within 'determinately' contexts; hence:

$$(\forall x)(x = a_i \rightarrow \Box\, x = a_i).$$

Let us assume, for *reductio ad absurdum*, that 'Kilimanjaro' is likewise a precise term. This tells us that we can use it to instantiate into 'determinately' contexts, obtaining this:

$$(\text{Kilimanjaro} = a_i \rightarrow \Box\, \text{Kilimanjaro} = a_i).$$

Putting the pieces together, we get this:

$$\bigvee_{i \leq N} \Box\, \text{Kilimanjaro} = a_i$$

But that's absurd. The only way a sentence of the form ⌜Kilimanjaro = a_i⌝ could be determinately true would be for a precise border of Kilimanjaro to be fixed, down to the last molecule. We conclude that 'Kilimanjaro' must be imprecise.

This argument relies on the assumption that a land mass is uniquely determined by its molecular composition. Unfortunately, this assumption isn't terribly plausible, since knowing the molecular composition of a mountain today won't determine, down to the last detail, what its molecular composition was a year ago. For the argument to go through, the a_i's have to be substitutable into 'determinately' contexts, which means they have to be fully precise, and to specify a body of land with full precision, you have to say enough to determine not just what its exact boundaries are today, but what its exact boundaries were throughout its history.

To make the argument serviceable, we need a way of characterizing a land mass more precisely, so that we determine its molecular composition at every time. How best to do this is a matter of metaphysical controversy, but the first thing that comes to mind would be to take the ultimate parts of a land mass to be either a temporal slice of an elementary particle or, if that's still not fine enough, a time-world slice of an elementary particle.[16] Then take a land mass to be a mereological sum of those.

Can we push the argument through with time-world slices of elementary particles in place of molecules? Two impediments present themselves. First, it was plausible to assume that individual molecules always have names. It's not credible to assume this for time-world slices of elementary particles, since there are uncountably many slices and countably many names. Second, since there are so very many slices, and even more sums of slices, what will take the place of

$$\bigvee_{i \leq N} \square \, a_i = \text{Kilimanjaro}$$

will be an infinite disjunction; and how can mere human thoughts and practices determine the truth values of infinitely long sentences?

The solution to these difficulties is to follow the standard procedure when we want to simulate infinitary logical operations by finitary means: Go metalinguistic. We take advantage of the fact that, in the

---

16 To precisely specify a referent for 'Kilimanjaro,' we have to determine not only what its parts are, but what its parts would have been if the comet Kohoutek had crashed on its summit; for this purpose, we have to look at worlds other than our own.

semantics we have been developing, variables function as rigid designators. Let $\{s_i : i \in I\}$ be a set that includes all mereological sums of time-
world slices of elementary particles in Tanzania. Then in any acceptable
model, any variable assignment σ that satisfies 'x is a land mass in
Tanzania' in the model will have to set $\sigma('x')$ equal to one of the s_i's. Let
$\mathfrak{A}$ be an acceptable model. Since '$(\exists x)(x$ is a land mass in Tanzania $\wedge\ x =$
Kilimanjaro$)$' is true in $\mathfrak{A}$, there must exist a variable assignment σ such
that σ satisfies '$x =$ Kilimanjaro' in $\mathfrak{A}$ and, for some i in I, $\sigma('x')$ is equal
to s_i. If 'Kilimanjaro' is a rigid designator, then it will follow by the
Evans argument that σ satisfies '$\Box\ x =$ Kilimanjaro' in $\mathfrak{A}$, hence that
'Kilimanjaro' denotes s_i in every acceptable model, which is absurd.

The argument here does not really rely on the assumption that the
physical objects are made up of time-world slices of elementary particles, since you can run the same argument under virtually any hypothesis you can think of about the ultimate constituents of physical reality.

The argument does, however, rely on mereology. Taken by itself,
the observation that 'Sparky is a part of Kilimanjaro' is indeterminate
doesn't tell us anything about the rigidity of 'Kilimanjaro,' because we
don't know anything about the rigidity of 'is a part of.' We do know
something about the rigidity of '=,' however, on account of Evans's
argument; so to deduce the irrigidity of 'Kilimanjaro,' we have to find
a deductive path from the indeterminacy of 'Sparky is a part of Kilimanjaro' to the indeterminacy of an appropriate identity statement.
For this, we need mereology.

To many people, myself among them, the principles of mereology
have seemed simply obvious. But one would like an argument, and an
argument is not easy to come by. David Lewis notes the extreme implausibility of a nontrivial precise classification of collections of time-
world slices of particles into those that do and those that do not satisfy
'$(\exists y)(y$ is composed of the members of x, and of nothing else).'[17] But it
isn't plausible to imagine a nontrivial imprecise classification either,
since "the only intelligible account of vagueness locates it in our thought

17 *On the Plurality of Worlds* (Oxford and Cambridge, MA: Blackwell 1986), 211-3.
See also Quine, *Theories and Things* (Cambridge, MA, and London: Harvard 1981),
8-13.

and language," and there isn't any place in the language of the phrase '($\exists y$)(y is composed of the members of x, and of nothing else)' where vagueness can creep in.[18] (Compare this to the nontrivial classification into those slices of particles that do and do not satisfy '($\exists y$)(y is a body composed of the members of x, and of nothing else),' a classification which is imprecise because 'body' is imprecise.) Lewis concludes that the classification is trivial, that is, ($\forall$ nonempty collection x of time-world slices of elementary particles)($\exists y$)(y is composed of the members of x, and of nothing else).

This is a good argument, but it isn't helpful in the present context, since it presupposes something we're trying to show, namely, that there isn't vagueness in the world, in addition to the vagueness that occurs in thought and language.

In the end, I don't have an argument for mereology, nor do I have an argument against vague objects that proceeds independently of mereology. What we get from Evans's argument is the conditional: If there are, indeed, precise objects in the great profusion mereology postulates, then there are not vague objects as well. If mereology is right, there are so many precise objects that they crowd all the available space, leaving no room for vague objects too. In view of the great credibility mereology commands, this is a good, though not an inescapable, argument against vague objects.

---

18   Lewis, *op. cit.*, 212

CANADIAN JOURNAL OF PHILOSOPHY
Supplementary Volume 23

Inscrutability

MARK RICHARD
Tufts University

Pick what seems a correct scheme of reference for a language, German say. Perhaps you have picked one which tells us such things as that

'Katz' refers in German to cats (and nought else)
'Hund' refers in German to dogs (and nought else).

Your scheme, given that it also accounts for German devices of sentence compounding such as 'und,' 'nicht,' and 'alle,' assigns truth conditions to German sentences.

Quine reminds us that it is possible to permute your reference scheme in such a way that the result assigns the same truth values to all German sentences, even though the permutation changes the reference of all of German's terms. For example, we can take 'Katz' to refer to undetached cat parts, 'Hund' to undetached dog parts, 'lauft' to be true of undetached parts of things that run, 'ist identische mit' to name the relation undetached object parts stand in when they are parts of the same object, and so on. Quine observes that it seems possible to do this without effecting the 'observational consequences' of German theories: a theory in German will be seen, under one interpretation, to be confirmed by some evidence iff it is so confirmed under the other.[1] Quine claims that nothing about the verbal dispositions of speakers provides a reason to prefer one reference scheme to the other. Thinking that semantical facts must be determined by such dispositions, he

---

1 For example: the theory we began with has 'ein Katz lauft' true iff a cat runs. The replacement theory has it true iff an undetached cat part is an undetached part of something that runs. The one condition obtains iff the other does.

concludes that it is indeterminate what the terms of a language should be said to refer to. That it is thus indeterminate is the claim that reference is inscrutable.

Some would appeal to causal considerations to defeat inscrutability: Reference, we are told, is grounded in causal contacts between applications of word and object referred to. It is not clear that this is much help. Touch a cat and you touch an undetached cat part. Smell a dog and you are causally in touch with the dog fusion, as well as any number of miscellaneous scattered objects which include the dogs. Once this occurs to one, it becomes somewhat plausible that there may not be *any* physical fact that distinguishes one of two incompatible reference schemes as *the* correct scheme. If we think that the physical facts determine all the facts, we will then find inscrutability a plausible if unsettling doctrine.

We might distinguish at least two theses which could be called the inscrutability of reference. There is the claim that for any language, there will be inequivalent accounts, adequate to all the facts, of the reference of the language's singular and general terms. Call this *weak inscrutability*. Then there is the claim that for any two languages, there will be in each inequivalent accounts, adequate to all the facts, of the reference of the other language's terms. Call this *strong inscrutability*.

The two claims aren't equivalent. The second thesis is analogous to the claim that translation between languages is indeterminate. But translation might be determinate, even if reference is weakly inscrutable. It's *in principle* possible that expressions be determinately synonymous, even though substantive claims about what they mean are indeterminate. Likewise, it is in principle possible that, although it is indeterminate to what two terms refer, it is determinate that they are co-referential — whatever it is we might say they are referring to, we must say they are referring to the same thing.[2]

In what follows, I grant, for argument's sake, weak inscrutability. I argue against strong inscrutability. After considering how the theses are to be formulated, I discuss a standard argument for the weak thesis. This sets the stage for an argument against what many see as the most distressing aspect of strong inscrutability — that no language can 'scrut' its own reference, since strong inscrutability implies that there

---

2 I blithely speak of predicates referring to their extensions throughout.

are inequivalent, yet adequate, accounts of reference-in-L in L itself. I argue that this should be rejected by anyone who allows that semantic phenomena are naturalistic phenomena. I then argue that facts about how speakers interpret one another are facts which, even from the perspective of 'radical interpretation,' constrain what can be said about the reference of terms. Such facts will in many cases, I argue, imply that there is not strong inscrutability between speakers.

I

By a reference scheme for a language L1 in a language L2 I mean, in the first instance, what's given by a collection of claims in L2 of a form suggested so:

> F1: Singular term 'a' refers in L1 to u
> F2: Predicate 'P' is true in L1 of the Fs (and naught else).

Such a scheme contains one clause for each simple term of L1, and thus provides the basis of a Tarskian account of truth-in-L1. I shall often speak of things which straightforwardly determine such schemes as themselves being reference schemes. In particular, I call mappings, of L1's simple vocabulary onto L2's vocabulary, reference schemes, as such mappings straightforwardly determine reference schemes in the first sense. I use 'interpretation' as a variant of 'reference scheme.'

It is often thought that the doctrine of inscrutability is the claim that, because of the sort of considerations reviewed in the first paragraphs of this paper, all claims about the reference of a language's terms are indeterminate. While the thesis involves the claim that there is an indeterminacy about reference, I don't think that this is exactly the indeterminacy Quine has in mind. Quine allows that talk of reference "makes sense"[3] and is "meaningful"[4] when properly relativized. The

---

3 W.V. Quine, *Ontological Relativity and Other Essays* (New York: Columbia University Press 1969), 50

4 Quine, *Ontological Relativity*, 48

relativization is to an arbitrarily chosen scheme for translating the terms of the language, of whose reference we speak. (Actually, there is a second parameter. I'll suppress it for a while.) I take it that saying that talk of reference is sensible and meaningful is intended to bestow the cachet of truth on (some of) it. The indeterminacy arises because there is supposedly nothing about the physical facts which justifies a preference among many incompatible translation manuals.

An obvious way to develop such a picture sees languages in which talk about reference is possible as extensions of languages initially innocent of semantic vocabulary. Adding semantic apparatus such as 'α refers in L to y' to an innocent language requires explicit or implicit presupposition of a 'translation manual' —a mapping of the vocabulary of languages about whose reference one is to speak onto the innocent language's vocabulary. Relative to this presupposition, truth can be sensibly bestowed upon the extended language's claims, that one or another term of a given language (covered by the translation manual) refers to such and such an entity. This is to say, limiting attention to expressions α which are unary predicates, that there is a relation REF($α$, L, y, M) which is as determinate as any physical relation; where M is the manual involved in extending an innocent language L1 to L2, L2's claim *α refers in L to y* is true iff REF($α$, L, y, M).[5] On this picture, claims about reference could be said to be true simply because their truth is 'built into' the language in which they are formulated. What is indeterminate is the choice among extensions of an innocent language: as far as there are facts to be faithful to, in introducing an expression with the function of 'refers,' there are many incompatible ways to introduce such.

Some will say that whatever the merits of such a picture, it is not Quine's; Quine is simply an instrumentalist about reference. Yet Quine *says* that talk of reference is meaningful if properly relativized. He speaks soberly of the ontological commitments of theories, and of reinterpreting an interpreted theory in various ways. His picture of epistemology naturalized, on which it is a "chapter of psychology and hence of natural science," is one where in epistemology we study

---

5 I will confuse use and mention as I do here whenever the confusion is easily resolved by those who are attuned to it in the first place.

how evidence relates to theory, and in what ways one's theory of nature tran-
scends any available evidence.... We are studying how the human subject of our
study posits bodies and projects his physics from his data...[6]

Taking such a passage at face value, one would expect epistemology-
cum-chapter-of-natural-science to deliver, *inter alia*, claims implying
that under certain conditions, subjects project theories with various
ontological commitments. Assuming that some such epistemological
theories are true, some true scientific theories entail that some people
accept theories committed to bodies. On Quine's account of ontological commitment, to say that a theory is committed to bodies is (roughly)
to say that the theory has a theorem of the form $\exists x F x$, where the predicate 'F' is true of an object (in the theory's language) only if the object is
a body. So, some true scientific theories have entailments which are
true only if claims about predicate reference are true.

As I am reading Quine, claims about reference are, or can be, true
parts of true and useful empirical theories. It is perfectly *true* that contemporary physical theory is committed to quarks. It is (probably) *true*
that people who accept theories committed to UFOs tend to be poor at
reasoning inductively. Claims about commitment and reference are,
on such a view, somewhat analogous to highly theoretical claims, which
have empirical import only in the context of a large theory. There is
nothing incoherent in holding that the claims are true while saying
that we *could* have adopted accounts of reference which, while prag-
matically impractical, were still as good as the one we have adopted;
had we adopted these, we would have not expressed truths about physical theory and UFO mania in terms of reference to quarks and UFOs,
but rather in terms of relations to other things and non-things.[7]

---

6 Quine, *Ontological Relativity*, 82-3

7 Perhaps it will be said that there is an incoherence here: How can (say) it be true
that theory T is committed to UFOs, and not some other entities (OFUs), while
it is also true (from some other perspective about reference) that T is committed
to OFUs, not UFOs? This would be incoherent if the notion of truth invoked
were not language relative. But for Quine, ascriptions of truth are language
relative.
    It would be incoherent to hold that T is committed to UFOs, but there is a
language we might speak in which one could truly say that T was not so

Field[8] and Davidson object to the idea that talk of reference is relative to a translation manual.[9] Davidson writes

> Quine proposes that reference be relativized to translation manuals. Hartry Field has pointed out that this won't work. For the natural way to state the conditions under which 'x refers to y relative to TM' holds is this: TM translates x as 'y.' This suggestion must be rejected because you cannot quantify into quotation marks.[10]

Of course you can, if the quantifier is substitutional; so far as I can see, all that is needed here is a substitutional quantifier. REF(α, L, y, M) is defined

(1) α is an expression of L & $\exists \beta (M(\alpha) = $ 'β' & $\forall x(x$ is in y iff x is a β)).

Recall that the REF relation is for simplicity restricted to α's that are unary predicates; 'y' is understood to range over sets. Translation manuals are thought of as functions mapping expressions of languages into those of the language of the definition.[11] If 'β' is interpreted substitutionally (with unary predicates of the language in which the

---

committed. So we must say, on a view like that which I am ascribing to Quine, that what (some of) the sentences of this other theory say is not what they appear to say, when translated in the natural fashion (i.e., homophonically). We will say that, in the sense of meaning in which meaning determines reference, 'refers' in those languages does not mean what it means in our language — it cannot, since it has a different extension. (It does not follow that there is no sense of 'meaning' in which 'refers' in the different languages may not have the same meaning. For instance, if we allow that there is a sense of 'meaning' on which expressions with similar 'inferential roles' have similar meanings, we may allow that 'refers' has similar meanings in languages in which it has disparate extensions.)

8   Hartry Field, 'Quine and the Correspondence Theory,' *Philosophical Review* **83** (1974)

9   There are a number of (in my opinion unsound) objections to such relativization due to Donald Davidson (in 'The Inscrutability of Reference,' *Southwestern Journal of Philosophy* **10** [1979]) which limitations of space forbid discussing here.

10   Davidson, 'The Inscrutability of Reference,' 231

11   This works only if no expression occurs in multiple languages. There are ways of individuating expressions — as constructions from sets of tokens, for example — which will achieve this.

definition is given as substitutends), this definition seems just right. For instance, it tells us that relative to a translation manual M1 which translates German's 'Katz' as 'cat,' 'Katz' in German refers to the set of cats, since it is of course true that

(2)   M1('Katz') = 'cat' & $\forall x(x$ is in the set of cats iff x is a cat);

(2) implies the existential generalization which, conjoined with "'Katz' is an expression of German," is equivalent to REF('Katz,' German, the set of cats, M1).

Quine often speaks of talk of reference as being doubly relative, to a manual and a background language.[12] The necessity for another parameter becomes clear once we recognize that we need to be able to talk (in our language L3) about an expression α of L1 referring to a set y relative to a manual M which translates L1 into a language L2 distinct from L3. To say that α so refers is to say that M translates α as β, and relative to the background language — which, recall, provides its own manual of translation, since such is presupposed by the introduction of 'refers' — β is translated as 'γ' and for any x, x is in y iff x is a γ. Since the background language is being exploited only for its resident translation manual, we might as well take the second parameter simply to be a translation manual; appropriating '*REF*' to name the new relation, we have

(3)   REF(α, L, y, M1, M2) $=_{df}$ α is an expression of L & $\exists b \exists \gamma(M1(\alpha) =$ b & $M2(b) =$ 'γ' & $\forall x(x$ is in y iff x is a γ)).

Here, b is an objectual variable ranging over expressions, 'γ' is a substitutional variable ranging over unary predicates of the object language.[13]

---

12 Sometimes, the relativization is said to be a background theory. I don't think it makes much difference, as long at the second parameter itself provides a translation manual.

13 Once the five-termed REF(α, L, y, M1, M2) is in place, we can use it to understand ordinary talk of reference: if my use of 'refers' presupposes M, then my use of 'α refers in L to y' is true as I speak it provided REF(α, L, y, M, M).
    Since the translation manual involved in the REF relation is simply a mapping of vocabulary to vocabulary, this account makes claims about reference

171

Above, I distinguished what I called weak from strong inscrutability. I close this section by giving a tolerably precise formulation of the two theses.

Inscrutability theses are claims that incompatible but (maximally) adequate ways of specifying the reference of a language are possible. A reference scheme for L1 in L2 is adequate if, given all the relevant evidence, acceptable principles for interpretation would sanction its use. That is to say: If theory T gives in L2 a reference scheme for L1, T is adequate if it would be assessed as adequate — would be assertible — relative to a perspective (i.e., a language and theory) which was privy to, and had a theory adequate to, all the relevant data.

Let us call such perspectives *idealized perspectives*, thinking of them as perspectives of idealized beings who have theories adequate to the observational data. Think of such perspectives in the first instance as lacking any semantic theories whatsoever, but as being extendable in various (not necessarily compatible) ways to contain adequate theories of reference and truth for the languages we speak. Any such perspective, once extended to contain a theory of reference for languages L1 and L2, can assess the adequacy of schemes of reference for L1 in L2. The perspective approves of a reference scheme R for L1 in L2 just in case the perspective assigns the same references to L1 expressions as it does to the L2 expressions with which R pairs them.

How, in this framework, should we explain inequivalence? Well, there are really two sorts of inequivalence involved in claims about inscrutability. Most obviously, for schemes of reference to be inequivalent they must assign different referents to names and disjoint

---

trivial. If we individuate languages in terms of their expressions (so that it is necessary that 'Katz' is an expression of German), then "'Katz' in German refers to the set of cats" says something necessary. What is not (wholly) trivial is the choice of how to extend an innocent language to one in which talk of reference is possible: as I shall argue below, different accounts of reference may have different empirical implications which will allow us to choose among them.

We could understand the claim that REF(α, L, y, M1, M2) in another way, however: We could interpret it as entailing the claim that M1 and M2 are empirically adequate manuals for translating from the relevant languages. I do not think anything in what follows depends on which understanding we adopt, and so I will stay neutral on whether this understanding is preferable.

referents to predicates, for all or most of such which occur in the language. Since it would seem that what referents a scheme assigns to a term is to be arbitrated, finally, only when we 'have all the facts,' this suggests measuring inequivalence of reference schemes in terms of whether they are assessed inequivalent in some idealized perspective. We can take the weak inscrutability thesis to be the claim that for any language L there is an idealized perspective p which can be extended in two ways, to provide interpretations of L which are, according to p, adequate but inequivalent.

There is another sort of inequivalence which seems to be at play in discussions of strong inscrutability: Those who have said that, for example, the reference of German is inscrutable to us have wanted to suggest that (for example) the German 'Hase' could be interpreted *in ways which seem to us obviously inequivalent*, say either with 'rabbit' or 'rabbit stage.' This sort of 'epistemic inequivalence' (for us) of English reference schemes for German doesn't seem to be a consequence of the 'ontic inequivalence' I just explained: maybe all the schemes which idealized perspectives find acceptable seem equivalent to us, though not to them.

There's scope for different formulations of the strong inscrutability thesis. For present purposes I will take it to involve both 'ontic' and 'epistemic' inequivalence, though I don't think anything in this discussion hangs on whether epistemic inequivalence is included. I take strong inscrutability to be the following claim: Suppose there is an interpretation R of L1 in L2 that is adequate according to some ideal perspective. Then there is another interpretation R^* of L1 in L2 and an ideal perspective p such that (i) p assesses each of R and R^* as adequate but inequivalent, and (ii) L2 speakers find R and R^* inequivalent.[14]

---

14 As noted above, the strong thesis is not a consequence of the weak one. Indeed, the weak thesis is consistent with the claim that there is *only one* adequate reference scheme for German in English — i.e., only one mapping of simple German terms onto English terms which, from an idealized perspective, preserves reference. For all that the weak thesis demands is that there be different stories to tell, from the idealized perspective, about what German and English speakers are referring to. This might be, even if there is, *in English*, only one adequate story which can be told about German reference.

II

Why should we accept the weak inscrutability thesis? Many standard arguments for inscrutability are variations on the following theme: (a) Semantic properties are either properties of whole sentences (such as truth conditions) or are determined by such properties. But (b) it is possible to permute a reference scheme for a language, which assigns one collection of extensions to its terms, into a scheme which assigns *any* disjoint extensions, without effecting what we say about the semantic properties of the language's sentences — for example, about their truth or assertability conditions. So, (c) even if we take the semantic properties of whole sentences to be determinate, a reference scheme is not determined; indeed, any story about the identities of the objects in the extension of a given predicate is consistent with an adequate semantic theory. An argument along these lines is suggested by Quine:

> A proxy function is any explicit one-to-one transformation, f, defined over the objects in our ... universe.... Suppose now we ... [reinterpret] each of our predicates as true rather of the correlates fx of our objects x that it had been true of. Thus, where 'Px' originally meant that x was a P, we reinterpret 'Px' as meaning that x is f of a P. Correspondingly for two-place predicates and higher ... We leave all the sentences as they were, merely re-interpreting. The observation sentences remain associated with the same sensory stimulations as before, and the logical interconnections remain intact.... [This illustrates] ... the unsurprising reflection that divergent interpretations of the words in a sentence can so offset one another as to sustain an identical translation of the sentence as a whole ... what I have called inscrutability of reference.[15]

I trust the idea about permutation is familiar. Suppose, for example, the universe is divided equally among ducks and pigs, and f maps the ducks 1–1 onto the pigs. The sentence

Q. A duck quacked

comes to be true provided something (which will in fact be a pig) is f of a duck that quacked.

---

15 W.V. Quine, *Pursuit of Truth* (Cambridge, MA: Harvard University Press 1990), 31-2

There is something wrong with this argument. A broad class of English sentences function as 'observation sentences,' with our acceptance of such being closely tied to our awareness of certain types of states of affairs or events. If I accept Q, this is normally because of my interacting with — my seeing and hearing — some duckish part of the environment, not with some piggish part thereof. Indeed, typically, when I accept Q, there is some duck (or duckish part of the environment) of which I think that it quacked. It is typically not the case there is some pig which I take to be *f* of a quacker.

Suppose that sentences of the forms *a is F* and *a is G* generally function as observation sentences. Then, for *some* way φ of thinking of what R assigns to G, an assignment of reference R to names and to predicates should validate principles (P1) and (P2):

(P1)   Someone's accepting *an F is G* is typically, and all else being equal, accompanied by her coming to think, of some *u* in R(F) that it is φ (unless such acceptance is brought about by a chain of reasoning).

(P2)   When someone is in the neighborhood of a *u* in R(F) which is also in R(G), that person typically, and all else being equal, accepts *an F is G*.

I trust the import of these is clear. (P1), for example, is an elaboration of the claim that, setting reasoning to the side, my accepting 'a duck quacked' is typically accompanied by my thinking, of something in the extension of 'duck,' that it quacked. To assign the permuted references to 'duck' and 'quacked,' and to allow that when I accept Q, there is a duck, but not a pig, of which I believe it quacked is, I think, inconsistent with (P1) and (P2).

More broadly: Given that certain sentences of a language function as observation sentences, there is a straightforward sense in which a reference scheme for a language commits us to a hypothesis about what interactions, with objects and properties, or with events or states of affairs involving such, bring a speaker to accept sentences. Such, at any rate, is the motivation for (P1) and (P2). And some such hypotheses, about the relation of speakers and events, can be ruled out by observing the speaker's interactions with her environment. For example, the permuted reference scheme commits us to the hypothesis that my tokening Q is typically brought about by my being aware of there being some pig which is such that it is *f* of a duck which quacked. To be aware of this is, *inter alia*, to be aware of a pig. It is simply not true that when I accept 'a duck quacked,' this is (typically) because of my interaction with some pig which has the property of being *f* of a quacking duck.[16]

If I am right, then claims about the reference of terms are not merely of instrumental utility. At least some can and should be evaluated empirically, by looking at how speakers' interactions with objects and their aspects correlate with their acceptance of sentences. Even if the choice of a reference scheme is not determined by the physical facts, empirical considerations may considerably narrow the range of acceptable candidates. And a reference scheme will have, relative to a physical theory, testable empirical content.[17]

Behind (P1) is the following line of thought. Observation sentences give expression to the observations we make of our environment; such observations are (in the main) observations of objects (and aspects thereof) with which we sensorily interact. When an observation counts among our beliefs (as it does when we accept an observation sentence which gives expression to it), that belief is a belief about those objects (and aspects thereof) of which the observation is an observation. But the belief a sentence expresses is about an object (or an aspect) only if

---

16 Surely there can be no serious objection to the idea that we can observe such interactions. If a duck quacks and that causes a goose to honk, there is a straightforward sense in which we observe that duck's quacking brought about the goose's honking. What is good for the goose, I would insist, is also good for interactions between speakers and the duck's quacking.

17 To what part of the permutation argument have I objected? It depends on what counts as a semantic property. If sentential properties like *being typically accepted because one heard a duck quack* are semantic, then the answer is that I'm objecting to premiss (b), which is false if what I said about principles P1 and P2 is correct. If the honorific 'semantic' is restricted to properties and relations such as *being true in L*, and *referring to x in L*, then my objection is that the argument isn't valid, since there are relations beyond these to which we can appeal to criticize a semantic theory.

the object is named by a term in the sentence or is in the extension of a predicate therein (or the aspect's extension is that of some predicate in the sentence). So, when someone accepts an observation sentence and thereby has a belief, her belief is one about objects which are, or are in, the extension of the terms in the sentence. This conclusion, I take it, licenses principles like (P1). Similar lines of reasoning can, I think, be used to establish (P2).

The premises of the argument just given border on banalities; so, therefore, do principles like (P1). But if what I have said is correct, granting (P1), banal or not, undermines the permutation argument, at least in as strong a version as Quine gives. Quine presumably rejects some of the humdrum premises from which I have deduced (P1), or my argument against the permutation argument. But which and why?

I believe, though I am not altogether sure, that Quine would accept the argument for (P1) I've given, while rejecting the way I've used (P1) to dismiss the permutation argument. In dismissing the permutation argument, I took it as given that it is interaction with ducks (or ducky things), not pigs (or piggy things) which brings about acceptance of Q; given that and (P1), one can argue against the acceptability of certain permuted reference schemes.

I imagine that Quine would respond that one can't take it as simply given that it is ducks (or ducky things), not pigs, that bring about acceptance of Q. At least, one can't accept this as given, if we are arguing about the question, 'How determinate is reference?' All that is obvious, I imagine Quine saying, is that our experience and education have given us a language and a theory which has, among its most central tenets, that it's ducks, not pigs, that cause us to accept Q. But the ducks and the pigs are simply posits of our theory; there are different theories possible (even if *we* cannot imagine such). The upshot is that if we hold our current theory fixed, then indeed, we can't contemplate an account on which 'duck' refers to pigs. But surely there are very different theories, which do just as well predicting how sensation and verbal behavior are correlated. But there is nothing to arbitrate a dispute about a semantic theory, beyond such predictive efficacy. So one must grant that there are adequate accounts which have us referring, with 'duck,' to things other than ducks.

One thing to note about this response is that it doesn't support the conclusion that there is an adequate theory which has our word 'duck' referring to pigs. If the objects of a theory are just posits thereof, then a theory which doesn't have substantial overlap with our theory will most likely be a theory which posits different objects than we do. We can agree, for argument's sake, that some such theories will not tell stories about reference which are the stories we tell. It doesn't follow that any such theory could coherently take the English sentence "'duck' refers to pigs" as true.

More importantly, I don't see why we should accept that the only criterion for evaluating a semantic theory is how well it correlates sensation or experience narrowly conceived with verbal behavior. At least, I don't see why we should accept this unless we have *already* accepted the view of reference of which the permuation argument is supposed to convince us. *Given* that observation is a causal interaction with the world, we will surely want to say that what we observe are things with which we interact. And, as the argument for (P1) is at pains to point out, what we should say about what we observe is tied to what we say about reference. So, *given* that observation is a causal interaction with the world, we can evaluate a reference scheme for a language by looking at what we know about what we do and do not interact with, when we make observations.

So far, I have said nothing against the first premise of the permutation argument:

(a) Semantic properties are either properties of whole sentences or are determined by such properties.

Behind this premiss is the idea that semantic facts supervene upon (i) the correlation between situations and sentences induced by our dispositions to accept such, and (perhaps) (ii) our inferential practices. What is worrisome about this thought is that the correlation in question is not a brute fact, but is itself something which seems to demand explanation. The natural way to explain it is in terms of relations, between words in sentences, and objects and aspects of the correlated situations. For example (if incredibly crudely), the fact that I tend to accept 'that's a cow' just when I am presented with a cow is to be explained, in part, by noting that it is the presence of cows (and cow-like things) which makes me have the kind of experience that 'calls up' 'cow.'

If we agree that the correlation in question is properly explained by appeal to such relations, why shouldn't we allow that what semantic facts supervene upon is not *merely* the correlation in question, but the world-word relations which determine them? What is obvious is not premiss (a), but a premiss like

(a′)   Semantic properties are *determined* by whatever determines properties (like truth and assertibility conditions) of whole sentences.

But (a′) and (b) don't imply (c).[18]

Still, to insist that it is (a′), not (a), which is acceptable is not to deny the weak inscrutability thesis. There are ever so many connections between my terms and various aspects of the environment. If I am interacting with a cow, I am interacting with a maximal instaneous temporal part of a cow — an MIT cow — too, as well as with the cow fusion. Looking at the jumble of connections my terms have to the world, one might argue, we see that there are various idealizations, simplifications, rounding offs, and explaining aways we could perform. What we identitfy as the reference scheme for my language depends upon which of these are selected and how they are carried out. None of the connections of my terms with the world favors one of these idealizations over the other. From an idealized perspective one sees a number of equally good, if different, stories to tell about reference.

Someone who argues in this way can accept both that word-world relations are (potentially) relevant to assessing a semantic theory, but still hold the weak inscrutability thesis. Such a person holds that the reason reference is inscrutable is not that semantically relevant word-world relations are non-existent, but that they are too anemic to

---

18 One finds in Davidson and Quine epistemological arguments which might be thought to be helpful in establishing (a). For example, if one accepts that semantic facts are determined by something 'accessible' to the child learning a language, one might be able to argue to (a). I shall ignore these; they have, in any case, been criticized elsewhwere. (See, for instance, Michael Friedman's 'Physicalism and the Indeterminacy of Translation,' *Noûs* 9 [1975].)

determine anything close to a unique scheme of reference. This strikes me as a reasonable position, one which may actually be correct.

III

Suppose we adopt it. Will we then be committed to the strong inscrutability thesis? Well, we are granting that world-word relations exist, and that they play an important role in explaining why we use our sentences as we do. Such relations, even if they are not strong enough to determine a unique scheme of reference, provide a basis for comparing languages, term by term, with one another. The semantically relevant relations terms of different languages bear to the environment may be very similar, even well nigh identical. If so, the terms in a straightforward sense must have the same semantical properties; though there may be different stories we can tell about what the reference of the terms are, the 'semantic indiscernability' of the terms requires that we treat them as co-referring.

This should be especially clear in the case in which a language talks of the reference of its own terms. As we understand Quine, α *refers in L to* β is true in L provided L's resident translation manual translates α with β. Formally, there is nothing to bar an extension of innocent English from adopting a bizarre translation manual, which maps, say, 'vixen' to 'part of the fox fusion which displays female characteristics.' But would such a manual be adequate?

Say that terms are semantically indiscernible provided their wordly relations are similar enough that, from any idealized perspective, they would be accorded the same reference. Now, suppose we are interpreting a language L1 in L2, and L2 has a term t_2 which is semantically indiscernible from L1's term t_1. Suppose L2 also has a term s which from some idealized perspectives is interpreted as co-referring with t_1, and from other such perspectives is interpreted as having a different reference. (So, s and t_1 could be related as Quine would have us believe 'Hase' and 'rabbit stage' are related.)

How shall we, in our project of interpreting L1 in L2 proceed? Is it a matter of indifference, whether we interpret L1's term t_1 with either of t_2 or s? Surely not. t_2 is in a clear sense a perfect match, semantically, for t_1. Their respective relations to the world are similar enough that, looking at the all the facts, we could not but say that they co-referred. If we think of absolute truth as what's had by a claim that would be vindicated in any perspective with an account adequate to all the facts, it is absolutely, determinantly true that t_1 and t_2 co-refer. But it is at best indeterminate whether t_1 and s co-refer — it's a matter of what perspective you take, as to whether they do. So surely our choice is made. We must prefer truth to indeterminacy, and prefer interpretations of L1 in L2 which interpret t_1 with t_2 to those which interpret it using s.

Say terms t_1 and t_2 of L1 and L2 are *congruent* when any acceptable interpretation of both of the languages (from an idealized perspective) assigns t_1 (in L1) the same extension as t_2 (in L2). The constraint I have just argued for — call it the congruence constraint — is that if you have terms congruent to those in the language you are interpreting, you must use such terms in your interpretation. More precisely: if a language L2 contains a term which is congruent with a simple term t of a language L1, then any acceptable interpretation of L1 in L2 interprets t with a term of L2 which is congruent thereto. The argument for the constraint presupposes that there are word-world relations which contribute to determining how a speaker's language represents her environment; in effect, the argument infers that when there is *great* similarily in these relations across languages, a semantic theory for one in the other should reflect that similarity. If the languages do a certain thing (try to refer) in the same way, a semantic account should reflect that.

Perhaps you are ready to grant the congruence constraint, but wonder how it could possibly do any work. Well, consider for the moment the hypothesis that there is a *very* twin Earth (vte).[19] Not only is vte a macroscopic duplicate of Earth, it is a microscopic duplicate too: Its streams and oceans are filled with H_2O, not XYZ; its tin cans, like ours, are made of aluminum, not molybdenum. Consider the project of interpreting English and very twin English from an idealized perspective. We can agree that English's 'pig' has alternative, inequivalent renderings in an idealized language; likewise for very twin English's

---

19 After writing an early version of this section in 1991, I discovered that Peter Unger (in *Philosophical Relativity* [Minneapolis, MN: University of Minnesota Press 1989], Chapter 1) has used the fiction of a very twin earth for purposes somewhat similar to those I use it.

'pig.' It doesn't follow that a theory which interprets English *and* its twin, but interprets them so that the languages' 'pig"s are interpreted inequivalently is just as good as a theory which interprets the 'pig"s alike. The languages surely should be seen as having the *same* semantics, even if it is indeterminate what that semantics is. We should give a naturalistic account of semantic phenomena. So we must take such phenomena as supervening on naturalistic phenomena. So when we ascribe different semantic properties, we need to be able to point to a relevant difference between the subjects of the ascriptions, that underlies the difference in the account. Since there is no such difference in this case, English's 'pig' is congruent with very twin English's. So, given the congruence constraint, an account of vte's English in earth's English must map its 'pig' to a congruent expression of earth's English. But this presumably rules out interpreting vte's 'pig' with 'momentary maximal pig event' or the like, since it will be possible to interpret the two languages so that vte's 'pig' and our 'momentary maximal pig event' do not co-refer.

One might object to the appeal to supervenience here. For Quine, to say that 'pig' refers in L to pigs is to say that 'pig,' L, and pigs bear a certain relation to one's (arbitrarily) chosen translation manual. So the facts about English reference supervene on the facts about English speakers *and their interpreter* (i.e., whoever is talking about English reference); the facts about vte reference supervene on facts about vte English speakers and their interpreter. (If you like: the supervenience base for the reference relation includes not just the speaker and her environment, but the interpreter of the speaker.) Now, given weak inscrutability, it must be possible for different interpreters to interpret English and vte English differently. And since we have different interpreters here, with one interpreter interpreting English one way and another interpreting vte English in another, there isn't the sort of isomorphism between the physical systems — interpreter + English speakers, interpreter + vte English speakers — necessary for a failure of supervenience. Since there are adequate interpretations of English and vte English which interpret them differently without a failure of supervenience, there will be a single intepretation which does so.

The last step in this argument is erroneous. Let I be an interpreter of both languages. Consider the physical facts about I and English speakers and about I and vte English speakers *before* interpretation begins.

There is no difference in these facts. The two 'physical systems' (I + English speakers, I + vte English speakers) are perfectly isomorphic. The facts in question surely include all the physical facts to which ascriptions of reference, by I to English speakers, and by I to vte English speakers, must be responsive. The adequacy of a translation manual, from each of the languages to I's, is determined by these facts. Since there is no difference in these facts, a manual which translated the languages differently would posit a difference in semantic facts where there was no physical difference, and thus, given that semantic facts are determined by physical ones, would be incorrect.[20]

Now, there are really two versions of the very twin Earth story. One of them, according to which there are two *distinct* planets, call them Earth and very twin Earth, in which ..., is science fiction. The other, according to which there are two planets, call them Earth and very twin Earth, in which ..., is fact. If we let Earth itself play the role of its twin and apply the congruence constraint, we immediately derive the superiority of certain interpretations of English within itself to others. For the canonical, disquotational interpretation of English in English maps each expression of the language interpreted to a congruent expression of the language of interpretation. (After all, in any comprehensive theory of the reference of English and English — that is, in any theory of the reference of English — the interpretation of an English-expression t will be the same as the interpretation of that to which the canonical scheme maps t.)

So by the congruence constraint, interpretations like the disquotational one in this regard — let us call them congruent interpretations — are to be preferred to ones in which some English terms are mapped to ones with which they are not congruent. But this assures that no two adequate interpretations I_1 and I_2 of English in itself are inequivalent. If I_1 and I_2 are adequate, then they are each congruent.

---

20 It should be noted that it is consistent with this that *once* I's manual is in place, there will be facts, about the relations between I and English and vte English speakers, which are relevant to translating from their languages into other ones. This will be relevant in the next section.

The last two paragraphs were prompted by objections from Vann McGee and Alex Byrne.

So, from any idealized perspective interpreting English, if t is an English term, the reference I_1 and I_2 assign t is assessed as the same. But then I_1 and I_2 can't be inequivalent. (They would have to be wholly or mostly disjoint, for most simple expressions, to be so.)

There are a number of objections one might have to this line of argument; I will address three.

(A) Let us return to vte. Some will say that anyone who takes weak inscrutability seriously will hold that an account which has English and very twin English referring to different things really *is* as good as one which has them co-referring, since the reference clauses of a semantic theory are truth valueless (or without empirical content).

But, first of all, this sort of instrumentalism about reference simply doesn't follow from weak inscrutability. It is one thing to say that the choice of reference schemes is not determined by the physical facts, and that the physical facts exhaust the facts. These claims do not imply that claims about reference are without truth value. There is a perfectly coherent story to tell, reconciling these views, that was sketched in section I. And as pointed out there, there is much reason to think that this story is Quine's story. Second of all, it is simply not true, at least if the arguments of section II have merit, that claims about reference are without empirical content. (Of course, they have such content only when embedded within a larger theory but this is presumably true of *any* claim.) Thirdly, claims about reference, if I am correct, imply claims about what objects speakers think about and what they think about them. Even if we are tempted by instrumentalism about reference, we should, I think, resist instrumentalism about thought. But if we assign different reference schemes to English and its very twin, then we are endorsing different hypothesis about what (sorts of) objects those speakers have thoughts about. But — essentially repeating the argument I just gave — we must see the facts, about what (sorts of) objects speakers have thoughts about as supervening on naturalistic facts which do not differ in relevant ways between Earth and its very twin. We thus cannot give differing accounts of English and very twin English reference, since we would then be endorsing distinct accounts of Earthian and very twin Earthian thought.

(B) A second objection grants that the congruence constraint does some work, if we take the 'logical syntax' of a language as fixed. But it insists that this is as much up for grabs as is the ontology of a language.

Consider Quine's example of the Japanese classifer. As Quine explains it, Japanese contains a variety of expressions, classifers, which are usually taken to attach to numerals. An expression which would naturally be translated as 'five oxen' looks something like this:

$$[\text{five}_{\text{numeral}}]+[\text{classifier}]+[\text{oxen}_{\text{noun}}].$$

Quine observes that there seem to be two ways to interpret such constructions: (a) treat the noun as a count noun, true of individual bovines, and treat the classifier as applying to the numeral, indicating something like 'objects in the animal world'; (b) treat the noun as a mass noun, true of the "totality of beef on the hoof," and take the classifier as applying to it, "to produce a composite individuative term, in effect 'head of cattle.'"[21]

If we think of Japanese as itself not containing any scheme of reference for Japanese in Japanese, there seem to be two ways to extend the language to include such, since there seem to be two stories we could tell about what its terms are, one corresponding to (a), the other to (b). Since they differ on what the terms of Japanese are, the congruence constraint seems inapplicable here, and inscrutability re-emerges.

In response: I would be loathe to say that there are not cases where the 'logical syntax' of natural languages is (apparently) up for grabs and arguably indeterminate. Anyone who has spent much time agonizing over the truth conditions for attitude ascriptions has surely on occasion felt despair over, say, whether there is a fact of the matter as to whether 'she thinks that Hesperus is a star' involves reference to a mental particular, mode of presentation, or some such. But I do not think that logical syntax is indeterminate enough to allow for arguments along the lines of Quine's. Fodor and Evans argue (in somewhat different ways) that by looking at the way in which speakers apply conjoined and unconjoined predicates one can garner evidence which rules out 'deviant' accounts of reference. While I do not think these arguments are successful in eliminating weak inscrutability, I am inclined to think that they succeed in showing that the logical syntax of garden variety predicates in natural language is tolerably determinant.

---

21 Quine, *Ontological Relativity*, 36-7

Ignoring certain subtleties, the idea behind Fodor's argument is suggested thus. Suppose that it's indeterminate whether Gerry's predicate 'rabbit' refers to rabbits or their undetached proper parts. Then there will be a parallel indeterminacy with regard to his 'rabbit ear.' Either both predicates refer to 'wholes' or undetached parts thereof. Now, if the predicates both refer to undetached parts, then there should be no reluctance on Gerry's part to assent to some tokens of 'that is a rabbit ear and a rabbit' when 'that' indicates one thing; for on the undetached parts interpretation this is sometimes true. (For example, a rabbit ear lobe is both a proper part of a rabbit ear and of a rabbit.) But Gerry will find sentences of the form in question inconsistent. The general strategy is to find a sentence of the form

(A1)   *a* is an *R* and *a* is a *S*

which would be consistent if the deviant reference scheme were correct (and '*a*' was unambiguous, 'and' meant conjuction, and what looks like predication in fact is such), but which no one thinks is consistent.

If the argument just rehearsed works — I think it does — it also rules out an interpretation of 'rabbit' as a mass term true of the totality of rabbit, with 'that is a rabbit' saying that a certain place is occupied by some of the rabbit mass. Presumably these sorts of considerations can be used to argue against Quine's alternative (b) above.

What such arguments do not do is show that once the logical syntax of the language is fixed, weak inscrutability disappears. Fodor notwithstanding, the argument has no force against the claim that it is indeterminate whether 'rabbit' refers to continuant rabbits or MIT rabbits, those instaneous regions of space time which contain all there is, at one time, of one rabbit, and which don't contain any space not occupied by said rabbit.[22] To apply the argument here, we need to show that there is some predicate S such that

---

22 Here is what Fodor says about temporal parts reference schemes:

> Notice that, in the normal course, a rabbit and its ears are contemporaries, so that a time slice that includes the one generally also includes the other. But 'rabbit' and 'rabbit's ear,' unlike 'time slice of a rabbit' and 'time slice of a rabbit's ear' are mutually exclusive. So the deviant ontol-

(A2)   *a* is a rabbit and *a* is an *S*

comes out true when 'rabbit' is interpreted as referring to MIT-rabbit, and *S* is interpreted in kindred fashion, though (A2) itself would be taken as inconsistent by a normal English speaker. I do not see that there is such an *S*. Pretty clearly, replacing *S* with 'rabbit ear' doesn't present a problem, since MIT rabbits and MIT rabbit ears are different things.[23] (The latter are *part* of the former, of course; but that is apparently true of rabbits and rabbit ears.) Evans gives other arguments against such interpretations, but they are, in my opinion, without force.[24]

---

ogy fails. [Jerry Fodor, *The Elm and the Expert* (Cambridge, MA: MIT Press 1994), 123, n.3]

It seems that Fodor is reasoning along the following lines:

A rabbit-ear-stage is (normally) part of a rabbit-stage.
So, (normally) there are things which are both rabbit-ear-stages and rabbit-stages.

But this argument is no better than one which identifies cars and carburetors, because the latter are parts of the former.

Some speakers — rabbit/rabbit body dualists of a sort — will blanch at the idea that

A3: *a* is a rabbit and *a* is a rabbit body

might be true. For such speakers, ambiguation of 'is a rabbit,' so that it sometimes refers to MIT rabbits, and sometimes to maximal sums of gen-identical MIT rabbits, is necessary. Since such speakers seem to be placing two objects in one place at one time, the resort to ambiguation of some sort for them is necessary anyway.

23 Appropriate adjustments in interpretation — for example, for the tenses — are understood.

24 Evans alleges a problem for an intepretation of 'rabbit' as a predicate of rabbit stages: It cannot deal with the tenses. Evans considers two Tarskian accounts, in which tense is treated as quantification over time. I will only discuss the second. Here, 't_u' names the time of utterance; $At(x, t_u)$, I take it, is something like a existence predicate, true of a stage and a time iff the stage is contemporaneous with the time. Then, taking some inessential liberties with Evans' presentation, the account runs so:

In sum: It's reasonable to think that the logical syntax of languages like English is (pretty) determinate. While this does not mean that there

---

T. 1. x satisfies *is F* iff At(x, t_u) and x satisfies F

 2. x satisfies *was F* iff for some time t' before t_u and some y co-membered with x, At(y, t') and y satisfies F

 3. x satisfies 'warm' iff x is a stage of a thing warm while the thing is warm.

Presumably these are truncations of claims to the effect that *relative to an utterance, or to an utterance time*, x satisfies a wff iff such and such obtains. Otherwise, T seems incoherent, since (for example), T.1 defines a temporally unrelativized notion of satisfaction as a temporally varying relation. (Evans's idea, I take it, is that a stage satisfies a *tensed* predicate only at the times it exists, though it 'satisfies' an untensed predicate such as 'warm' or 'rabbit,' 'absolutely' or at every time.) I will henceforth so understand the proposal, and take it in a slightly generalized form, as defining satisfaction, of a wff by an object, relative to an arbitrary time. So understood, and writing $u[\phi]t$ for *relative to t, u satisfies ϕ*, the proposal runs

T. (1) $u[is\ F]t$ iff (At(u,t) and $u[F]t$)

 (2) $u[was\ F]t$ iff $\exists t'\exists u'(\ t'<t$ and u' is co-membered with u and At(u', t') and $u\uparrow F]t'$)

 (3) $u[warm]t$ iff u is a warm stage.

What is wrong with T? According to Evans,

> We are supposing that an object satisfies the tensed predicate 'was warm' iff it is a stage latter in the life of some object than some stage which satisfies the simple predicate. But this does not get the truth conditions right. 'A rabbit was running' may be true even though there is no stage of a rabbit latter than some running stage — the running stage might have been the last. (Gareth Evans, 'Identity and Predication,' *Journal of Philosophy* **72** [1975], 361)

But there is an obvious response to this. Note first that the form

Quantifier phrase+tense+predicate

apparently suffers from a scope ambiguity, between subject and tense, as witnessed by sentences such as 'The president was a Republican.' In standard tense logic, accounting for this is straightforward, since predicates are treated as open sentences and tenses as sentence operators; the two readings may then be regimented somewhat so

P1. was(the president$_x$ (x is Republican))

P2. the president$_x$ (was(x is Republican))

is no inscrutability, it does imply that, if the congruence constraint is correct, then languages like English can 'scrut' their own reference in a way the strong inscrutability thesis implies they cannot.

If there is an ambiguity here, there is one in 'a rabbit was warm' as well, between readings which, on a first pass, might be regimented so

R1: was(a rabbit$_x$ (x is warm))
R2: a rabbit$_x$ (was (x is warm))

A subtlety arises, since in T the tenses are (apparently) being treated as expressions which modify adjectives (and perhaps noun phrases) to yield a verb phrase. In the context of a proposal like T, either the tenses need to be *syntactically* ambiguated (so that there is a 'was' which applies to adjectives and a 'was' which applies to sentences), or we need to reformulate T.1 and T.2 so that 'is' and 'was' are understood as applying to something sentential (with the status of 'x is F'), or we need to reformulate the syntax in some more dramatic way.

However, the issues here are purely syntactic, not semantic. If we think of the tenses in proposal T as applying to sentences — and thus think of the 'F' in T1 as ranging over something with the status of open sentences — we can regiment the ambiguity in 'a rabbit is warm' as above. If we then extend T in the obvious way, by adding

(4) $u[a\ N_x(F)]t$ iff $\exists u'(At(u',t)$ and $u\uparrow N]t$ and $u\uparrow F]t]$
(5) $u[rabbit]t$ iff u is an MIT rabbit

we assign readings R1 and R2 these truth conditions: Relative to t,

R1: For some t' before t, there is a u which exists then which is an MIT rabbit and is a warm stage.
R2: For some u which exists at t and is an MIT rabbit, there is an earlier co-slice which is a warm stage.

R1 of course is the reading which Evans says T cannot capture.

I believe that the treatment given here, and its obvious relation to a tense logical treatement refutes Evans's odd claim ('Identity and Predication,' n. 15) that "treating tenses as operators requires an ontology of persisting things."

Considerations of space prevent me from discussing other claims which Evans and Fodor make about 'deviant' reference schemes. I must, however, remark that Evans's objections to re-interpretations which look upon predicates as designating properties seem to me completely without merit, ignoring as they do the possibility of treating a language in a way parallel to the way we treat the first order predicate calculus when we interpret it by mapping its sentences onto the sentences of an (interpreted) version of predicate functor logic.

(C) One might object that the congruence constraint is too restrictive. Take a predicate P, say 'rabbit.' Presumably there is some predicate Q — say, 'continuant rabbit' (i.e., 'rabbit which is an object which is wholly present at any time it exists') — which we can all agree *is* co-extensive with 'rabbit,' but which is *not* guaranteed, in the relevant sense, to be co-extensive with it. For let us suppose that we all in fact agree that it is *true* that something is a rabbit iff it is a continuant rabbit, and thus true that something satisfies P iff it satisfies Q.

If we grant weak inscrutability, and allow that a good illustration of possible alternative ontologies is given by the contrast between continuant and MIT rabbits, we seem committed to saying that P and Q are not congruent. So by the congruence constraint, we are to prefer accounts of reference (of English in English), which tell us that 'rabbit' refers to rabbits, to ones which tell us that 'rabbit' refers to continuant rabbits. But this is absurd, given that it is *true* that rabbits are continuant rabbits: if that *is* true, then the *reference* of P and Q are the same, and so the two accounts are equally correct.

So long as I am granting the weak inscrutability thesis, I deny the premiss that accounts of reference which (from a particular perspective) assign the same reference to terms must be equally correct accounts (even from that perspective) of those terms' reference. First of all, I am inclined to reason as follows. Consider the claims

(a)   'duck' is true of something in my language iff it is a duck
(b)   'duck' is true of something in my language iff it is a continuant duck
(c)   'duck' is true of something in my language iff it is an MIT duck.

If we are granting the weak inscrutability thesis, then claims (b) and (c) fail, in some sense, to have a determinate truth value. After all, they can be assessed as true or false only relative to an arbitrarily chosen background theory (according to Quine) or relative to arbitrary identification of my language (Davidson). Relative to some choices, (b) comes out true, (c) false; relative to others, they reverse truth value. In this, they presumably contrast with other sentences, such as

(d)   Either there are ducks or there are no ducks,

or, for that matter,

(e)   Ducks normally have wings.

Arguably, both of these are 'absolutely' or 'determinately' true, in the sense that they will be assessed as such relative to any perspective with an an adequate account of me and my linguistic behavior.

I take it that in this regard, (a) patterns with (d) and (e), not with (b) and (c): The reference of 'duck' is inscrutable not because there is a good theory which fails to entail that (a) is true as I use it; rather, it is inscrutable (roughly) because of the facts about (b) and (c). Because of this, it seems to me hardly arbitrary to prefer theories which entail (a), but not (b) or (c), to those which entail, say, (a) and (b). After all, the former sort of theories are (all else being equal) in a clear sense *determinately* correct; the latter, having indeterminate consequences, are not.

Secondly, matters of *correctness* to one side, I have argued that as semantic theories, congruent theories are better theories than non-congruent theories. A congruent theory provides a better interpretation of the language being interpreted than a non-congruent one, since the congruent theory will interpret object language expressions with ones which match, in relevant respects, the object language's indeterminacy. If the reference of the object language is indeterminate, but we are none the less called upon to account for what its expressions refer to, we do best if we match, in our interpretation, the object language's indeterminacy in all relevant respects. And this, of course, is what a congruent interpretation does.

IV

Let A and A' be individuals (or homogenous linguistic communities) speaking languages L and L'. Suppose that A and A' each has and employs a single, established, (more or less) conventional way of interpreting the other's linguistic behavior. Suppose, in fact, each interprets by employing a scheme of reference for the other's vocabulary. Let each of these interpretations satisfy all the constraints on interpretation which Quine or Davidson offer — let each, for short, be Q-

Mark Richard

adequate.[25] Note that if two people have Q-adequate ways of interpreting one another, then, by the lights of advocates of inscrutability
like Quine and Davidson, they must be said to understand one another's linguistic behavior.

A and A"'s situation is not unusual. A might be me, A' some English
speaker familiar to me, with each of our schemes — ignoring the complications of context sensitivity — more or less homophonic, so that
each of us presupposes something along the lines of

(R)   The other's use of 'rabbit' applies to rabbits.

It will simplify matters a bit — and I think it is harmless — if we
both ignore indexicality and assume that each reference scheme is the
inverse of the other. Then we may say that A and A' use a single 'scheme
of interpretation' — i.e., a bijection of primitive vocabulary of one language onto the other, which can be used in an obvious way to arrive at
two theories: one characterizes truth-in-L' in L, the other truth-in-L in
L'. Say, when A and A' are so related, that they are engaged in *mutual
interpretation*.

I'm going to argue that the fact that two people (or communities)
are engaged in mutual interpretation constrains in a significant way
what can be said about the reference of the terms of their respective
languages. I'll argue that our mutually interpreting each other generally *removes* any inscrutability of reference between L and L': there won't
be an acceptable account of L-reference in L' at variance with the scheme
A' uses to interpret A; and vice versa. Though this does not show that
in general the reference of one language will be scrutable in the other, it
reduces the scope of inscrutability. And it implies that the strong inscrutability thesis is false.

There is a simple argument that there is no inscrutability between
the languages of individuals who are engaged in mutual interpretation under a scheme R. (1) If the speakers of L and L' are engaged in

25 The exact criteria vary between Davidson and Quine, and vary for each across
    writings; see, for instance, Quine, *Word and Object* (Cambridge, MA: MIT Press
    1960), *Pursuit of Truth*; Davidson, 'Radical Interpretation,' *Dialectica* 27(1973). So
    far as I can see, such variation is not relevant to the present argument.

mutual interpretation, then they understand each other, and thus their theories of each other's languages are correct. So, (2) no theory which is completely adequate to the facts will imply that the speakers of L and L' fail to have adequate accounts of one another's reference. So, (3) there can't be an ideal perspective which can be extended to adequately interpret L and L' in two ways, with the reference of L's terms seen as distinct from the reference of their image under R. For if there were, there would be a theory adequate to all the facts that implied that L and L' speakers didn't understand each other. So there is no inscrutability between L and L'.

To put the argument more simply: Suppose we begin accepting the strong inscrutability thesis. Then, presumably, we say that understanding someone is having a Q-adequate way of interpreting her. So if L and L' speakers have a Q-adequate way of interpreting one another, they have all the (semantic) facts right. So there can't be a correct story to tell, according to which they have got the (semantic) facts wrong, because (say) they are misinterpreting each others' uses of 'rabbit.'

Though I think someone like Quine or Davidson must grant premiss (1), some will reject it because they are realists about reference. They will say that having a scheme of interpretation which satisfies Quine and Davidson's constraints doesn't guarantee getting the reference right, and that getting the reference right is necessary for understanding. But I don't need a claim *quite* as strong as (1) for the argument. If we hedge (1) so that it is the claim that *normally* mutual interpreters understand each other, we can still infer hedged versions of (2) and (3) which begin with 'normally.' That is enough for my purposes. Presently, I will offer reasons for thinking that a (suitably) hedged version of premiss (1) is in fact true, and ought to be acceptable even to someone realistic about reference.

Let me defend the argument by responding to some of the many objections which might be brought against it.[26]

---

26 Two responses which I should perhaps mention, are these: (a) One could shrug and say that it is in fact indeterminate what one says — this is a consequence of inscrutability — and so it must, strictly speaking, be indeterminate whether I understand you, given that I picked one of a number of (mutually exclusive) tenable stories to tell about what you said. (b) One might challenge the inference from

(A) Some may think the argument does not really refute the strong inscrutability thesis. Suppose that you and I have come to mutually interpret each other under scheme R. Now, consider us *before* we come to so interpret one another. Weak inscrutability tells us that inequivalent

---

it is determinate that I understand you, by using a scheme which interprets you as saying that Jones is surfing

to

the truth value of my use of 'you said that Jones is surfing' is determinate.

The motivation is that determinate understanding is simply a matter of having an acceptable interpretation scheme. But such schemes will, because of inscrutability, issue in claims about what is said which don't have a determinate truth value.

In my view, (b) isn't coherent. It requires that we make sense of a situation in which we can correctly say something like this: Richard understands your utterances. In particular, he understands your utterance of 'Jones is surfing' to say that Jones is surfing. But it is not true that your utterance says that.

(a) is coherent. But it is, in my opinion, without credible motivation. First of all, it simply does not follow from the inscrutability thesis — i.e., from the relatively uncontroversial thesis that there are different schemes of reference one could give for your and my languages — that it must be indeterminate whether or not I understand you. Suppose that our respective languages are so related that, while it may be indeterminate what our uses of 'Jones' and 'is surfing' refer to, it is determinate that whatever one refers to, the other does. This is consistent with the weak thesis. And it seems to imply that, if I interpret your 'Jones is surfing' with my own, I understand you.

Furthermore, the response in fact constitutes a retreat from the official position of Davidson and (perhaps) of Quine, according to which there really are semantic and intentional phenomenon, such as understanding. It is one thing to say, as Quine and Davidson appear to, that there are different, but equally good ways for one person to understand another's linguistic behavior. It is quite another to say that there is no such thing as understanding another's linguistic behavior, or that it is never 'strictly speaking' true that I understand you. It is one thing to say, as Davidson and Quine do, that there are different acceptable accounts of what a person is referring to, since we can make changes in what we say the person believes to adjust for the variations in the account we give of their language; it is another to say that no matter what we might say, about what a person believes and what he means, there is a perspective, adequate to all the facts there are, from which it must be said that we have gotten it wrong.

accounts of my reference and of yours are possible. Either of us could (to make it concrete) have been construed as referring to rabbits or their stages with 'rabbit.' So, I could have correctly interpreted your 'rabbit' with scheme R as referring to rabbits, or with a scheme R' as referring to stages. But then there is a scheme, R', inequivalent to R, which gives a correct interpretation of you, contrary to the conclusion of the argument.

This response is fallacious. It infers that R' in fact has a property P (interpreting you) from the fact that in certain circumstances (those in which I do use it to interpret you) R' would have had P. That is, the argument is analagous to this one: The Elks club *could have* adopted the bylaws of the Masons to determine who was elegible for membership; so there is a set of laws different from those of the Elks club which *can* be used to determine who is eligible for membership in the Elks club.

(B) One might say: Dismissing response (A) in this way does not explain *how* mutual interpretation serves to fix reference; the suggestion that it does is mysterious. For the Elks club to adopt one set of bylaws as opposed to another is, indeed, to *adopt* or *fix* which laws govern their practice. Thus the adoption excludes the applicability of other laws. But my interpreting you under R, instead of R', does nothing to help *fix* to what you or I are referrring with 'rabbit.' Thus, the analogy with the Elks club fails, and it remains mysterious how we can accept the argument.

It *is* plausible, that adopting a scheme of reference to interpret you helps fix the reference of my terms. Think of the case in which you and I come to mutually interpret one another under a scheme R. In this case, we have a successful practice of communicating with each other, one so successful that there is nothing about our dispositions to behavior, verbal or otherwise, which in any way undercuts it. The success of this practice is based, in part, on each of us presupposing that our use of 'rabbit' is true of something iff the other's use of 'rabbit' is true thereof. Each of us, in adopting and continuing to use the scheme R, undertakes and maintains a commitment to recognizing that our use of the term applies to an object iff the other's use does. Since the interpretation of our words is, in some sense, up to us, such a commitment has at least *prima facie* efficacy: Unless something overrides it, our terms *will* have the same interpetation. In advancing premiss (1), or at least a hedged version thereof, I am suggesting that if the scheme *R* we use to interpret one another provides a Q-adequate account, for each of us, of the other's linguistic behavior, then (normally) nothing overrides the commitment. The same sort of argument, I think, makes it plausible to say that my interpreting you with a Q-adequate scheme *R* constrains the interpretation of my terms, so that whatever you refer to with term *t* is what I refer to with *t*'s image under *R*.

It will be said that I have conceded everything of interest to the advocates of indeterminacy and inscrutability. Consider the doctrine of translational indeterminacy. Surely what Quine meant, in saying that translation is indeterminate, is just that there are ways we *could* have translated German into English which, though wildly different from our actual practices, are just as good. And you, the objector continues, have conceded just this sort of thing at the level of reference — that we *could* have interpreted German reference in a wildly different but adequate way.

The objection offers a modal formulation of strong inscrutability and translational indeterminacy. But what is packed into the modal here? If someone tells us

(1)   A' could have correctly interpreted A's use of 'rot' as referring to yellow

this is of no moment if what is meant is, say,

(2)   A might have used 'rot' in the way she in fact uses 'gelb,' and had she, A' could have correctly interpeted A as referring to yellow with 'rot.'

If (1) is of interest, it is because it is the claim that

(3)   Whatever in fact determines the semantic properties of A's use of 'rot' might have been as it actually is, and A' could still have correctly interpeted A as referring to yellow therewith.

Given that social relations, like those in which mutual interpreters stand, are relations which help determine the semantic properties of expressions — so that changing them is typically changing the semantic properties of a word — we have no reason to accept (3), and so no reason to accept (1), interpreted in an interesting way.

Perhaps it will be said that the fact that A' could have interpreted A differently *is* of interest because it shows that interpretation is extremely arbitrary. Now, why would such arbitrariness be of philosophic importance? I think someone like Quine would answer thus: If it is indeed arbitrary, how one person interprets another, this goes to show that what those people mean or are referring to isn't (within the bounds of the arbitrariness) fixed by anything. The arbitrariness in question shows that *really*, there aren't such things as synonymy, identity of reference, and the like; indeterminancy and inscrutability are indicators of the irreality of semantic properties and relations.

But this line of argument is, I think, fallacious. For it to be good, it would have to be true that the sorts of relations which people bear to each other when they (colloquially speaking) share a language were *irrelevant* to the meaning and reference of their shared vocabulary. It seems to me simply absurd to think that these are so irrelevant. I trust that anyone with even a smidgen of sympaythy for doctrines such as Putnam's, about the division of linguistic labor, will agree, at least as far as reference goes. But anyone who agrees with this should agree that the defense of the significance of (1) we are currently contemplating, which presupposes that these relations are semantically irrelevant, must be rejected.

We have the feeling that facts about mutual interpretation are somehow irrelevant to inscrutability because we tend to work with an idealized picture of interpretation, on which it is a one-way affair, carried off without appreciable effect on the natives or their quaint practices. We think of the matter, that is, in the idealized manner of the second chapter of *Word and Object*. This, in my opinion, is a mistake. In fact, the more seriously we take the possibility that reference is underdetermined, the more seriously we ought to take the idea that the natural course — indeed, part of the purpose — of interpretation is to invest the languages involved with new semantic properties. Imagine that we are looking at *L1* and *L2* from an idealized perspective. We see that each aspires to a unique mapping of its predicates onto sets of objects, but neither has the resources to effect it. A natural strategy for at least winnowing down the possibilities is for *L1* and *L2* to join forces, semantically linking their vocabularies by agreeing that this *L1* predicate and that *L2* predicate are to be interpreted in the same way, as are this pair of predicates, and so on. With such linkage, whatever constraints there are on mappings of *L1* vocabulary onto extensions will apply to *L2* predicates, and vice versa. With any luck, some small improvement in the slack between theory and interpretation will be achieved. It is natural to think of mutual interpretation, though it is also instituted for other purposes, as having this sort of effect.

(C) Some will wonder whether the fact, that individuals have a Q-adequate interpretation scheme, really requires them to presuppose, of one another, that their terms have the same reference or application.[27] Imagine a group whose members have fixed the reference of their terms by 'internal,' unverbalized demonstrations: each does things like say to herself "By 'aardvark' I mean that sort of thing." Such a group's members can certainly have a Q-adequate scheme for interpreting one another. But if we allow that their individual reference schemes can have priority, so far as reference determination is concerned, we must admit that having a Q-adequate scheme does not assure that its users use the terms it concerns with identical reference. For what is to prevent the members of the group from having demonstrated different objects or kinds when, for example, fixing the reference of 'aardvark'?

There are two ways in which one might reply to this objection. First off, one might question whether the example in fact makes it plausible that (normally) speakers, who have Q-adequate interpretation schemes, can be coherently seen as referring to different things. The example is one in which speakers begin by determinately referring to different things with 'aardvark,' in virtue of their differing properties and relations; they then enter into social relations which (*prima facie*) are inconsistent with (all of them) continuing to refer in the way in which they did. The example, that is, is one in which there is a conflict among already operative 'reference determiners.'

---

27 The objection that follows and its example are based upon comments by Brian Loar, though he should not be held responsible for the form I've given it in. Other members of the Rutgers Philosophy Department pushed similar lines of objection.

As I see it, normally this sort of conflict is not present where we have Q-adequacy — at least it is not present if we take the weak inscrutability thesis seriously. In the normal case, we do not find that, absent the existence of a Q-adequate interpretation scheme, the properties and relations of speakers suffice to determine that they refer to a particular thing with 'aardvark'; it is, instead, indeterminate to which among a range of things they refer. Suppose that this is so, and that the range of candidate referents for 'aardvark' among members of the general population is roughly the same. Suppose further that I am correct in saying that adopting a Q-adequate reference scheme involves undertaking a commitment to recognizing that, for instance, my use of 'aardvark' applies to just what yours does. Then normally, when we have a Q-adequate interpetation scheme, there will be something that, *prima facie*, commits us to co-referring, and nothing which pulls in another direction. It would seem to follow that normally, Q-adequate interpretation will be accompanied by co-reference.

So runs the first response. Now, a rejoinder to this response is that it does not really address the point behind the objection, that our adopting a Q-adequate reference scheme need not involve our presupposing our words apply to the same things. Consider again the community of (initally) solitary mental demonstrators. It is true that its members can be assumed to be disposed to say things like "we all mean (refer to) the same things with 'aardvark'," just as our own is. But nothing turns on whether the members of the community are *right* about this. In particular, there are no community goals or purposes, which the common language is supposed to serve, which would be frustrated if community members were wrong — as they in fact are — in thinking that they were all talking about the same things. So why think that identity of reference is really presupposed in this case?

But there *are* any number of things which the members of a linguistic community like our own think their language enables them to do, and which they would be unable to do, if the presupposition that community members shared a reference failed. Let me point to four.

(a) We assume that we are able to argue about what there is or isn't, and to assess one another's ontological commitments. Suppose you say that there are rabbits, rivers, or real numbers, and I deny it — that is, you seriously utter 'there are rabbits' (or whatever), and I just as seriously utter 'there are no rabbits' (whatever). Or suppose that you say that I, or my theory, is committed to rabbits, rivers, or reals, and I deny it. There is no engagement here if our sentences merely differ in truth value in our respective idioms; there is no engagement, even if our sentences ('there are rabbits,' 'there are not rabbits') are necessarily divergent (because, say, you refer to continuant rabbits, I to their stages, and the existence of either necessitates the existence of the other).

Ontological disagreement or evaluation presupposes the existence of a shared language, or at least of a shared semantics for some of the language. Such, I take it, is the burden of Quine's remarks on imputations of ontology. If we are to argue about what there is, we must both be able to refer to it. Since we obviously think that we can do this, and intend to use our language to do this, we have an example of something we think we are able to do with our language which we could not, if our presupposition of shared reference failed.

(b) Our conversational practices apparently presuppose that we use terms with a common reference. Consider the following dialogue:

A: Smith went to the store yesterday and got some worms.
B: Indeed. And when he came home, he used them to catch some fish.

Given that B's 'he' is anaphoric on A's 'Smith,' the success of B's contribution to the conversation apparently depends upon 'he' picking up the reference of A's 'Smith.' (It certainly can't be the case that such pronouns are generally 'pronouns of laziness' in any straightforward sense, since we can have anaphoric linking to indexicals.) But then, in general, what A refers to with 'Smith' will have to be the same (sort of) thing B would refer to therewith. For suppose, for example, that A refers to a continuant person therewith, while B refers to a stage, or sum thereof. Then there will be a corresponding difference in the extensions of those of A and B's predicates which are sensibly predicated of 'Smith': A's will have continuant extensions, while B's will have stages (stage sums) as extensions. So, unless A and B co-refer with proper names, B's contribution will be false, even if, in fact, Smith did use the worms to catch some fish.

(c) If A seriously utters 'Smith is sad,' B can generally correctly say 'A said of Smith that he is sad.' If A seriously utters 'dogs bark,' B can generally correctly say 'A said of dogs that they bark.'[28] Now the exact semantics of B's envisioned utterances is a matter of some delicacy. But on most views — including, I think, Quine's own — if there is a coherent semantics for *A said of a that it is F*, the truth of B's utterance of such will imply that A uttered a sentence of the form α *is G*, and the reference of *a* as used by B is that of α as used by A. Something analagous will be true of ascriptions which are '*de re*' with respect to a set, species, or attribute. If so, then something we obviously think we can do — say what objects and relations others are thinking about — requires intersubjective referential identity.

(d) Above I pointed to one sort of disagreement — about what there is — which we think we can quite generally have with those with whom we have a Q-adequate scheme of interpretation, but which we could not have, if we did not have referential agreement. I am tempted to say that, quite generally, we cannot disagree with one another if our words do not share reference.

If I yell 'a puppy is crossing the street,' and you scream 'a rabbit is not drowning in the well,' we do not disagree, even if my utterance is false and yours is true. Suppose that B uses 'puppy' to refer to rabbits and 'is drowning in the well' to pick out things crossing the street, and A uses 'puppy' and 'drowing in the well' as do we. It does not seem to me that when A shouts 'a puppy is drowing in the well' and B screams its negation they are thereby disagreeing. Even if A and B utter sentences which (say things which) are necessarily divergent, this does not in and of itself mark a disagreement: If you affirm Fermat's Last Theorem, and I deny the Four Color, we are, necessarily, at odds. But we need not disagree. (After all, I may go on to affirm Fermat, and you to deny Four Color.)

The question is, what more is needed for disagreement? An obvious candidate is referential isomorphism between a sentence affirmed and one denied; if that is correct, then the job is done.[29] For if we cannot

---

28 This last sentence is, I think, ambiguous, and may have some readings which don't in any interesting sense follow from the fact that A's expressed a belief with 'dogs bark.' But there is a reading which does follow.

29 This is probably too simple minded. If I utter 'no rabbit is crossing the road,' I am disagreeing with someone who utters 'a rabbit is crossing the road.' But it is

disagree without sharing reference, we cannot communicate without sharing reference, for (I claim) without (the possibility) of disagreement there is no genuine communication.[30] However, it might be said that this is stronger than it needs to be. For example, someone might propose that A and B disagree provided they utter sentences which they know diverge in truth value, or know are necessarily exclusive. If this is sufficient for disagreement, then — since the knowledge in question does not seem to exclude subsentential referential divergence — agreement in reference is not required for disageement.

While the proposed account of disagreement is not altogether implausible, it presents a problem for anyone who wants to say that disagreement is normally disconnected from referential agreeement. Suppose that a pair of normal English speakers disagree: one says 'a rabbit is crossing the road,' the other says 'it is not the case that a rabbit is crossing the road.' On the proposed account of disagreement, they must know that their sentences as uttered are incompatible; if they are normal speakers, they surely do know this. But how exactly does it come to be the case that they know it? If we were to press them, they would presumably tell us that the reason the sentences can't both be true is (*inter alia*) because they are both talking about the same things when they use 'rabbit' and the other terms. But if this is (part) of the ground for their belief, then it is not at all clear that A and B can be said to know that their utterances are incompatible unless they *are* referring to the same things with 'rabbit.'

The upshot is that, even given the possibility of disagreement without shared reference, given the presuppositions which in fact accompany linguistic acquisition, our being able to disagree with each other requires that our words share their reference.

(D) Some will say that a theory which assigns different references to my 'rabbit' and yours *does not* (at least need not) contradict a theory,

---

not clear that I am denying the sentence 'a rabbit is crossing the road.' I certainly didn't *utter* it.

So far as I can see, this sort of issue, as interesting as it is, is irrelevant to the issues at hand, and so I propose to ignore it.

30 I grant this is hyperbolic, though I think it is true.

which sees the terms as co-referring. On this response, the parts of the theories which impute reference to terms don't 'state facts'; they are of merely instrumental utility. The parts of the theory which 'state facts' and can actually contradict one another are those parts which say things like

(M):   My use of 'there is a rabbit in Massachusetts' is true iff there is a rabbit in Massachusetts.

But nothing has been said which shows that a contradiction arises here.

The discussion of section II undercuts this response. And if its principles (P1) and (P2) are correct, the response cannot be sustained. For suppose A, as he puts it, thinks

(1)   A''s use of 'duck' refers to ducks.

Then A is sanctioned by (P1) to think, on hearing A' utter 'a duck quacked,' something which A would put so:

(2)   There is some duck that A' is thinking about.

Suppose, now, that someone in an ideal perspective, B, interprets A's use of 'duck' to refer to Fs and A''s use of 'duck' to refer to Gs. Then B will, knowing that A' uttered 'a duck quacked,' be sanctioned by (P1) to think something which B will put so:

(3)   There is some G that A' is thinking about.

But by B's lights, this is not how A interprets A'. As B understands A, what A is getting at with (2) is that A' is thinking, not about Gs, but Fs. So, according to B, A has gotten things wrong.

This shows, I think that there is a genuine conflict between the (implications) of the reference schemes which A and B use to interpret A'. They can't both be right. And if this is so, the response we are considering fails.

(E) One might still be worried about the transition from (1) to (2) in the argument. Why think that if I understand you, then I must have the reference of your terms right? This response will sound queer to those who are realistic about reference, but, in the current context, it is a fair enough question. So let me try to answer it.

Suppose for the moment that principles like the following are correct:

(I):   One (literally) says that Jones is surfing only if one refers to Jones and says of him that he is surfing — i.e., uses a predicate true of the surfers and therewith says that Jones is among them.

Suppose further that I interpret you using a certain scheme of reference *R*, determining therewith to what you refer and what you say of the things to which you refer. Given this, it is hard to see how I could correctly interpret you as having said that Jones is surfing if I didn't have the reference of your terms correct. For suppose that I correctly interpret you as having said that Jones is surfing, but

(4)   'Jones' as you use it refers to Jones

is wrong. By (I) and the fact that you said that Jones is surfing, you must have referred to Jones. But, I presume, there are facts about your use of your language which will constrain what can be taken, in your utterance of 'Jones is surfing,' to refer to Jones — constrain it enough, in fact, so that if your utterance of 'Jones' didn't refer to him, then nothing therein did. (If the arguments of Evans and Fodor discussed above do show that logical syntax is (more or less) determinate, this is almost certainly so.)

I think considerations like this make it plausible that *if* principles like (I) are correct, then the fact that I correctly interpret you by using a certain scheme of reference implies that the scheme is correct. It remains to make it plausible that we must accept principles like (I).

A start at this is simply to point out that principles like (I) *are* presupposed by our day to day individuation of what's said. If I mumble 'jurnesisinhawaiisurfin' it goes without saying that, if in doing that, I *didn't* refer to Jones, then whatever I did, I didn't say that Jones was in Hawaii. This sort of thing goes without saying because it goes without saying that (i) what we say is a matter of what objects we are talking about, and what we are saying about them, and (ii) what we are talking about, and what we are saying about it, is a matter of what our words refer to and what they predicate.

Some will respond that there are different ways to individuate what an utterance says: Referential identity gives one scheme of individuation, 'ideological similarity' another, and 'motivational similarity' yet a third. I will grant, for argument's sake, that there are schemes of statement individuation which employ the second two factors. But I question whether these factors without the first are sufficient for identity of what is said. Let the motivational and ideological powers of 'pseudoepherine is good for colds' for you be as similar as you like to those of 'oxymetazoline is good for colds' for me. (If neither of us knows much about the chemistry of cold medications, they can be well nigh identical.) It is simply wrong for me to report your utterance of 'pseudoepherine is good for colds' as saying that oxymetazoline is good for colds, for such a report has you talking about oxymetazoline when you were not. This strongly suggest that if a speaker literally says that oxymetazoline is good, then she referred to oxymetazoline. That is, it strongly suggests that principles like (I) are correct.

(F) One may think that I am begging a question. To invoke the fact that two people mutually interpret each other, it will be said, is to invoke intentional facts, about what those people believe and intend about their own and others' linguistic behavior. But advocates of inscrutability have been led to it because they thought that what determines semantic facts is limited to the kind of evidence available in 'radical translation' or 'radical interpretation.' And in such interpretation, one is not privy to such intentional information. So argues Davidson:

> The evidence cannot consist in detailed descriptions of the speaker's beliefs and intentions, since attributions of attitudes, at least where subtlety is required, demand a theory that must rest on much the same evidence as interpretation. The interdependence of belief and meaning is evident in this way: a speaker holds a sentence to be true because of what the sentence ... means, and because of what he believes ... radical interpretation should rest on evidence that does not assume knowledge of meanings or detailed knowledge of beliefs.[31]

Though I disagree with Davidson about the scope of what determines semantic facts, I do not think I am committed to saying that interpretation presupposes 'detailed knowledge' of the contents of

---

31 Davidson, 'Radical Interpretation,' 134-5

intentional states. It is surely plausible to think that what is available to the radical translator makes it determinate, that, for example, you and I interpret one another's linguistic behavior — that is, that each of us has *some* way of interpreting the other's utterances as things with truth conditions. After all, the fact that I hold my own sentences true is information available to the radical interpreter. Surely she can also know that I hold your sentences true, and that I take the conditions under which they should be held true to be somehow correlated with the conditions under which my own should be.

But, I think, facts about the way in which I 'process' utterances — facts such as the fact that I routinely call up my *rabbit* lexical entry when I hear you utter 'rabbit' — can determine that, *given* that what I do when I process your utterances is interpreting you, I am in fact interpreting you using a particular scheme of reference, in my language, for yours — that is, using a particular mapping of your vocabulary onto mine.

If this is correct, then what is available to the radical interpreter, along with perfectly determinate facts about linguistic processing, can suffice to determine that I use a particular scheme of interpretation. I recognize that advocates of inscrutability usually deny that 'sub-personal' facts, like those about processing, have a bearing on interpretation. But surely such facts about processing are facts. We have good reason to think that they bear on interpretation. I disagree with Davidson and Quine, as to whether such facts can help narrow the range of interpretations of a language. I am not, in invoking them, begging a question about the determinacy of intentional states.[32]

---

32 It might be said that the response in (F) undercuts the motivation in (B). (B) offers a partial explanation for how it is that my interpreting you in a certain way R can cause my terms to have certain semantic properties. The explanation is in terms of such interpretation having certain intentional effects, or, at least, being accompanied by certain intentional states ('committments,' which are, *inter alia*, combinations of intentions and beliefs). But (F) claims that the proposal I am making does not require us to see semantic facts as being determined by anything other than non-intentional phenomena and 'very basic' intentional phenomena. But wouldn't the intentional states involved in the committements be 'non-basic'?

Assuming it is not going to completely discredit the passage from Davidson cited in the text, a response to this worry would need to show that the commit-

(G) Someone might object to the proposal I have made along the following lines. Suppose three pairs of individuals, A and B, B and C, and A and C, each have Q-adequate schemes for interpreting one another. We may suppose they all speak what are syntactically identical dialects of English, and that A and B, and B and C, use a single homophonic scheme of interpretation R. This is consistent with A and C using a non-homophonic scheme, say one under which each interprets the other's 'rabbit' with 'rabbit stage' and interprets the other's 'rabbit stage' with 'rabbit.' (One assumes that A, B, and C don't often get together to talk rabbits.)

The problem this might be alleged to cause is the following. Given the proposal I have made, it would seem that it must be true that

(a)   'rabbit' as used by A and 'rabbit' as used by B co-refer
(b)   'rabbit' as used by B and 'rabbit' as used by C co-refer.

But these seem to imply

(c)   'rabbit' as used by A and 'rabbit' as used by C co-refer.

---

ments in question are determined by non-intentional and 'very basic' intentional phenomena. I think this could be done, if we count as 'very basic' intentional phenomena such things as wanting (and intending) to be able to argue with and convey information to others. (The sort of desire I have in mind is general, not specific — wanting that for many p, I am able to argue about p, *not* wanting to be able to argue about p, where p is some fixed proposition.) For one might argue that, (1) all else being equal, people who have a common goal and are behaving in a way w such that one would, on reflection, recognize w as being the most likely way, given how things stand, to achieve the goal have a committment to continue to behaving in way w. But (2) people who are engaged in mutual intepretation have a mutual goal (being able to argue and inform) and a way of behaving (mutually interpeting) which satisfies this condition. So, (3) all else being equal, such people are committed to continuing to mutually interpret in the way in question.

If some such argument is sound, it derives the existence of the *prima facie* committment from the existence of general goals and the fact of mutual interpretation. And if such are derivable therefrom, they are determined thereby. So if what's said in (F) is correct and the general goals are 'very basic' intentional phenomena, the worry is put to rest.

And (c) seems unlikely, or worse, given that A and C use the non-homophonic reference scheme indicated above (and can be expected to find 'no rabbit is a rabbit stage' well nigh analytic).

By itself I don't think this is a terribly serious problem. It dissolves the moment we allow that 'rabbit' as used by A, B, or C might have more than one use — that A, for example, might be using it one way when speaking to B (speaking the idiom he uses to communicate to B), and another way (speaking another idiom) when speaking to C. Once we admit this, (a) and (b) need some sort of relativization, perhaps along the lines indicated by

(a′)   there is a language spoken by A and a language spoken by B such that what 'rabbit' refers to in one is what it refers to in the other,

or perhaps just

(a″)   there is a language spoken by A and B in which 'rabbit' occurs.

So far as I can see, any one who admits that having a Q-adequate way of interpreting someone is understanding her needs to say something along these lines. And the relativized versions of (a) and (b) don't lead to trouble.

This may seem initially bizarre. I have but a single 'rabbit' entry in my mental lexicon; so, it might be said, I have command of at most one word spelled r-a-b-b-i-t. But if I speak two languages in which 'rabbit' means (or refers to) different things, I must have two words 'rabbit.'

But why think the relation between lexical entries and words is one-one, and not one-many? I speak German and I speak English. It is a bold hypothesis indeed that I have two 'Empedocles' entries, one in my German dictionary, one in my English. Someone could be like me, but be embedded in communities such that 'Empedocles' referred, in the two linguistic communities, to different things, though she was not aware of it. It may be hard to say what such a person thinks, when she utters to her German friends 'Empedocles liebt.' But it is not hard to say to what she is referring: Given that she is speaking German, she is referring to what 'Empedocles' refers to in that language.

It might be thought that admitting that speakers may be understood as speaking many languages, when they in some sense appear to be speaking one, is tantamount to allowing the strong inscrutability of reference. Isn't it inscrutable, in the case of C, whether he is speaking the language he shares with A or with B? Won't it in fact be indeterminate what languages he speaks?

The alleged inscrutability does not follow. Suppose we say that what determines what languages a person speaks are various, broadly social, relations, interpretative and otherwise. Oversimplifying *enormously*, we might identify a language with what is shared by a maximally large group of individuals all of whom are able to adequately interpret one another under a single reference scheme. (That is, roughly speaking: for any three members of the group a, b, and c, if b interprets a's use of word w with word w', and c inteprets b's use of w' with w'', then a interprets c's use of w'' with w. More generally, if R is the reference scheme a and b use to interpret each other, and R^* is the one that b and c use to interpret each other, then the reference scheme a and c use can be obtained by composing R with R^*.) Then there is no reason to think in a case like that of A, B, and C that it is indeterminate what languages C speaks. The situation of A, B, and C is not one in which it is indeterminate, as to whether C speaks the A-C language or the A-B language; his sentences are determinately part of both. Furthermore, it will often (though not invariably) be obvious that only one of these languages is appropriately identified as the language of a particular utterance of C. When this is so, it is determinate that C should be taken to be speaking, on that occasion, a particular language.

Of course these remarks are promissory notes, to be cashed out only when we have a more adequate sketch of what it is for individuals to share a language. I think it is possible to give such, but that is beyond the scope of the current discussion. What I have tried to do here is only to show that granting the weak inscrutability thesis will not lead us to say that one is unable to determinately specify the reference of the terms of other languages. If what I have argued is correct, then since we sometimes do manage to successfully interpret each other — to enagage in mutual intepretation — the strong inscrutability thesis is simply false.[33]

---

33 Thanks, for comments, objections, and discussion, to Jody Azzouni, David Braun, audiences at Yale and Rutgers Universities, and an MIT reading group.

CANADIAN JOURNAL OF PHILOSOPHY
Supplementary Volume 23

Skepticism about Meaning: Indeterminacy, Normativity, and the Rule-Following Paradox

SCOTT SOAMES
Princeton University

Quine and Kripke's Wittgenstein both present "skeptical" arguments for the conclusion that there are no facts about meaning.[1] In each case the argument for the conclusion is that (i) if there are facts about meaning (and propositional attitudes), then they must be determined by some more fundamental facts, but (ii) facts about meaning (and propositional attitudes) are not determined by any such facts. Consequently there are no facts about meanings (or propositional attitudes). Within this overall framework, Quine and Kripke's Wittgenstein differ substantially — both in their reasons for thinking that facts about meaning (and propositional attitudes) are not determined by other facts, and in their responses to the alleged elimination of these facts. Despite this, I believe that their arguments fail for essentially the same reason; each equivocates about what it means for one set of facts to determine another. Once the equivocation is eliminated, the arguments lose their plausibility.

---

1 In discussing 'Kripke's Wittgenstein' I have in mind the philosophical position presented by Saul Kripke in chapters 2 and 3 of *Wittgenstein On Rules and Private Language*, (Cambridge, MA: Harvard University Press 1982). Kripke presents this position both as an interpretation of the leading ideas of Wittgenstein's *Philosophical Investigations* and as a philosophical point of view of independent interest. My discussion of the position will be concerned only with its content and merits, not its origin. The question of whether the position outlined by Kripke is an accurate interpretation of Wittgenstein is not directly relevant to my discussion.

Kripke's Skeptical Argument

I begin with Kripke's Wittgenstein. His argument is based on an undeniable truism: What we mean by a word is not exhausted by the cases in which we, or those who have taught us the word, have actually used it. Rather, what we mean somehow determines the correct application of the word to an indefinite range of new, so-far unencountered, cases. Kripke's skeptical argument challenges us to explain how this comes about. What is it about us that determines that the word, as we now use it, already applies in a definite way to cases we have not yet considered? If we mean anything at all by the word, then something must determine this, for otherwise we would be free to apply the word in new cases in any way we liked, without changing its previous meaning (or saying anything false). But surely we are not free to do this. So, if it is a fact that we mean so and so by a given word *w*, then some fact about us must determine in advance how *w* properly applies in new cases. This much seems undeniable. The surprise comes when we examine potential candidates for such a determining fact and find that none fills the bill. Because of this, the skeptic concludes, we have no choice but to admit that it is not a fact that we mean anything by *w* after all.

Kripke uses '+' to illustrate the point. This symbol, as we normally understand it, stands for the addition function, which assigns a unique natural number to each of infinitely many pairs of natural numbers. Thus, its range of application far exceeds the (relatively) small number of cases in which we have actually used it in computing sums. Consequently if we really do mean the addition function by '+,' then something about us must determine that when '+' is applied to a pair of numbers we have not previously considered it always yields the sum of those numbers, rather than nothing, or the result of applying some other arithmetical operation. But, the skeptic argues, nothing about us does determine this.

Wait a moment, one might object: Isn't the skeptic's position self-defeating? In setting up the case, he uses the words *sum* and *the addition function* to pick out a certain function, which he himself seems to characterize as applying in a definite way to infinitely many pairs of arguments. The problem, of course, is that if he is right, this is precisely the sort of thing that cannot be done. Thus, doesn't his own argument presuppose the falsity of its conclusion?

The short answer is that, yes, in my opinion, there is an important sense in which the skeptic's argument is self-undermining; if one succeeds in stating the argument, or in using it to justify one's belief in the conclusion, then that very act falsifies the conclusion.[2] The real challenge is to find where the argument goes wrong; and to do this it is helpful to have a formulation which is not (immediately) self-defeating. Kripke provides one. In his formulation we assume that there is no doubt about what we *now* use our words to mean. In particular, we all agree that at present we use '+' to stand for the addition function, which applies in a definite and prescribed way to infinitely many cases. All arithmetical facts about this function, including all results of applying it to particular numbers, are taken as given, and are not in dispute. What is in dispute is what we meant by '+' *in the past.*[3]

Here we face the familiar problem. Although I performed lots of calculations in the past using '+,' there are infinitely many pairs of arguments that I never applied it to. Pick one such pair — say, 68 and 57. Doing the calculation now, I will tell you '68 + 57 = 125.' Everyone grants that this is arithmetically correct. However the skeptic raises the question whether it is correct in a certain metalinguistic sense.[4] Is it the case that in the past I used the '+' sign to denote a function that gives 125 as value to the pair of arguments 68 and 57? More generally, is it the case that in the past I used '+' to denote the same function I now do, the addition function?[5] If so, then some fact about my past

---

2 Stating the skeptic's argument is not just a matter of uttering the words, but rather involves taking up genuine propositional attitudes toward the contents expressed by those words.

3 The advantage of this way of formulating the problem is that it allows us to take the meanings of the words we use in stating the argument for granted while the argument is being given and evaluated. Hence we do not have to rely on the meanings of certain words in stating the argument while at the same time questioning what those words mean.

4 Kripke introduces this sense of metalinguistic correctness on 8.

5 The skeptic's challenge is made graphic by his suggestion that perhaps in the past I used '+' to denote not the addition function but the quaddition function, where the latter differs from the former in assigning the value 5 to all pairs of arguments greater than any arguments I had explicitly used in calculations. It is assumed, for the sake of discussion, that 68 and 57 are such a pair.

understanding of the '+' sign must have determined that '125' was the right answer to the question 'What is 68 + 57?' even though I had never considered that case. The skeptic challenges us to find such a fact.

Certain natural responses are immediately disqualified. If, outside the context of the skeptical challenge, one were asked what past facts determined what we meant by a particular word, it might be natural to answer that the determining facts were facts about the beliefs and intentions connected with our use of sentences containing the word. For example, one might claim that my having meant addition by '+' is a consequence of the fact that in the past when I used sentences containing '+' I did so with the intention of communicating my belief concerning the result of *adding* certain numbers, rather than the result of applying some other function. Because of this, it was addition that I meant by '+.'

Whether or not such a response is true, it is of no help in dealing with Kripke's skeptical challenge. The skeptic raises a question about the content of the words we use. He does so knowing all the nonintentional facts there are about our past uses of the word — our linguistic performances, our behaviour, and so on. Any attempt to answer his question by citing our past beliefs and intentions will be met with a mere reformulation of the original challenge. Granted, in the past we used the words $9 + 16 = 25$ to express a belief. But what belief? A belief about addition, or a belief about some other function? To settle this question we must find some fact that determined the contents of our past beliefs and intentions. But this is just our original problem all over again. Having started by challenging us to find facts that determined the content of our words, the skeptic continues by challenging us to find facts that determined the contents of our mental states. Thus, if we are ever going to be able to answer the skeptic, we will have to find facts that determine content in general — linguistic and otherwise.

The same sort of difficulty plagues other natural responses to the skeptic. For example, in the case of '+' it is probably true that for most of us coming to understand the term was associated with learning a rule or algorithm for applying it. When confronted with a new calculation, we simply apply the algorithm and obtain the desired result. Since, in principle, the algorithm applies to infinitely many cases, it might seem ideally suited to answering the skeptic. One might say, for example, that the fact about me that determined that in the past I used '+' to stand for a function that assigns the value 125 to the arguments 68 and 57, even before I performed the actual calculation, was simply the fact that the algorithm I associated with '+' gives the result 125 in that case. The same point obviously can be made for all other cases. Thus, one might say, the fact that I meant *addition* by '+' was determined by the fact that the algorithm I associated with it in the past always yields the *sum* of the arguments to which it is applied.

But what is an algorithm anyway? Is it a collection of symbols (the symbols we use to express it), or is it the content of those symbols (what those symbols express)? If we think of the algorithm as just a collection of symbols, without any particular interpretation, then it won't determine the value of any function at any argument, and so will provide no answer to the skeptic. If, on the other hand, we think of the algorithm as the content of the symbols used in stating it, then the skeptic will question whether we did associate that content with '+' in the past. He does not doubt that in the past we associated the same symbols with '+' as we do now — symbols which, under their present interpretation, express an algorithmic content that determines the addition function. However he does doubt that we interpreted those symbols in the past in the same way we do now. In particular he doubts that, as we interpreted the symbols of the algorithm in the past, they provided a procedure that always yields the sum of a pair of numerical arguments.

Our problem, then, is this. We think that our understanding of '+' determines how it applies to an indefinitely large range of cases, even though at any given time we have considered only a small number of these. Thus, the fact that we mean one thing by '+' rather than another cannot consist simply in the uses we have already made of it in particular calculations. What then does it consist in? A natural thought is that it consists in associating '+' with a linguistic rule that determines its correct use. However this only postpones the problem, since we can now ask what our understanding of the symbols used in formulating the rule consists in. At some point this process of using symbols to interpret other symbols must stop. And when it does, we have to face the skeptic's challenge directly. In general, if we ever mean anything by any expression, then there must be some expressions whose meanings are not determined either by the particular occasions we have used them in the past, or by any linguistic rules we have associated with them, or by any introspectable, content-bearing, mental images or psychological representations that may accompany their use.[6]

This realization leads to a different attempt to answer the skeptic — one that Kripke calls the dispositional view. Applied to '+,' it says that for us to use '+' to denote one function rather than another is for us to have certain mental and behavioural dispositions. Specifically, in the past I used '+' to denote the addition function in virtue of the fact that I was disposed when asked any question of the form *What is m + n?* to answer by giving the sum of *m* and *n*. Thus, even though in the past I never was asked the question *What is 68 + 57?*, if I had been asked, I would have answered *125* — just as I do now . Although the particular calculations I have performed have changed over time, my dispositions to answer arithmetical questions in specific ways has not. Consequently, the dispositionalist concludes, I meant the same thing by '+' in the past as I do now.

Paraphrasing Kripke, we may take (D) to be a preliminary statement of the dispositional analysis of '+.'

(D)   One uses '+' to denote a 2-place numerical function f iff for all natural numbers m, n, and z, and numerals $\underline{m}$, $\underline{n}$, and $\underline{z}$ denoting

---

6   Kripke's skeptic raises a challenge about content-bearing (i.e. intentional) facts. The challenge is to locate non-content-bearing (i.e. nonintentional) facts that determine the content-bearing ones. In attempting to meet this challenge, the nonintentional facts that one is allowed to appeal to are not restricted to behavioural facts, publicly observable facts, or even physical facts. Mental images, representations, feelings, and sensations can all be appealed to, provided that their 'interpretations,' or contents, (if any) are not taken for granted, but are themselves given a thoroughly non-intentional explanation.

In certain cases, it is quite plausible to suppose that factors such as linguistic rules or representations really do play a role in determining the meanings of some expressions. A case in point is '+' itself. However in this, as in other cases, the role is dependent upon a prior explanation of the contents of the relevant rules, algorithms, images, or representations.

them, one is disposed to answer z when asked the question ⌜What is $\underline{n} + \underline{m}$?⌝ iff $f(m,n) = z$.[7]

It is worth noting that on this account, the fact about me that determined what I meant by '+' was an intentional fact that is itself subject to skeptical worries of two different sorts. First, the disposition to *answer* a question in a certain way is a disposition to *assert* a certain proposition in answer to the question. But what, the skeptic will demand, justifies our characterizing an event that consists of my producing a numeral z in response to the utterance of an interrogative sentence, ⌜What is $\underline{n} + \underline{m}$?⌝, as my answering the question — by asserting the proposition that n + m = z — as opposed to emitting a mere verbal reflex, or giving an arbitrary response without meaning anything? A thoroughgoing skeptic about meaning and propositional attitudes would not take this for granted. Consequently our statement of the dispositional view already presupposes more than the skeptic would allow. Second, in order to use the analysis to determine the function meant from my verbal performances one would have to be given the denotations of the numerals and other symbols used in questions and answers. These are just as subject to skeptical doubt as the interpretation of '+.'

For these reasons, the dispositional analysis (D) stated here is itself too intentional to succeed as a response to the skeptic. However, I will put this objection aside temporarily in order to review two other objections discussed by Kripke — the error and finitude objections. After looking at these, our worries about the intentionality built into (D) will resurface in the discussion of Kripke's normativity objection.

The error objection is that the analysis does not make room for dispositions to misapply the expression. Since, according to it, any answer I am disposed to give to a particular query, ⌜What is $\underline{n} + \underline{m}$?⌝, is definitive of what I mean by '+,' all such answers must be correct. But this is wrong. One can mean addition by '+' even if one is disposed to make a few systematic mistakes in particular cases, and hence is disposed to give incorrect answers to some questions of the form ⌜What is

---

7 Kripke, 26

$\underline{n}$ + $\underline{m}$?'. The finitude objection is that the analysis cannot account for the fact that our dispositions are finite, and will give out before the application of the term does. Certainly, one can mean addition by '+' despite the fact that at some point the numbers to be added get too large for us to deal with. When this happens we have no dispositions to answer the relevant questions 'What is $\underline{n}$ + $\underline{m}$?', even though the addition function denoted by '+' continues to be defined.[8]

For these reasons the dispositional analysis, in the form we have stated it, is surely inadequate.[9] Nevertheless, it is difficult to resist the idea that our dispositions to apply a term in particular cases play some

---

8 Both the error and the finitude objections can be generalized to cover dispositional analyses of other terms. In this connection, it is important to note that the finitude objection to the dispositional analysis of '+' is just one instance of a more general objection. The objection is that a term may apply to certain objects even in cases in which those objects are, for one reason or another, epistemically inaccessible to us, and hence are not objects about which we have any normal dispositions. In the case of '+' the infinity of natural numbers ensures that at some point they will get too big for us to consider. In the case of other words the reasons for epistemic inaccessibility may be quite different.

9 One possible response to these objections would be to give up the dispositional analysis for '+,' while retaining it for simpler notions like 'successor,' in terms of which '+' could then be defined. Certainly, there is less room for error in applying the successor function than in applying the addition function. However, some room for error may remain, and, in any case, the finitude objection still seems to apply. Another possibility, considered by Kripke, is to reformulate the analysis so as to appeal to idealized dispositions — dispositions to answer questions 'What is $\underline{n}$ + $\underline{m}$?', not in just any circumstances, but in certain idealized circumstances, in which one scrupulously 'checks' one's work, and in which one's mental capacities have somehow been enhanced to allow one to consider arbitrarily large numbers. Kripke's criticism of this response is telling. In order for the analysis to be non-circular, one must not characterize the idealized dispositions in a way that presupposes in advance what we mean by '+.' For example, they cannot be characterized as dispositions to answer the relevant questions when we have been provided with sufficient mental capacities to allow us to correctly *add* any two numbers. However, if our characterization of the ideal dispositions is non-circular, then we will have little reason to be confident that they will in fact determine the desired function. It is also worth noting that the finitude and error objections cannot be overcome by appealing to the dispositions of the entire linguistic community of which the speaker is a part. These

role — perhaps along with other factors — in determining what the term means. With this in mind, we turn to Kripke's normativity objection. Applied to the dispositional analysis, it is designed to show how far from providing an answer to the skeptic the analysis really is. Applied more generally, the normativity objection is seen as the most fundamental obstacle to any analysis that attempts to answer the skeptical challenge.

The objections to the dispositional analysis based on error and finitude show that my dispositions to calculate with '+' do not correspond perfectly to the addition function. The normativity objection maintains that even if my dispositions did correspond perfectly to the addition function, that would not be enough to show that I meant addition by '+.' The mere fact that I am now, and have been in the past, disposed to answer a question in a certain way does not show that I should answer it in that way. But it is a crucial aspect of meaning something by a term that one has adopted a standard to which one tries to adhere, and which provides a basis for judging responses to be correct or incorrect. Kripke contends that the dispositional analysis doesn't provide such a standard.

According to Kripke, the main reason that it doesn't is that it fails to explain how I can be *justified* in giving one answer rather than another when presented with a previously unconsidered calculation.[10] The

---

dispositions are just as subject to the objections as are the dispositions of an individual.

These considerations constitute serious obstacles to the dispositional analysis. I do not maintain that they rule out all possible reformulations. Perhaps there are reformulations of the analysis that are capable of avoiding the error and finitude objections. Even if this is so, the normativity arguments will remain, and will, I suspect, require appeal to some factors over and above dispositions. See below.

10 A relevant passage is the following:

To a good extent this reply *[the dispositional analysis]* immediately ought to appear to be misdirected, off target. For the skeptic created an air of puzzlement as to my *justification* for responding '125' rather than '5' to the addition problem as queried. He thinks my response is no better than a stab in the dark. Does the suggested reply advance matters? How does it *justify* my choice of '125'? What it says is: "'125' is the response you are

picture that emerges from his discussion is something like this: The skeptic gives me a new calculation that I have never done before. He asks me *What is 68 + 57?* I answer that 68 + 57 = 125. The skeptic asks me to cite some past fact that justifies this answer, in the sense of showing that it is the answer I ought to give provided that I am now using '+' with the same meaning as I did in the past. In effect, the skeptic is imposing the requirement that no fact will suffice to answer his challenge unless we can conclude from that fact that I ought to give '125' as answer to the question *What is 68+57?*, provided that I now intend to use '+' with the same meaning as I did before.

Let me formulate this requirement as follows:

(N_E)   If the fact that F determined that (in the past) one meant addition by '+,' then knowing that F would, in principle, provide one with a sufficient basis for concluding that one ought to give

---

disposed to give, and (perhaps the reply adds) it would also have been your response in the past." Well and good, I know that '125' is the response I am disposed to give (I am actually giving it!), and maybe it is helpful to be told — as a matter of brute fact — that I would have given the same response in the past. How does any of this indicate that — now *or* in the past — '125' was an answer *justified* in terms of instructions I gave myself, rather than a mere jack-in-the-box unjustified and arbitrary response? (23)

The emphasis here on justification echoes the way in which Kripke initially sets up the skeptical problem.

In the discussion below, the challenge posed by the skeptic takes two forms. First, he questions whether there is a *fact* that I meant plus, not quus, that will answer his skeptical challenge. Second, he questions whether I have any reason to be so confident that now I should answer '125' rather than '5.' The two forms of the challenge are related. I am confident that I should answer '125' because I am confident that this answer also accords with what I *meant*. Neither the accuracy of my computation nor of my memory is under dispute. So it ought to be agreed that *if* I meant plus, then unless I wish to change my usage, I am justified in answering (indeed compelled to answer) '125' not '5.' An answer to the skeptic must satisfy two conditions. First, it must give an account of what fact it is (about my mental state) that constitutes my meaning plus, not quus. But further, there is a condition that any putative candidate for such a fact must satisfy. It must, in some sense, show how I am justified in giving the answer '125' to '68 + 57.' (11)

the answer '125' to the question *What is 68 + 57?*, provided one
intends to use '+' with the same meaning it had in the past.

It is important to understand what must be presupposed in order for
this requirement to make sense. The reason one ought to answer '125'
is that, if one did mean addition by '+,' then '125' is the *correct* answer
to the question *What is 68+57?*; and the correct answer is the answer
one ought to give. The reasoning here is as follows: If knowing that *F*
allows us to conclude that in the past one meant addition by '+,' then it
allows us to conclude that the sentence *68 + 57 = 125* means that the
sum of 68 and 57 is 125, and hence is true iff the sum of 68 and 57 is 125,
provided, of course, that one is now using '+' with the same meaning
as before.[11] Next we appeal to the arithmetical fact that 125 *is* the sum
of 68 and 57, which the skeptic grants, and is not in dispute.[12] From
these two facts, one about meaning and one about numbers, it follows
that the sentence *68 + 57 = 125* is true, and hence that one speaks the
truth if one responds '125' to the question *What is 68+57?* Since the
skeptic's requirement clearly presupposes that one ought to speak the
truth in this case, it follows that one ought to answer '125.' In this way
knowledge of the putative meaning-determining fact that *F*, together
with undisputed knowledge of nonlinguistic facts and the general presumption that one ought to speak the truth, provide a basis for concluding what answer one ought to give to the question *What is 68+57?*

---

11 I am here taking the meanings of the other symbols — the numerals and identity
sign as given. This simplification does not affect the point at hand.

12 On page 11 Kripke insists *"Neither the accuracy of my computation nor of my memory
is under dispute. So it ought to be agreed that if I meant plus, then unless I wish to
change my usage, I am justified in answering ... '125,' and not '5.'"* Similarly, on page
13, in explaining why he sets up the paradox as a metalinguistic problem about
the past use of an expression, Kripke says that when this is not done, *"some
listeners hear it as a skeptical problem about arithmetic: "How do I know that 68 + 57 is
125?" (Why not answer this question with a mathematical proof?) At least at this
stage, skepticism about arithmetic should not be taken to be in question: we may assume, if we wish, that 68 + 57 is 125."* I take these passages to indicate that in
Kripke's formulation of the paradox, my present (true) belief that 68 + 57 = 125
can be appealed to (without further justification) in attempting to meet the
skeptic's demand that I show how I am justified in thinking that '125' is the
answer required by my past understanding of the term.

Applying the normativity requirement (N_E) to the dispositional view yields the first premise, (P1), of an obvious normativity argument.

(P1)   If one's past dispositions to answer questions ⌜What is $\underline{n} + \underline{m}$?⌝ determined that one meant addition by '+,' then knowing one's past dispositions to answer such questions would, in principle, provide one with a sufficient basis for concluding that one ought to give the answer '125' to the question *What is 68 + 57?*, provided one intends to use '+' with the same meaning it had in the past.

The normativity objection to the dispositional analysis consists in (P2).

(P2)   Knowing one's past dispositions to answer questions ⌜What is $\underline{n} + \underline{m}$?⌝ does not, in principle, provide one with a sufficient basis for concluding what answer one ought to give to any such question, provided one intends no change in meaning.

Together, (P1) and (P2) entail that no matter how closely my past dispositions to answer questions of the relevant form may, in fact, have corresponded to the results of applying the addition function, those dispositions did not determine that in the past I meant addition by '+.' Thus, if (P1) and (P2) are correct, then the dispositional response to the skeptic is incorrect.

Much of Kripke's discussion is aimed at supporting (P2), which is itself quite plausible. Suppose I had amnesia and didn't remember what I meant by '+' in the past. When asked, at present, to calculate '68 + 57' I might feel inclined to give the answer '125.' Still, I might wonder whether this answer was justified, in terms of what I meant by '+' in the past. Would it be sufficient to be told that this was the answer I was disposed to give in the past? It doesn't seem that it would, for I might wonder whether in the past this was one of the calculations on which I was disposed to make mistakes. A similar observation holds regarding the point of view of someone viewing me from the outside and wondering whether my present answer of '125' is correct. Simply being given a specification of the relevant past dispositions is not enough to allow such an observer to conclude that my present answer accords with my past meaning or intentions.

Since (P2) is true, and since (P1) and (P2) entail that the dispositional response to the skeptic is false, the success of the argument against the dispositional view depends on our evaluation of the Normativity Requirement (N_E), and the particular instance of it given in (P1). How plausible are these principles? Quite plausible, it seems, provided that we understand what it is for one empirical truth to determine another in accord with the following constraint.

(Det_E) P determines Q only if, given P, one can demonstrate Q without appealing to any other empirical facts — i.e. only if Q is an apriori consequence of P.

With this understanding of determination, (N_E) and (P1) will hold.[13] If the claim that in the past one meant addition by '+' were an apriori

---

13 Is it necessary, in order for the Normativity Requirement (N_E) to play its proper role in the skeptic's argument, for the meaning-determining fact that F to provide the basis for an apriori, demonstrative inference to the relevant conclusion, or would it be enough for the fact that F to provide the basis for any sort of inference to the conclusion? Although the point is arguable, there are reasons for opting for the stronger interpretation. First, Kripke's skeptic seems to be looking for nonintentional facts that both metaphysically necessitate and epistemologically demonstrate the relevant meaning facts. Nonintentional facts that have meaning facts as apriori consequences would, presumably, do this; whereas nonintentional facts which provide only the basis for an empirical inference to the meaning facts presumably would not. Second, when we cast our net wider, and include nonintentional facts other than the dispositional facts presently under consideration, the skeptic's claim that meaning facts are not apriori consequences of any such set of facts remains plausible, whereas a corresponding claim, to the effect that meaning facts cannot be inferred from nonintentional facts, even by an empirical inference to the best explanation, say, is not nearly so plausible.
   A different question about the normativity requirement is whether, as it is currently stated, it is too weak. Perhaps, in addition to being required to have meaning facts as apriori consequences, meaning-determining facts should also be required to be readily accessible to the speaker — so that the speaker is in a position to draw the relevant conclusions from those facts. I have no objection to this strengthening of the requirement; all the philosophical points I want to make regarding (N_E) would hold for this strengthening of (N_E). My reason for preferring the weaker version in the text is that it leads to a conclusion of greater generality. I am indebted to George Wilson for a discussion of this point.

consequence of the relevant dispositional truths, then knowing those dispositional truths would, in principle, make it possible to conclude that in the past one meant addition by '+.' But then, since it is accepted as uncontroversial that 125 *is* the result of adding 68 and 57, one could conclude that '125' is the correct answer to the question *What is 68 + 57?*, and hence is the answer that one ought to give, provided one intends to use '+' with the same meaning as it had in the past.

It is worth emphasizing that on this account the substantive constraint placed on the meaning-determining fact F by the normativity requirement (N_E) is that, in principle, knowledge of F must allow one to demonstrate that in the past '+' was used to mean addition. This is essentially a descriptive matter. The normative prescription about what answer one ought to give in a particular case results from (i) the descriptive fact about what one meant, (ii) the arithmetical facts involving the addition function, and (iii) the normative presumption that one should speak the truth. The substantive requirement on F is just that knowledge of it be sufficient to demonstrate the first of these.[14]

---

14 The point here is a general one, and applies to versions of the rule-following paradox involving all sorts of different words. For example, consider a word like 'fossil,' which applies to concrete physical objects. Given some object o, the normative prescription regarding whether one should apply 'fossil' to o depends on (i) the meaning of the word 'fossil,' (ii) the nonlinguistic facts about the nature of o — i.e. whether or not it is a fossil and (iii) the general presumption that one should apply a term to an object only if doing so would involve speaking the truth. As Michael Thau has emphasized to me, examples like this highlight the need for (ii) over and above (i) particularly clearly.

There is, however, another issue involving facts like (ii) that is worth mentioning, even though I don't have sufficient space here to go into detail. Suppose I apply the word 'fossil' to a certain object o, and then I am challenged by a skeptic to justify this new application of the word. Suppose further that part of my response involves citing some fact F about my past use of the word. Imagine for the sake of argument that knowledge of F does allow me to demonstrate that in the past I used the word to mean fossil. Still, this by itself doesn't justify my application of the word to o, even if I am now using the word with the same meaning as before, and it is granted that I ought in this case to speak the truth. To complete my justification I have to show that I am justified in thinking that o is a fossil. And how am I to do that? Perhaps the explanation of what it is for me to think that o is a fossil is simply for me to understand the

The advantage of this way of construing the normativity objection is that the resulting argument against the dispositional analysis turns out to be sound. However, there is a corresponding disadvantage — the conclusion thereby established is weak. Suppose that the proposition that one meant addition by '+' really isn't an *apriori consequence* of true propositions about one's past dispositions to calculate. For all we know it might still be a *necessary consequence* of those propositions. And if it is, then there is an important sense in which what one means is determined by facts about one's dispositions. Despite all that has been shown up to now, facts about meaning may yet turn out to be meta-

---

word 'fossil' and be disposed to apply it to *o* on the basis of some reasonable, empirical examination of, or inquiry about, *o*. If so, then the justification for my thinking that *o* is a fossil may amount to little more than my now understanding the word 'fossil' and being disposed, after appropriate investigation and reflection, to apply it to *o*.

If this is the situation, then in some ultimate sense I may have no justification for applying the term to a new item *o*, other than my own confident, informed, and reflective inclination to do so, plus my status as a competent user of the term. This does seem to be an important part of what Wittgenstein was trying to show in his deployment of the rule-following paradox, and it is also present in Kripke's discussion. Moreover, there are, I think, cases in which something like this point is correct. However, this observation about justification does not undermine the response given in the text to Kripke's version of the skeptical paradox; nor does it lead to any defensible skepticism about meaning.

What it may do is point to an alternative route to one of Wittgenstein's conclusions about language — a route that does not require any fundamental, skeptical recasting of our ordinary conception of meaning. The conclusion is that, at least in some cases, the explanation of a speaker's understanding of a term *T* (including his ability to apply it to newly considered objects) does not involve associating *T* with an independently apprehended property *P* (and judging those objects to have *P*). Understanding a term, or using it to mean a certain thing, is not always like deciding to attach a new proper name to an object with which one is already familiar. See my 'Semantic Competence,' *Philosophical Perspectives* 3 (1989) 575-96, at 587-91 for a brief discussion of this idea. This idea is discussed in more detail in my, 'Facts, Truth Conditions, and the Skeptical Solution to the Rule-Following Paradox,' *Philosophical Perspectives* 12 (1998), forthcoming.

I am indebted to James Pryor and Michael Thau for helpful discussions of the material in the footnote.

physically necessary consequences of facts about dispositions, even if they are not apriori consequences of such facts.

However, this is not all that Kripke has to say about the normativity objection to the dispositional analysis, as is indicated by his discussion of the following example.

> Assuming determinism, even if I mean to denote *no* number theoretic function in particular by the sign '*,' to the same extent as it is true for '+,' it is true here that for any two arguments *m* and *n*, there is a uniquely determined answer *p* that I would give (I choose one at random, as we would normally say, but causally the answer is determined). The difference between this case and the case of the '+' function is that in the former case, but not in the latter, my uniformly determined answer can properly be called 'right' or 'wrong.' (p. 24)[15]

Kripke's idea can be made more graphic by imagining that as a result of some special brain surgery, I might be programmed to verbally respond to an utterance of the interrogative sentence *What is x * y?* by uttering a definite numeral z for each pair of numerals x and y used in the question. For any pair of numerals you give me, using '*,' I will respond by uttering a definite numeral. Because of this we may presume that some definite function *f* on the natural numbers corresponds to the verbal responses I am disposed to give to interrogatives containing '*.' Despite this, it might still be that I don't *mean* anything by '*.' My responses may be nothing more than verbal reflexes. I might notice that I always give determinate responses to queries using '*.' But I don't regard these as correct or incorrect — since I don't intend to assign any meaning to '*.'

The point here is that, by themselves, mere verbal dispositions to respond to interrogative sentences involving a symbol, either '+' or '*,' are not enough to endow it with meaning — even if the dispositions can be seen as corresponding to a definite function. Since it is possible to have these dispositions without meaning the function, meaning the function is not a necessary consequence of having the specified dispositions. Some other element must be present in order for us to have genuine meaning. So far, we haven't found it.

---

15 See also Kripke's discussion in footnote 18, 24.

It should be noticed that in giving this argument, we have quietly replaced Kripke's original formulation (D) of the dispositional analysis with some nonintentional understanding of it. In the original formulation, the allegedly meaning-determining dispositions were characterized as dispositions to *answer* arithmetical questions, presumably by *asserting* that a particular number is the value of the relevant function at a given pair of arguments. By contrast, in Kripke's '*' example I don't mean anything by '*'; I do not *assert* anything or *answer* any question. Here the dispositions — both with '*' and with '+' — are characterized simply as dispositions to utter specific numerals when prompted by utterances of particular interrogative sentences containing '*' or '+.'

When dispositions are characterized in this way, Kripke's discussion of the '*' example can be seen as constituting a second normativity argument against the dispositional analysis. Like the first, it is based on a general requirement, in this case (N_M).

(N_M) If the fact that F determined that (in the past) one meant addition by '+,' then in any possible world in which it is the case that F, one means addition by '+'; hence, in any possible world w in which it is the case that F, '125' is the answer one ought to give to the question *What is 68 + 57?*.

Applied to the nonintentional version of the dispositional analysis, this general requirement yields (P1').

(P1')   If a certain complex dispositional fact — namely the fact that in the past one was disposed to verbally respond in such and such ways to utterances of interrogative sentences ⌜What is $\underline{n}$ + $\underline{m}$?⌝ — determines that (in the past) one meant addition by '+,' then in any possible world w in which that dispositional fact obtains one means addition by '+' in w, and hence ought to answer '125' to the question *What is 68 + 57?*

The second normativity objection to the dispositional analysis (formulated nonintentionally) is (P2').

(P2') It is possible *not* to mean addition (or anything at all) by '+' even though one is disposed to verbally respond in such and such ways (the ways mentioned in (P1')) to utterances of interrogative sentences ⌜What is n + m?⌝

From (P1') and (P2') it follows that the fact that in the past one was disposed to verbally respond in the ways mentioned in (P1') to utterances of interrogative sentences ⌜What is n + m?⌝ does *not* determine that (in the past) one meant addition by '+.'

The argument is clearly valid. Moreover, the discussion of the '*' example shows that (P2') is true, provided that the dispositions spoken of are nonintentionally stated and restricted simply to the production of numerals in response to utterances of interrogative sentences. (P1') is also true, provided that the determination relation it speaks of is constrained by the following principle.

(Det$_M$) P determines Q only if Q is a necessary consequence of P

We have, then, two versions of the normativity objection. One version, the necessary-consequence version, incorporates (Det$_M$); the other version, the apriori-consequence version, incorporates the earlier requirement, (Det$_E$), on the determination relation. Both versions are sound, and establish their conclusions, when applied to the nonintentional form of the dispositional analysis. However, recognition of the difference between the two gives rise to an important question. If, in addition to the verbal dispositions already considered, we cast our net wider, so as to include more and more nonintentional facts, will the two versions of the normativity objection continue to apply together, or will they come apart at some point?

In order to investigate this question, we let T be the set of nonintentional truths about my dispositions to produce numerals in response to questions ⌜What is n + m?⌝. In our discussion of the '*' example, we have seen that it is possible for all members of T to be true even though I don't mean anything by '+,' because my responses are not real answers but only verbal reflexes. Are there other nonintentional truths which, together with T, would change this result? Suppose we formed a new set, T', which included all members of T together with all additional nonintentional truths about my dispositions to verbal behaviour involving '+' — for example, dispositions covering cases in which I 'check and revise' my work, dispositions to insist on one and only one 'answer' for any given question, dispositions to strive for agreement between my own answers and those of others, and so on. Would it be possible for all members of this larger set T' to be true, even though I didn't mean anything by '+'?

I should emphasize that I am not here trying to identify all the relevant verbal dispositions; nor am I trying to characterize them precisely in a thoroughly nonintentional way. Rather I am assuming that some such characterization is possible, and I am asking whether, by taking a broad enough look at such a characterization of our linguistic behaviour and dispositions, we would at some point reach a stage in which we were confident that anyone conforming to all those facts meant something by his words? Is there a possible world in which all one's nonintentionally characterized dispositions to verbal behaviour, including those just mentioned, match my dispositions in the actual world, yet one does not mean addition, or anything else, by '+'? If so, how is this possible? Would the result change if we enlarged the set of potential meaning-determining truths still further to include not only all truths about my dispositions to verbal behaviour, but also all truths about (i) the internal physical states of my brain, (ii) my causal and historical relationships to things in my environment, (iii) my (nonintentionally characterized) interactions with other members of my linguistic community, (iv) their dispositions to verbal behaviour, and so on? Is there a possible world in which someone conforms to all those facts — precisely the facts that characterize me in the actual world — and yet that person does not mean anything by '+'?

I think not. Given my conviction that in the past I did mean addition by '+,' and given also my conviction that if there are intentional facts, then they don't float free of everything else, I am confident that there is no such a world. Although I cannot identify the smallest set of nonintentional facts about me in the actual world on which meaning facts supervene, I am confident that they do supervene. Why shouldn't I be? I start out convinced that in the past I meant addition by '+.' Next, I imagine some large set of nonintentional facts about the past remaining fixed, so that they obtain in some possible world w. I then ask whether the individual who corresponds to me in w — the individual who is the focus of the fixed nonintentional facts in w — means something by '+.' The answer, of course, is that since I meant something in the actual world, he means something in w. And if he means something by '+,' surely he means what I meant by '+' in the actual world — addition.

Of course, this won't convince the skeptic. He isn't willing to grant that I meant anything in the past. He wants to be shown that there is a nonempty set of meaning facts about which the question of supervenience can be raised; and he won't be satisfied until I specify a set of nonintentional truths from which the existence of such meaning facts can be demonstrated. In effect, he demands that I establish that purported truths about what I meant are apriori consequences of nonintentional truths the existence of which we both accept.

But why should I acquiesce in this demand? It would be very interesting if it turned out that I could refute the skeptic using only uncontroversial premises that even he accepts. However this is not generally required of responses to skeptical problems, and I see no special reason to require it in this case. What is required is that I rebut any skeptical challenge that purports to show that our ordinary, pretheoretic beliefs about meaning conflict with other fundamental beliefs in a way that makes our beliefs about meaning unsustainable. In general, the power of skeptical views lies not in their rejection of what we commonly take for granted, but in their finding reasons for such rejection that arise directly from other fundamental convictions of ours. If the skeptic can find such reasons, he can show that our own most deeply held views are sufficient to undermine the beliefs (about meaning) that he challenges.

Has Kripke's skeptic about meaning done this? I don't think so. He has insisted that if I meant anything in the past, then what I meant must be determined by nonintentional facts; and I have agreed, provided that the determination relation is one of necessary consequence. I grant that if I meant anything in the past, then what I meant must be a necessary consequence of nonintentional truths about me, my environment, my community, and so on. But it is not evident that there is a problem here, since none of the skeptic's arguments show that such a relation fails to hold. Indeed, they scarcely even attempt to show this. Instead, they try to establish that no collection of nonintentional truths will allow us to *demonstrate* the truth of the relevant intentional claims. This, I have suggested, is tantamount to an attempt to convince us that claims about meaning (and propositional attitudes) are not apriori consequences of any set of nonintentional truths.

On this point it must be admitted that the skeptic has a strong case. The task of deriving claims about meanings (and propositional attitudes) from nonintentional truths, together perhaps with apriori definitions of intentional notions like meaning and belief, is daunting. I don't know how to give such a derivation, and I am not sure that any is possible.[16] Consequently, I am willing to grant that the skeptic might be right in maintaining that claims about what I meant are not apriori consequences of nonintentional truths.[17]

If it were clear that any necessary consequence of a set of claims *P* was also an apriori consequence of *P*, then this admission would provide the skeptic with just what he needs; for then he could force me to admit that claims about meaning may not be necessary consequences of nonintentional truths. That would conflict with my conviction that meaning facts must supervene on nonintentional facts, and so would threaten my pretheoretic commitment to meaning facts. However, this argumentative strategy fails. Thanks to the work of Kripke and others, it has become clear that many necessary consequences of propositions are not apriori consequences of them. Consequently, my admission that claims about meanings may not be apriori consequences of nonintentional truths need not undermine my belief that they are necessary consequences of those truths.

Could the skeptic undermine my claims about past meanings by appealing directly to the thesis that if there are facts about what I meant

---

16 One important reason why it is difficult to be certain on this point is that it is not completely clear what apriori definitions of intentional notions are possible. For a good discussion of this issue, and an argument for the conclusion that facts about meaning (and belief) are not apriori consequences of nonintentional facts, see Alex Byrne, *The Emergent Mind*, unpublished dissertation, Princeton University, 1993.

17 If the required epistemological relationship between the nonintentional truths and the claims about meaning were weakened to include empirical inferences to the best explanation, then the skeptical thesis that meaning claims are not epistemological consequences of nonintentional truths would be far more questionable. In any case, Kripke's skeptic does not argue in this way. (See note 13 above.)

in the past, then they must be apriori consequences of nonintentional truths? I don't think so. That thesis is not one of my beliefs about meaning, pre-theoretic or otherwise. Since the skeptic has done nothing to establish it in its own right, his challenge fails.

To sum up, the general form of the skeptic's argument is the following:

P_1 If in the past there was a fact about what I meant by '+' , in particular, if there was a fact that I meant addition by '+,' then either:

(i) this fact was determined by nonintentional facts of such and such kinds — facts about my past calculations using '+,' the rules or algorithms I followed in doing calculations involving '+,' my past dispositions to respond to questions ʿWhat is $\underline{n}$ + $\underline{m}$?ʾ, the totality of my past dispositions to verbal behaviour involving '+,' etc.

or

(ii) the fact that I meant addition by '+' was a primitive fact, not determined by nonintentional facts.

P_2 Nonintentional facts of type (i) did not determine that I meant addition (or anything else) by '+.'

P_3 What I meant by '+' was not a primitive fact.

C_1 Thus, in the past there was no fact that I meant addition (or anything else) by '+.'

C_2 By parity of reasoning, there never was a fact about what I, or anyone else, meant by any word; *ditto* for the present.

In my view, the argument suffers from equivocation. If the determination relation is one of necessary consequence, then P_3 is plausible, but P_2 is not.[18] If the determination relation is one of apriori consequence, then P_2 is plausible, but P_3 is not. What makes the argument seductive is the failure to distinguish these alternatives. Once this distinction is made, the argument loses much of its force. There is no in-

---

18   Given an appropriately broad listing of nonintentional facts in P_1.

terpretation in which P_1, P_2, and P_3 are jointly true; nor do I know of one in which they are even jointly plausible.

Quine's Indeterminacy Thesis

I will now try to show that Quine's arguments for the indeterminacy of translation (and inscrutability of reference) suffer from a similar defect. We may begin by noting the relationship between Kripke's skeptical problem and Quine's. Kripke sets up the challenge as that of specifying nonintentional facts which determine that what I mean now by '+' is the same as what I meant by '+' in the past. This can be rephrased as the challenge of specifying nonintentional facts which determine that a translation from '+' as I used it in the past to '+' as I use it now is correct, whereas a translation from '+' as I used it in the past to, say, 'quus' as I use it now (to stand for the quaddition function defined in note 5) is incorrect. Quine's question is a generalization of this challenge: What nonintentional facts determine that it is correct to translate an expression A, as used by a person p, or a community c, as meaning the same as an expression B, as used by a person p', or community c'? Like Kripke's skeptic, Quine answers that in a wide range of cases there are no meaning-determining facts.

Quine's position can be set out as a series of theses. The first of these is The Underdetermination of Translation by Data, which is an instance of his view that empirical theories of all sorts typically are underdetermined by observational evidence.

> *The Underdetermination of Translation by Data*
> Let L_1 and L_2 be arbitrary languages, and let D be the set of all observational truths (known and unknown) relevant to translation from one to the other. For any theory of translation T for L_1 and L_2, compatible with D, there is a theory T', incompatible with T, that is equally well supported by D.[19]

---

19 The strength of this thesis, as well as the more general thesis of the underdetermination of empirical theories by observational data, depends on one's conception of what it is for a class of data statements to support a theory.

This thesis can be fleshed out by saying a little about what theories of translation are, and what Quine takes the evidence for them to be. First consider theories of translation. A theory of translation for two languages correlates individual words of each language with words or phrases of the other language; this correlation is used in the theory to correlate the sentences of the two languages.[20] Any system of establishing such correlations can be counted as a translation manual, or theory. We may take such a theory as yielding (infinitely many) theorems of the form:

> Word or phrase w in L_1 means the same as word or phrase w^* in L_2.
> Sentence S in L_1 means the same as sentence S^* in L_2.

According to Quine, the empirical data relevant to theories of translation are statements about the stimulus meanings of sentences. The stimulus meaning of a sentence S (for a speaker at a time) is a pair of classes — the class of situations in which the speaker would assent to S, and the class in which the speaker would dissent from S. Stimulus meanings are particularly important in evaluating translations of what Quine calls 'occasion sentences' and 'observation sentences.' An occasion sentence is one assent to, or dissent from, which depends on the

---

For present purposes I will follow what appears to be Quine's latitudinarianism on this subject. Theories, together with auxiliary observational statements, make (entail) observational predictions. (Which statements count as observational for this purpose will not be an issue here.) A set of such observational predictions supports a theory to the extent that the theory, supplemented by true auxiliary observation statements, entails the members of the set. Two theories (appropriately supplemented with auxiliary observational statements) that entail the same members of the set, are equally well supported by the set.

20 I am assuming, in order to simplify the argument, that words are the minimal meaning bearing units, that languages contain finitely many such words, and that the translation of the infinitely many phrases and sentences of the two languages is the result of (i) the translation of the words that make them up plus (ii) combinatorial principles specifying the translations of syntactically complex expressions in terms of the translations of their parts.

speaker's current observation. An observation sentence is an occasion sentence for which assent or dissent depends only on observation — with no, or only a minimum in the way of, background information required. For example, 'He is a bachelor' is an occasion sentence, since assent or dissent in a given case depends on whom the subject is observing; but it is not an observation sentence in Quine's sense because whether or not one assents in a particular case depends in part on having special background information about the person perceived. 'That is red,' on the other hand, does not depend (to the same extent) on having such background information, and so counts as an observation sentence for Quine. Quine's way of approximating this intuitive notion of an observation sentence within his behaviouristic framework is to define an observation sentence in a language L to be an occasion sentence for speakers of L the stimulus meaning of which varies little from one speaker to another.

The stimulus meanings of observation and occasion sentences play a prominent role in Quine's conception of the main observational predictions made by translation theories. These predictions are summarized by the following three principles for extracting testable claims from theories of translation (which otherwise wouldn't entail any such predictions via their form alone):[21] (i) if a translation theory states that an observation sentence S in L_1 means the same as a sentence S^* in L_2, then the theory predicts that the two sentences have the same stimulus meanings in their respective linguistic communities; (ii) if S and S' are occasion sentences of L_1, and if a translation theory states both that S means the same in L_1 as S^* in L_2 and that S' means the same in L_1 as $S^{*'}$ in L_2, then the theory predicts that S and S' have the same stimulus meaning in L_1 iff S^* and $S^{*'}$ have the same stimulus meaning in L_2; (iii) if a theory translates an expression n of a language L as meaning the same as 'not' in English, then adding n to sentences of L must reverse stimulus meaning; similar claims are made regarding other truth functional operators. On this conception, the observational data for theories of translation consist mainly of behavioural evidence regarding the stimulus meanings of occasion sentences.

---

21 See chapter 2 of *Word and Object* (Cambridge, MA: MIT Press 1960).

Quine also considers a possible constraint relevant to the translation of what he calls standing sentences — sentences assent to, or dissent from, which is independent of current sensory stimulation. The possible constraint is that sentences assented to (dissented from) in every situation by the community of speakers of L_1 must be translated onto those assented to (dissented from) in every situation by the community of speakers of L_2. But this constraint is itself problematic, and, in any case, adding it would not significantly change the overall picture. It is clear that if the observational data for theories of translation are restricted to behavioural evidence of the sort Quine has in mind, then profoundly different theories of translation will be supported equally well (in his sense) by all observational data, known and unknown, in virtually all interesting cases.

For example, the set of all behavioural data concerning the stimulus meanings of sentences for me, past and present, is equally compatible with theories of translation which claim that (i) the term 'rabbit' as used by me in the past means the same as the term 'rabbit' as used by me now, (ii) the term 'rabbit' as used by me in the past means the same as the phrase 'set of undetached rabbit parts' as used by me now, or (iii) the term 'rabbit' as used by me in the past means the same as the phrase 'temporal stage of a rabbit' as used by me now. Since the expressions 'rabbit,' 'set of undetached rabbit parts,' and 'temporal stage of a rabbit,' as used by me now mean, and refer to, different things, alternative translation theories that map these different expressions onto the term 'rabbit' as I used it in the past conflict with one another, and can be regarded as incompatible. Quine concludes from this that theories of translation are underdetermined, in the sense defined above, by the observational data for them.[22]

---

22 When Quine speaks of different , *incompatible* theories (or 'theory formulations') all equally supported by the same possible observational evidence, he seems to have in mind *logically incompatible* theories (or theory formulations). (See 'On the Reasons for Indeterminacy of Translation,' *Journal of Philosophy* **67** (1970) 178-83, at 179; and 'On Empirically Equivalent Systems of the World,' *Erkenntnis* **9** (1975) 313-28, at 322.) However, despite the obvious difference in meanings between 'rabbit,' 'set of undetached rabbit parts,' and 'temporal stage of a rabbit' as I use them now, the following claims are not *logically* incompatible: (i) the term 'rabbit' as I used it in the past means the same as the term 'rabbit' as I use

Since empirical theories of all sorts are typically underdetermined by the observational evidence bearing on them, the extension of this result to theories of translation is not, in itself, a radical development. What makes it striking is Quine's use of it as the basis for the truly radical doctrine of the Indeterminacy of Translation.

The Indeterminacy of Translation
Translation is not determined by the set N of all truths of nature, known and unknown. For any pair of languages, there are incompatible theories of translation for those languages that accord equally well with N. All such theories are equally true to the facts; there is no objective matter of fact on which they disagree, and no objective sense in which one is true and the other is not.[23]

---

it now (ii) the term 'rabbit' as I used it in the past means the same as the phrase 'set of undetached rabbit parts' as I use it now, (iii) the term 'rabbit' as I used it in the past means the same as the phrase 'temporal stage of a rabbit' as I use it now. Consequently, translation theories making these different claims need not be *logically* incompatible with one another.

Logical incompatibility will result if translation theories are embedded in larger background theories containing the following claims: (a) Rabbits are not sets of undetached rabbit parts & sets of undetached rabbit parts are not temporal stages of rabbits & rabbits are not temporal stages of rabbits ; (b) 'Rabbit' (as I use it now) refers to an object iff it is a rabbit & 'set of undetached rabbit parts' (as I use it now) refers to an object iff it is a set of undetached rabbit parts & 'temporal stage of a rabbit' (as I use it now) refers to an object iff it is a temporal stage of a rabbit; (c) if two words refer to different things then they don't mean the same; (d) if a means the same as b & a means the same as c, then b means the same as c. Let T_1 be a translation theory containing statement (i), T_2 be a translation theory containing statement (ii), and T_3 be a translation theory containing statement (iii). The union of T_1, T_2, and a set containing (a)-(d) is logically inconsistent; as are corresponding unions involving the other relevant combinations. The justification for appealing to these auxiliary claims is that (a) states an obvious fact and (b)-(d) are axiomatic to any overall theory that makes significant use of the concepts of meaning and reference.

23 See Quine, 'Reply to Chomsky,' D. Davidson and J. Hintikka, eds., *Words and Objections* (Dordrecht: Reidel 1969), 303.

This doctrine is a consequence of two more basic Quinean views.

> *Physicalism*
> All genuine truths (facts) are determined by physical truths (facts).
> *The Underdetermination of Translation by Physics*
> Translation is not determined by the set of all physical truths (facts), known and unknown. For any pair of languages, there are incompatible theories of translation for those languages that accord equally well with all physical truths (facts).

Quine's route to the Indeterminacy of Translation is as follows: He begins with the behaviourist premise that since we learn language by observing the linguistic behaviour of others, the only facts relevant to determining linguistic meaning must be publicly observable behavioural facts — in particular facts about stimulus meaning. But his discussion of the Underdetermination of Translation by Data shows that these facts do not determine which translations of our words are correct, and so do not determine what our words mean. It follows that *no* physical facts determine word meaning or correct translation. In the presence of the doctrine of Physicalism this means that claims about what our words mean — e.g., claims like *'rabbit' as I used it in the past means the same as 'rabbit' as I use it now* — never state genuine facts, and never count as expressing genuine truths. Hence, the Indeterminacy of Translation.

How persuasive is this argument? Many object, quite correctly, to its behaviourist premise, which allows Quine to move from the Underdetermination of Translation by Data to the Underdetermination of Translation by Physics.[24] However, there is another, more fundamental, point to be made. The contents of Quine's central claims are unclear.

---

24 In this paper I will assume, without argument, that Quine's behaviourism about language is false. It is noteworthy, however, that the appeal of the indeterminacy thesis, and the challenge posed by it, have been strongly felt by many philosophers who have not been prepared to accept behaviourism independently. My task here is to diagnose the source of that appeal, and defuse the challenge felt by those philosophers.

In particular, it is unclear precisely what determination relation is invoked in the three central theses of Physicalism, the Underdetermination of Translation by Physics, and the Indeterminacy of Translation. Because of this, equivocation threatens. On certain construals of the determination relation Physicalism is plausible; on other construals the Underdetermination of Translation by Physics is plausible; but there is no construal on which both Physicalism and the Underdetermination of Translation by Physics are plausible, and no interpretation in which the Indeterminacy of Translation can be sustained.

What is it for one set of claims to determine another? It is not for the claims in the second set to be logical consequences of the claims in the first. Certainly translation theories are not logical consequences of the set of all physical truths. But this is trivial, since whenever an empirical theory of any interest includes vocabulary not found in the truths of physics it will fail to be a logical consequence of those truths. For example, not all the truths of chemistry and biology are logical consequences of the set of true sentences of the language of an ideal physics. But chemistry and biology are supposed by Quine to be determined by physics; so the determination relation cannot be that of logical consequence. If it were, Physicalism would obviously be false.

A different way of specifying the determination relation would be to say that a set P of statements determines a set Q of statements iff it would be (metaphysically) impossible for all the statements in P to be true without all the statements in Q being true — i.e. iff Q is a (metaphysically) necessary consequence of P. On this construal physicalism is quite plausible; it states that all genuine truths (facts) supervene on the physical truths (facts). However, the Underdetermination of Translation by Physics now turns out to be implausible. The point here parallels the one made in response to Kripke's skeptical argument about meaning. Prior to any skeptical argument, Kripke's or Quine's, we naturally assume at the outset that there are facts about meaning and translation of the sort the skeptic denies. Given this conviction, we may ask directly whether a physically identical twin — someone (in a physically identical possible world) whose utterances, behaviour, brain states, causal and historical relations to the environment, and interactions with other speakers completely and exactly matches mine (in the actual world) — could mean by 'rabbit,' what I mean (in the actual world) by, say, 'set of undetached rabbit parts.' The natural answer to this question is 'No.' Hence on this interpretation of the thesis of The Under-determination of Translation by Physics, it should be rejected.

The thesis could, of course, be saved if it could be shown both that (i) theories of translation are not apriori consequences of the set of physical truths, and that (ii) whenever a claim is not an apriori consequence of a set of statements it is not a necessary consequence of those statements. As we shall see something like (i) is reasonably plausible. Thus if one were confused about the relationship between necessity and aprioricity, or if one failed to distinguish them, one might wrongly conclude that both Physicalism and The Underdetermination of Translation by Physics are jointly true, when determination is taken to be necessary consequence. The error here is the implicit reliance on the false claim (ii) — that any necessary consequence of a set of statements is an apriori consequence of that set. Once this error is removed there is no plausible route to the theses of the Underdetermination of Translation by Physics and the Indeterminacy of Translation, on the interpretation in which determination is construed as necessary consequence.

In light of this, it may be worthwhile to put the notion of necessity aside and examine a more epistemological conception of the determination relation. One might say that a set P of claims determines a set Q iff it is in principle possible, given the claims in P, for one to demonstrate the truth of the claims in Q, appealing only to logic and obvious apriori principles or definitions. The idea here is that for P to determine Q is for P to provide a theoretical basis for establishing Q that is absolutely conclusive, and that rules out any possibility of falsehood. In effect, determination is here construed as apriori consequence.

On this construal, the thesis of the Underdetermination of Translation by Physics is both interesting and plausible. Given the total set of behavioural evidence about stimulus meanings of the sort Quine identifies, I cannot absolutely establish that what a speaker means by one of his terms is what I now mean by 'rabbit,' as opposed to what I now mean by 'set of undetached rabbit parts' or 'temporal stage of a rabbit' (even if the speaker is me in the past). The claim that a speaker means one of these things rather than another is not an apriori consequence of the total set of claims about Quinean stimulus meanings. Moreover, it is hard to see how adding more behavioural facts (beyond Quinean facts about stimulus meaning), or more physical facts — about the neurological events in the person's brain or his physical interactions with his environment — would, by itself, change the situation. Thus, it may turn out that theories of translation are epistemologically under-determined by the set of all physical truths.

But how serious would this be? Is there some reason to believe that all genuine truths must be not just necessary consequences, but also purely apriori consequences, of the set of all physical truths? As far as I can tell this is not one of our pretheoretic convictions; nor has Quine given a theoretical explanation of why it must be maintained.[25] Hence, if theories of translation do turn out to be underdetermined by physics in this epistemological sense, such a result should be taken to show that the corresponding epistemic version of Physicalism is false, even though the metaphysical version of Physicalism, in which the deter-mination relation is that of necessary consequence, remains true. Cer-tainly, such a position is preferable to the radical and paradoxical rejection of facts about meaning and reference implied by Quine's In-determinacy thesis.[26]

---

25 It is important not to confuse what is a genuine pretheoretic conviction — namely that we do know what our words, and those of our neighbors, mean — with what is not such a conviction — namely that we arrive at this knowledge by deriving true claims about the meanings of our words, and those of our neighbors, as apriori consequences of purely physical truths. Whereas the former claim is clearly true, the latter is almost certainly false.

26 Quine's doctrines of Physicalism, the Indeterminacy of Translation and the In-scrutability of Reference entail that claims of the sort, *Person P's word w refers to rabbits (as opposed to sets of undetached rabbit parts, etc.),* are not determined by the totality of physical facts and so do not express genuine truths; *ditto* for any open formula *P's word w refers to x* relative to an assignment of an object as value of the variable 'x.' Given Quine's usual understanding of the existential quanti-fier, one can conclude from this that $\exists x$ *P's word w refers to x* never expresses a genuine truth. Supposing that it is nevertheless meaningful, we may conclude that ~$\exists x$ *P's word w refers to x* will always be true; in effect, no one's words ever refer to anything. This is eliminativism about reference (as ordinarily under-stood). Pretty paradoxical, especially for someone who clearly is attempting to use words to refer to, and make claims about, things.

Quine nowhere explicitly acknowledges such starkly paradoxical conse-quences of his views. The closest he comes is in the essay 'Ontological Relativ-ity,' in Quine, *Ontological Relativity* (New York and London: Columbia Univer-sity Press 1969), 26-68, at 47-51. There he notes the paradoxical consequences of

If this is right, there may be an interesting epistemological construal of the determination relation according to which the Underdetermination of Translation by Physics is true, while Physicalism and the Indeterminacy of Translation are false. However, this point must be qualified by a complication that I have neglected up to now. In order to derive any empirical theory T from the set of truths of physics, one must appeal to theoretical identifications, or bridge principles, relating the vocabulary of T to the vocabulary of the underlying physics. What conditions must these identifications or bridge principles satisfy in order to be available for such derivations? Is it enough that they be true, or must they also be apriori (or necessary)? In my epistemic characterization of the determination relation, I allowed only obvious apriori truths and definitions. With this understanding the Underdetermination of Translation by Physics is at least plausible (though it has not, of course, been demonstrated).

However, with this same understanding, Physicalism is threatened, not just by theories of meaning or translation, but by ordinary instances of theoretical reduction, such as the reduction of the biological concept of a gene to a physical construction involving the concept DNA. The relevant theoretical identity statement relating the two seems to be an empirical, a posteriori truth. Thus, if bridge principles relating the biological vocabulary to the physical vocabulary are restricted to apriori definitions, then our theoretical identity statement will be excluded, and the derivation of genetics from physical theory will be placed in jeopardy. Surely no one would conclude from this that genetics in particular, or biology in general, fail to state genuine truths; rather, if a choice has to be made, we will reject the (strong) epistemological version of Physicalism.[27]

---

applying the Indeterminacy and Inscrutability doctrines to our (present) selves, and attempts (unsuccessfully) to avoid these consequences by invoking his mysterious doctrine of reference relative to a coordinate system (48) and "acquiescing in our mother tongue" (49). Unfortunately, space limitations prevent me from providing a thorough discussion of these passages here.

27 This result could be avoided if it could be shown that there are genuinely apriori semantic definitions of 'gene' and 'DNA' from which, together with the set of purely physical truths, the theoretical identification of genes with DNA can be

In light of this, we could opt to weaken the epistemological determination relation so as to allow P to determine Q provided that Q is a logical consequence of P together with bridge principles, or theoretical identities, consisting of any truths — contingent, aposteriori, or otherwise — that relate the vocabulary of P to that of Q.[28] On this weakened

---

derived. Since I am not certain whether this is possible in principle, I am not certain that the case of genetics provides a genuine counterexample to the strong epistemological version of physicalism. By the same token, I am not certain that no genuinely apriori semantic definitions of notions like meaning and reference exist from which, together with all physical truths, claims about meaning and reference can be derived.

28 This conception of determination is closely related to familiar conceptions of theoretical reduction, which are used by Michael Friedman in 'Physicalism and the Indeterminacy of Translation,' *Noûs* 9 (1975) 353-73, to characterize Quine's theses of Physicalism and the Indeterminacy of Translation. There Friedman recognizes two kinds of reduction, strong and weak. Strong reduction is reduction in the classical sense. A theory T_2 is classically reducible to a theory T_1 iff the theorems of T_2 are logical consequences of T_1 together with a set D containing a 'definition' for each primitive predicate of T_2. A 'definition' is a universally quantified biconditional establishing the extensional equivalence of an n-place primitive predicate of T_2 with a corresponding formula of arbitrary complexity of the language of T_1.

The same point can be expressed in another way by noting that the 'definitions' appealed to in a reduction can be taken as establishing a mapping D from primitive predicates of T_2 onto coextensive open formulas of T_1. Given this, we may define the notion of an n-place (primitive) predicate P of T_2 being *satisfied by an n-tuple in an arbitrary model* M *relative to a mapping* D as consisting in the image of P under D being satisfied by that n-tuple in M. Classical (strong) reduction obtains when there is a mapping D such that every model of T_1 is a model-relative-to D of T_2. (See Friedman 357-8.)

Weak reduction is just like strong reduction except that the mapping D associates each primitive predicate of T_2 with a set of corresponding open formulas of the language of T_1. The set of formulas D associates with each primitive predicate P must be coextensive with P — i.e., as a matter of fact an n-tuple will satisfy P iff it satisfies at least one formula in the image of P under D. The notion of an n-place (primitive) predicate P of T_2 being satisfied by an n-tuple *in an arbitrary model* M *relative to such a mapping* D is then defined as consisting in there being at least one member of the set of formulas associated with P by D being satisfied by that n-tuple in M. As before, reduction obtains when there is a mapping D of this sort such that every model of T_1 is a model-relative-to D of

epistemological conception the usual reduction of the notion of a gene to DNA will pose no difficulty for the thesis of Physicalism. However, on this weakened conception, even theories of translation will be determined by the set of physical truths.

To see this let Sx be some formula specifying a set of physical facts satisfied by me and only me — so that Sx is true relative to an assign-

---

T_2. (Weak reduction differs from strong reduction only in cases in which the sets associated with the primitive predicates of T_2 are infinite.)

Friedman's stated reason (358) for allowing weak reduction to count as a genuine type of theoretical reduction is to make room for positions such as functionalist theories of mind which identify each token of a mental type with a particular physical realization, while recognizing arbitrarily many different ways in which the given type *might be physically realized*. Note, however, the modal notion here. Its use in characterizing the relevant functionalist theories points up a modest puzzle having to do with Friedman's position. Reduction, as he officially characterizes it, does not require the 'definitional' mapping D to pair the predicates of T_2 with formulas, or sets of formulas, that are intensionally equivalent to them in any sense. In particular D is not required to produce pairs that are extensionally equivalent in arbitrary counterfactual, or apriori imaginable, circumstances. Because of this the different merely possible, or merely imaginable, ways in which a mental type might be physically realized are, strictly speaking, irrelevant to the existence of 'definitional' mappings D satisfying Friedman's stated conditions for reduction. Since, as far as I know, physicalist functionalists never maintain that there actually exist infinitely many physically different kinds of realizations of a given mental type, they presumably ought to be reasonably confident in asserting the strong reducibility (in Friedman's official sense) of their theories to physics. Why then is there a need for the notion of weak reducibility? Does Friedman's use of the notion reflect an implicit desire to require the 'definitional' mappings in genuine reductions to provide more than actual coextensiveness? Do they also have to provide coextensiveness in all counterfactual (or in all apriori imaginable) situations as well? If so, then couldn't we define the determination relations needed to evaluate Quine's theses directly in terms of necessary, or apriori, consequence, as above?

Putting these and other subsidiary issues aside, I would like to acknowledge the essential correctness of some of Friedman's central points. In particular, he makes a plausible case for interpreting Quine's thesis of the Indeterminacy of Translation as the doctrine that theories of translation are not reducible (in either his strong or his weak sense) to the set of physical truths. He then argues for the correct (but understated) conclusion that Quine has given no compelling argument for the Indeterminacy Thesis, understood in this way.

ment of me as value of x, and is false relative to other assignments. It doesn't matter what this formula looks like — whether it is complex, whether we can identify it as applying just to me, etc. It only matters that it exists. For completeness we may suppose that it includes a specification of all physical facts about me relevant to my use of language — facts about my present and past brain states, facts about my behavioural dispositions, facts about my physical interactions with the environment, including causal and historical relations connecting my uses of individual words with other speakers and things, and so on. Let Lx be a similar formula applying uniquely to a certain Spanish speaker, Luisa. (For the sake of simplicity, suppose that I am a monolingual speaker of English and Luisa is a monolingual speaker of Spanish.) Now imagine a claim of the following sort, exhaustively listing the translation of the finitely many individual words of my language into words and phrases of Luisa's language.[29]

TSL: $\exists x\ \exists y$ [Sx & Ly & for all words w (of English) and words or phrases w^* (of Spanish), w as used by x means the same as w^* as used by y iff (i) w = 'woman' and w^* = 'mujer,' or (ii) w = 'headache' and w^* = 'dolor de cabeza,' or ...

A corresponding claim lists the translation of the finitely many individual words of Luisa's language onto words and phrases of my language; similar claims may be imagined for each actual pair of language users — past, present and future. Since it is extremely plausible to suppose that there are only finitely many such pairs of speakers, it seems safe to assume that some extremely long and complicated general formula of the following sort exists which encompasses all the individual cases.

---

29 In this discussion I ignore certain practical complications such as the fact that some speakers speak more than one language, the fact that words of the language may be ambiguous, and the possibility that sometimes there may be no translation of a word in one language onto a word or phrase of the other language. Although these are real factors in translation, they are peripheral to Quine's philosophical claims about translation.

GT: For all speakers x and y, and for all words w in x's language and words or phrases w^* in y's language, w as used by x means the same as w^* as used by y iff (i) Sx & Ly &(w = 'woman' & w^* = 'mujer,' or w = 'headache' & w^* = 'dolor de cabeza,' or ...; or (ii) Lx & Sy &(w = 'semaforo' & w^* = 'traffic light,' or ...; or (iii) Sx & Gy & ...; or ...

GT may be regarded as a bridge principle providing a coextensive physicalistic counterpart of the predicate *means the same as* applied to words and phrases in theories of translation. Next we need a general bridge principle that encompasses the combinatorial rules used in theories of translation to combine translations of parts into translations of whole sentences. Presumably there are only finitely many such combinatorial rules for each pair of speakers. If, as we are assuming, there are only finitely many such pairs of actual speakers, these rules can in principle be exhaustively listed. This list together with GT can then be used to formulate another bridge principle that provides a coextensive physicalistic counterpart to the predicate *means the same as* as used between sentences in theories of translation. But then, theories of translation will be derivable from the set of all physical truths together with these bridge principles, and so will count as determined by physics in our weakened epistemological sense.

It might, of course, be observed that this trivialization just shows that stronger conditions are needed to characterize the required determination relation. Two possibilities suggest themselves. First, it might be claimed that what we want is not just a reduction of theories of translation to physical truths, but rather a single reduction to the set of physical truths of all theories making use of semantic notions such as meaning and reference. Surely, if these notions are legitimate they will have significant theoretical uses well beyond theories of translation in the narrow sense considered here. The fact that a trivial reduction is theoretically possible when translation theories are considered in isolation does not show that such a reduction is possible in a context which is properly more inclusive.

The point is well taken. But the problem with this suggestion is that it takes us far beyond Quine's own discussion, and into uncharted waters. Before we can make any progress on the question of whether a single physicalistic reduction of all legitimate uses of semantic notions is theoretically possible, we need a reasonably precise and exhaustive characterization of the range of theoretical uses of semantic notions. Until we have this, we can't evaluate the case for skepticism about meaning (and reference) because no sufficiently articulated case for skepticism about these notions has even been made.

The second possible response to the trivial reduction sketched above is to stick to a physicalistic reduction simply of translation theories, but to claim that what is wanted are bridge principles that provide definitions yielding physical formulas coextensive with their nonphysical counterparts in all counterfactual circumstances. The bridge principles in the trivial reduction do not satisfy this demand, since, for example, someone could have meant the same by a particular term as I do by 'woman' even though that person did not satisfy the physical predicate identifying any actually existing individual.

I have no quarrel with this strengthened, modal constraint on the determination relation. However, two points should be noted. First, if, unlike Quine, we grant the legitimacy of modal notions, then we can characterize determination directly in terms of necessary consequence. But then, as I have maintained above, we have reason to believe that theories of translation *are* determined by the physical truths. Second, if one insists characterizing determination in terms of a strengthened reduction relation that requires physicalistic formulas which are necessarily coextensive with the predicates and other vocabulary items used in the theories undergoing reduction, then it is not clear what our attitude should be towards the resulting strengthened versions of Physicalism and the Underdetermination of Translation by Physics. On this interpretation the latter thesis requires the existence of physical formulas (or sets of formulas)[30] necessarily coextensive with the predicates *expression E as used by x means the same as expression E' as used by y* and *sentence S as used by x means the same as sentence S' as used by y.*

---

30 On this interpretation Friedman's relation of weak reduction, strengthened by the requirement that the mapping from predicates in T_2 to *sets* of formulas of the language of T_1 produce pairs that are *necessarily* coextensive (in the sense of note 28), should count as a genuine instance of determination in the sense presently under consideration.

Are there such formulas (or sets of formulas)? There may well be, though it is hard to say for sure. Certainly Quine has given no compelling arguments to the contrary. Thus, on this interpretation, the case for the Underdetermination of Translation by Physics has not been made.

A similar point can be made regarding Quine's other premise — namely Physicalism — in the argument for Indeterminacy. On the present strengthened interpretation of the determination relation, it is not evident what we should think of the resulting version of Physicalism. I have already granted the truth of a weaker version of Physicalism, which states that all genuine truths must be necessary consequences of the physical truths. Is it obvious that we should add the further requirement that they be logical consequences of the Physical truths plus definitions that provide necessarily coextensive physical translations of all vocabulary items used in genuine truths? Since this point hasn't been established, the present interpretation of the determination relation is one in which neither of the two premises for the Indeterminacy Thesis has been secured. In light of this, the conclusion to be drawn is that Quine's argument for the Indeterminacy of Translation, like Kripke's skeptical argument about meaning and following a rule, fails to provide a compelling challenge to our pretheoretic convictions about meaning and translation.

This does not foreclose the possibility that something could be done to strengthen, or revive such a skeptical challenge. But surely the burden of proof is on those who wish to persuade us to adopt a radically skeptical attitude toward our ordinary semantic notions. Although I do not believe that any skeptical challenge of this sort could succeed, that has not been the burden of my argument. Instead, I have tried to defuse the particular skeptical arguments of Kripke and Quine by showing that their initial power is due in substantial part to an equivocation about what it is for one set of claims to determine another. Once this equivocation is removed, the original skeptical arguments lose their force, and it becomes highly dubious and problematic that any nonequivocal replacements could be found that would provide good reasons for a thorough-going skepticism.[31]

31 The ideas in this paper date back to seminars I gave in the summer of 1988 at the University of Washington, and in the fall of 1988 at Princeton University. These ideas were refined and elaborated in my fall semester seminar of 1993 at Princeton. An early version of the first section of this paper, on Kripke's account of the rule-following paradox, was presented in June of 1995 at the *Instituto de Investigaciones Filosóficas de la Universidad Nacional Autonoma de Mexico*. Later versions of the paper were presented at the Department of Philosophy, Wayne State University on October 13, 1995, the Chapel Hill Philosophy Colloquium on October 29, 1995, the Division of Humanities at the California Institute of Technology on November 3, 1995, the *Instituto de Investigaciones Filosoficas de la Universidad Nacional Autonoma de Mexico* on January 26 and 29, 1996, the Department of Philosophy at Rutgers University on March 7, 1996, the Department of Philosophy at Reed College on March 20, 1996, and the Department of Philosophy at the University of California at Berkeley on April 25, 1996. It was also presented at my fall semester seminar in 1996 at Princeton. I would like to thank the participants at all those presentations, and seminars, for their comments. In addition, I would like to thank James Pryor, Michael Thau and George Wilson for reading and commenting on earlier drafts of the paper.

Notes on Contributors

John P. Burgess received his Ph.D. from the Group in Logic and Methodology at Berkeley in 1974, and shortly afterwards came to Princeton, where he has been Professor and Director of Undergraduate Studies in the Department of Philosophy since 1986. He has published extensively in logic and philosophy of mathematics journals and anthologies, and is co-author with his colleague Gideon Rosen of *A Subject with No Object: Strategies for Nominalistic Interpretation of Mathematics*.

Richard Cartwright is professor of philosophy, emeritus, at the Massachusetts Institute of Technology. Earlier he taught at the University of Michigan and Wayne State University. He has published articles in philosophical journals, some of which are reprinted in his *Philosophical Essays*.

Vann McGee is a professor in the department of linguistics and philosophy at MIT. He is also editor, along with Krister Segerberg, of the *Journal of Philosophical Logic*. Research interests include philosophical logic, philosophy of language, and philosophy of mathematics.

Terence Parsons received his B.A. degree in physics from the University of Rochester and his Ph.D. in philosophy from Stanford University. He has taught at the University of Illinois (Chicago), the University of Massachusetts (Amherst), and at the University of California, Irvine since 1979. He has worked in philosophical logic, philosophy of language, and metaphysics, and recently in the history of medieval semantics. He is the author of *NonExistent Objects*, a book on Meinongian metaphysics, and *Events in the Semantics of English*, on the semantics of natural language.

Mark Richard is Associate Professor and Chair of Philosophy at Tufts University. He is the author of *Propositional Attitudes* (Cambridge

University Press, 1990) and numerous articles in philosophy of language, philosophy of logic, and philosophy of mind.

Nathan Salmon is a professor of philosophy at the University of California, Santa Barbara. He is the author of numerous articles in analytic metaphysics and the philosophy of language. His book, *Reference and Essence* (1981), was awarded the Gustave O. Arlt Award in the Humanities by the Council of Graduate Schools in the United States. Salmon has been a staunch defender of Millianism about proper names. His *Frege's Puzzle* (1986) presents a detailed response to the problem of substitution failure.

Scott Soames is a professor of philosophy at Princeton University. He is author of many articles in the philosophy of language, and of the forthcoming book *Understanding Truth* (Oxford University Press).

George Wilson is a professor of philosophy at Johns Hopkins University. He has written on the philosophy of language, the theory of action, and aesthetics (film and literary theory). His two books are: *Narration in Light: Studies in Cinematic Point of View* (Johns Hopkins Press, 1986) and *The Intentionality of Human Action* (Stanford University Press, 1989).

Index

CANADIAN JOURNAL OF PHILOSOPHY
SUPPLEMENTARY VOLUMES

Shipping costs: Canada/U.S.A., $5.00 single copy; international, $9.00 single copy.
Unless otherwise indicated, outside Canada, prices are in U.S. dollars.
Canadian orders must include 7% GST. All prices subject to change without notice.

Orders to: UBC Press, University of British Columbia,
6344 Memorial Road, Vancouver, B.C., V6T 1Z2 Canada
Telephone: (604) 822-5959; Fax orders: 1-800-668-0821